TRANSFORMERS

TRANSFORMERS

*The Artists
of Self-Creation*

REVISED EDITION

Jacquelyn Small

BANTAM BOOKS
NEW YORK · TORONTO · LONDON · SYDNEY · AUCKLAND

TRANSFORMERS
A Bantam Book / published by arrangement with the author

PRINTING HISTORY
DeVorss & Company edition published 1982
Bantam edition / October 1992

Book design by Stanley S. Drate/Folio Graphics Co., Inc.

Library of Congress Cataloging-in-Publication Data
Small, Jacquelyn.
  Transformers : the artists of self-creation / by Jacquelyn Small.
  — Rev. ed.
      p.   cm.
  Includes bibliographical references and index.
  ISBN 0-553-37000-6
  1. Self-actualization (Psychology) 2. Self-perception.
I. Title.
BF637.S4S56   1992
158'.1—dc20   91-10347
                                                            CIP

Published simultaneously in the United States and Canada

PRINTED IN THE UNITED STATES OF AMERICA

FFG   0   9   8   7   6   5   4   3   2   1

To each of you who has shared so deeply with me in the workshops and seminars we've experienced together. This book is an outpouring of the knowledge, experience, and endorsement I have gained from my work with you. On many levels, you are its author.

Contents

BOOK TWO

THE PRACTICAL WORK OF THE TRANSFORMER

Foreword

There is an innate urge in human beings to become what we *can* be, not what we are at the moment. This drive is so deep, so basic, that people throughout history frequently have given their lives to answer it. The goal is to awaken from our ordinary, slumbering consciousness to the glorious possibilities awaiting us. This process of waking up is what *Transformers* is about.

Modern life is stacked against this process. The ebb and flow of daily existence favors remaining asleep, not waking up. Our daily existence has become almost synonymous with *attachment*—attachment to family, career, status, wealth, power, drugs, and alcohol—materiality in all its expressions. But today, more people than ever realize that these attachments are a poor substitute for answering our higher callings, responding to the inner voice of the soul.

Today, more than ever, we need wise guides to assist in this process, someone who knows the tortuous twists and turns of the path toward waking up. Throughout history, such teachers have always arisen. Jacquelyn Small is such a guide; she is someone who has been there, someone who has come through.

Jacquelyn Small's work has made an enormous difference in the lives of thousands of people. I have followed her writing and activities for years, and I have participated in her workshops. I honor and admire her contributions immensely. She embodies genuine wisdom and compassion in her teaching, which shine through in this book. Jacquie is a true *bodhisattva*—one who sees perfection in every person and place, who does not have to retire into solitude and trance to know these things, and who will not rest until she has assisted everyone else to realize their own enlightenment.

For anyone who has ever felt the "tug from in front," that undeniable urge toward something higher, *Transformers* will come as a gentle, wise offering.

—LARRY DOSSEY, M.D.
Author of *Meaning & Medicine, Recovering the Soul,*
and *Space, Time & Medicine*

Preface to the Revised Edition

Transformers was first written for therapists who were making the shift from conventional psychotherapy to transformational or spiritual therapies that include working with both the ego and the soul. Today, I see that therapists are not the only ones working with others who are seeking psychospiritual guidance. All of us at some point are asked to be present for another who is searching for clarity or peace of mind. I've learned through writing this book and utilizing its principles in my own life that some people just naturally spark changes in the life of another. Not because they intend to, but just because they are who they are: carriers of transformational energies who affect others *just by being themselves*. There is no logical explanation for this phenomenon, except to say that some people are so real, they shake up others who are trapped in stagnant patterns or in living a lie. And some people are so naturally loving and nonjudgmental, we simply trust them with our darkest secrets, and in their presence we open and share in ways that lead to healing and wholeness.

So whether you are actually serving in a helping profession, or just happen to be one of those that others seek out when in need, this book will be a familiar companion. It will remind you of things you already know in your heart, but perhaps have never had verified by an external voice. In this new edition, I've broadened the language and concepts to include us all—those of us who are therapists, counselors, teachers, and professional advisers, as well as all seekers of Self-knowledge who are making the journey that eventually carries us "home," that place we all share as one Humanity.

JACQUELYN SMALL
Austin, Texas
November 1991

Acknowledgments

In appreciation of the great world teachers whose inspiration created this synthesis . . . Hermes, Pythagoras, Solomon, Plato, St. Francis, Sri Aurobindo, Gurdjieff, Hermann Hesse, Alice Ann Bailey, Carl Jung, Roberto Assagioli, Elisabeth Haich, Abraham Maslow, and the unsurpassable Jesus, the Christ.

And, more tangibly, my thanks to the persons who helped me bring this book into concrete form: my editors Toni Burbank and Jan Johnson, whose creative insights and editing make this book's true message shine through.

I'm also grateful for the support I received from those who work with me both objectively and subjectively in the expression of our shared vision and life's purpose.

TRANSFORMERS

Introduction

Some of you aren't fitting in too well with your usual groups anymore. And you're beginning to lose interest in what most people find quite entertaining. Your ordinary routines have become just that—too ordinary. And painfully so. And you don't know exactly what has happened; while you were looking the other way, something in you just seemed to shift. And now, you are only fascinated by one thing, really: your own experience of personal transformation, and finding others to share this journey with you. And it's not because you have the vaguest idea where this journey will lead! It's simply because this is all that preoccupies you these days. You've probably become a puzzlement to many of your old friends, and even to yourself.

You may be aware of a gnawing dissatisfaction with what you see around you, at home, at work, in your family, in the world at large. And you find that you are quietly (or not so quietly) looking for some new role or setting where you can express your truth in a more straightforward manner. You want some cause, some *feeling* to catch ahold of you and fill you with awe—to bring you a life's work with meaning and sacred purpose in which you can sound your own note. It's as though from somewhere deep inside, you've heard a wake-up call—and now you are becoming obsessed with responding to this deeper urge. So with a growing urgency you're searching out the new, expanding beyond your ordinary reference points, seeking a voice or a written word that resonates. And you cannot rest until you find it.

Well? Hello. . . . You are indeed awakening. . . . You are deepening into the human psyche, moving toward your own fulfillment and completion as a human soul. And, although you may have feared you are alone, you are not. There are others like you just waiting to greet you. You're about to realize how valuable and spiritually prepared you already are. For your time has come: You're becoming part of the conscious circle of Humanity. You are a Transformer.

Discovering the meaning and spiritual purpose of our human experiences is the reawakening, the transformation we all seek. Meaning, we discover, is another word for God. It is curative in nature, for it gives the true Self its sense of wholeness, a feeling that we are all going somewhere together that is more fulfilling and absolutely meant to be.

Just before Abraham Maslow's death he wrote that he had discovered there were two types of people who self-actualize: nontranscenders and transcenders, "those who were clearly healthy, but with little or no experience of transcendence, and those in whom transcendent experiencing was important and even crucial." The first type of person seemed "practical, realistic, mundane, capable and secular," while the other was motivated more by a unity consciousness and a sense of destiny, having had "illuminations or insights or cognitions which changed their view of the world and of themselves."[1]

Transformers fall into the "transcender" category, for they can no longer comply so easily with the ordinary routines of the mundane life as most people seem to do. Instead, they have become captivated by the inner life—a larger life—and with the transcendent qualities, aligning with the mystical viewpoint, from which saints and sages have spoken to us throughout human history.

Mystics are those who have always understood that there's more going on here than meets the eye. Transformers are people who are becoming committed to "the more." They have experienced some type of inner shift in consciousness that now is causing them to become catalysts for their own and others' move toward becoming fully themselves. Whether conscious of this fact or not, people who carry

"Transformer consciousness" are like magnets who just naturally attract others who are also changing and growing. They are guides, not because they are "experts" on other people, but because they are travelers along the same path and have become familiar with the terrain of the inner process of awakening. Meeting them is like finding a big brother or sister, someone who can validate our new longings and experiences. They stir old and familiar, yet still vague, memories. They feel like members of our real family from someplace we call "home."

Several years ago, Marilyn Ferguson reported a research study describing a certain group of people who are quietly but powerfully bringing about a social transformation.[2] These people have no titles, no organizations, no outstanding identity. Instead they are held together by a unity consciousness and a common vision. They recognize each other and need no words to communicate their coherent understanding of the new world view that is, among other things, synthesizing the left brain and the right, the science of the West with the perennial wisdom of the East.

Through a series of inner transformational experiences, they merge within themselves the practical and the mystical views of reality, transcending the dichotomy between these alleged opposites. They awaken to the value in *all* of life's experience—even our painful mistakes—and are more concerned with process and patterns than with content and specific events. She calls them "conspirators." Transformers often function this way, whatever setting they find themselves in, be it politics, religion, education, mental health, the business world, home life, or ordinary social activities.

While studying with physicist Fritjof Capra in 1983,[3] I became convinced that we are indeed undergoing the most dramatic paradigm shift in consciousness that we've experienced on this planet for ages. In Jean Houston's terms: "It is so far-reaching in its implications that one might call it evolution consciously entering into time, the evolutionary potential asserting itself. It needed a certain critical mass, a certain merging of complexity, crisis, and consciousness to awaken. Now it is happening."[4]

How We Got Here

Ever since the seventeenth-century philosophers Descartes and Newton infiltrated our thinking, Western civilization has operated under a false notion with three parts: 1. that a material world exists independently and apart from human consciousness; 2. that the human mind can know this material world "objectively"; and 3. that what we know we can, therefore, control. Humanity *against* nature (including our own human nature), rather than humanity participating in harmony with all nature, has been the result. This mechanistic, deterministic world view, based on the old physics, pervades every aspect of our lives today. We've labeled it "the American way," technology, and materialism.

Our technological advances over the past three hundred years have so dramatically improved our outer world that we have tended to accept this materialistic, concrete model of reality as the only reality. We've completely forgotten that how we inwardly experience our world truly determines how we feel and act. Our psychological states and spiritual yearnings are much closer to the "truth" about us than the comforts and discomforts of the furnishings with which we surround ourselves. One evidence of that truth is that today there is little, if any, talk of objective reality, even from scientists themselves.[5]

In the early eighties, Fritjof Capra was being described as the scientist at the "top of the pyramid" in his ability to communicate the current scientific revolution. He views the paradigm shift as a merging of East and West, a rise in the feminine principle (after two thousand years of patriarchal society), the end of the fossil fuel age, and a move away from the mechanistic world view of Descartes and Newton to "a globally interconnected world in which biological, psychological, social and environmental phenomena are all interdependent."[6]

Capra, and now many other adherents of the new physics and the emerging fields of transpersonal psychology and the healing arts,[7] feel that the current major crises in our country are all facets of the same problem: We are still stuck in the materialistic world view begun by the once relevant but now outgrown Cartesian-Newtonian assumptions; we see what is considered "normal" from the old paradigm-bound viewpoint that no longer explains reality. Our emerging scientifically explored "reality" has not only outgrown this viewpoint, it is completely inconsistent with it! When quantum/relativistic physicists began studying the basis of life in the subatomic structures, they discovered what the ancients have always known: that matter, indeed all form, simply does not exist as anything solid. Life is relationship, fluctuation, and dynamic flow. And our conscious participation in life is the vital key to our well-being as human souls.

Consciousness (denied by the Cartesian-Newtonian physics) may be the connector in life's events that creates realness, say the modern quantum/relativistic physicists. We are paradoxical creatures: not just biological machines, but also unlimited fields of consciousness, able to co-create realities and effectively impact the world we inhabit.

In the words of physicist/photographer Jane English, "Over the past 300 years changes in consciousness have lagged far behind the theoretical and technical changes. . . . Great effort was made to remove the 'contamination' of subjective experience from scientific work. Scientists lost touch with the mystical aspect of their work and instead came to value the ability to predict and control the material world."[8]

The material world does indeed exist. But it is just one half of reality, the *created* side. It is the part that has manifested in a concrete, physical form. The more subtle realms of reality, however, where our psyches reside, are the spirit of humankind, our co-creative essence. They are much more

the "determiners" of our experience than the external conditions studied by science.

Unfortunately, materialism has permeated all areas of
life in the United States, especially our scientific efforts, to
the near exclusion of the deeper, nonmaterialistic side of
truth. Human core qualities greater than our egos' intellects—self-transcendence—are downplayed or even scoffed
at by many. Yet these intrinsic qualities, according to Abraham Maslow, turn out to be the most species-like for the
human being. No other portion of the life chain carries these
traits.[9]

We can, therefore, conclude that science has not been
able to study the *root* of human nature, the characteristics
that literally make us human! Why? Because scientific meth-
odology cannot harness these nonmaterialistic qualities in an
experimental laboratory. By its own definition, science must
stick to what it can observe through the physical senses. And
by our own nature, we are spiritual beings. Our root consciousness resides beyond the scope of science's empirical
lens.

What Can Be

The two functions of our spiritual nature are the power to
create and the power to experience meaning and purpose.
These provide us with a reason to live. This is our human
consciousness, which can be defined as the illuminator of
meaning, spiritual purpose, and light upon the darkness and
neutrality of the material world and the inner psychic realms.

As we learn more and more about the basis of life from
the new model of reality emerging from the marriage of
science and spirituality, we are rediscovering that healing is
not something bestowed on us from without. Healing origi-
nates from deep within the psyche, gradually pushing its
positive, life-giving energies toward the surface of our lives
to manifest in our outer appearance as a final result.

Among other things, this paradigm shift affects the health/mental health field for both care-givers and consumers in every possible way. In the new way of thinking, the conditions of health, rather than the symptoms of disease, are stressed. Process, pattern, vision, symbolism, paradox, and the flow replace the outworn emphasis on specific events, outward form, and modification of the parts. Holistic healing, intuition, warmth, love, and a focus on spirituality replace diagnostics, labeling, testing, and prescribing.

In the words of an American doctor observing a Tibetan physician while visiting an American hospital: "I know that I, who have palpated a hundred thousand pulses, have not truly felt a single one."[10]

Only Transformers can bring about the manifestation of this new vision in health care and in all areas of our lives, for they carry a consciousness that gently, but confidently, invites others to break out of old stereotypes and risk being themselves. Transformers have undergone the personal transformation that must be experienced consciously to be understood. Reformers, who try to mold and shape others, believing they have the power and the authority to change them, cannot do this work. They are holding their own selves away from the journey into Self that teaches us the new ways. Consequently, all they can do is judge it from the outside, offering criticisms that are based on an outmoded mechanistic model of reality, other peoples' thinking which they have memorized and adhere to. Don't expect reformers to understand; they cannot get hold of it intellectually. "It" can only be experienced from within.

The mechanistic world view and reformer consciousness cannot make us healthy because they miss the point of who we are: conscious beings passing through an experiential evolutionary process, creative and fluctuating in nature, able to transcend to new levels anytime we fall into entropy. We are never victims of our past, but instead, are capable of being in charge of our own destiny. If we continue to focus obsessively on the objects in our lives, or worse, treat ourselves and each other as objects, our real lives will happen while we're looking the other way.

This means we must move away from reductionistic, analytical therapies and self-help methods to the more intuitive and synthesizing ones, drawing more on the feminine principle that is receptive, creative, expansive, inclusive, inward, and spontaneous. Movement, music, breath work, integrative body work, meditation, yoga, prayer, sacred ritual, journaling, dreamwork, the mystical and esoteric traditions, Taoism, Gestalt therapy, Sufism, Christian mysticism, the Gurdjieff system, Psychosynthesis, body/mind medicine, homeopathy, and all the transpersonal therapies fit with the new.

Approaches that label and diagnose from the viewpoint of "the professional," behavior modification, and Freudian analysis are fading away. A person's truth is to be drawn from his or her own inner Self, with guidance when needed. Therapists and teachers become guides instead of "experts" and must be able to tolerate where their clients or students are in their personal evolution, which can only happen when the ones guiding are familiar with these places within themselves. Counselor training in the coming age will emphasize inner work to elevate one's level of *being*, as opposed to memorizing and practicing labeling systems and techniques, which elevate knowledge level only.

Psychology, which has fought long and hard to become a science, with its emphasis on defining the Self materialistically, has missed the point. Viewing the Self as merely a personality (personal mask) seeking constant ego gratification, psychology fails to provide answers to the deeper questions we have about meaning and purpose in our lives. When these deeper questions continue to go unanswered, we get scared and sicken, often with an addiction of some kind.

It is paradoxical to note that Western psychologists as a group lack interest in the psyche (soul), the very unit of analysis they have professed to study (Psychology literally means the study of the soul!). They focus instead on the vehicle of the psyche, its outer covering, our personality.

Sri Aurobindo has said this most eloquently:

> *I find it difficult to take these Western psychiatrists at all seriously . . . yet perhaps one ought to, for half-knowledge is a powerful thing and can be a great obstacle to the Truth. . . . They look from down up and explain the higher lights by the lower obscurities; but the foundation of these things is above and not below. . . . The significance of the lotus is not to be found by analyzing the secrets of the mud from which it grows; its secret is to be found in the heavenly archetypes of the lotus that blooms forever in the Light above.* [11]

We are so ingrained with this philosophy of our destiny that we will have to undergo a radical change in consciousness before we can break through this veil of partial truths. Until we can comprehend the difference between personality and essence (the soul), we cannot begin to know the Self.

Opening Ourselves to What Can Be

The study of human consciousness and the process of addiction are intrinsically related. The anxieties and sometimes terrors of experiencing the expansion of our consciousness to include more and more of the unknown nearly always frighten us. And predictably, our fears will take us into the addictions, which block our awareness and temporarily provide a pseudo ease as the old gives way to ever-increasing newness. These fears, simply put, must be faced if we are to grow.

A redefinition of Self is currently being explored by theories at the growing edge of the human sciences—theories that go beyond personality (the home of the ego) into the essence of the individual. The study of essence has been relatively ignored by science because our essence is our soul.

And a scientist would say the soul belongs only to the realm of the softer, unprovable stuff of religion and metaphysics.

This essence, however, turns out to be the authentic unifying center behind our personality. It is the knowing Self, residing in a realm beyond concrete reality, which bases its choices on the essentials about us—our unique mission and purpose in life. Essence is the seat of our vision, our hope, creativity, intuition, spiritual yearnings and purpose, love, wisdom, and all the other qualities that really give our lives meaning.

Essence puts us in touch with the true powers of being human. All the human virtues lie within the realm of this amazing superconscious energy field, a place where all of humanity merges. Learning to elicit a response from this incredible knowing Self is vital in letting go of self-defeating, mechanical addictions and meaningless habits that occur on the personality level in our daily lives. Understanding essence puts us in touch with our power. *Experiencing* essence obviates neurosis and addiction. From our essence, we are able to self-create in cooperation with a Higher Power, or God.

This felt sense that we are co-creators is the first step in the act of Self-creation and gives us a strong feeling of a higher identity. We begin to have powerful thoughts, with ideas that are bigger than we are. These seed thoughts become planted in our consciousness, take root and grow, drawing to themselves everything they require to be sustained. They move us on past the little self we were before.

▲ **A seed thought is an idea whose time has come that takes hold and changes our reality.**

This book is about the process of Self-creation, which is the inner work we do that teaches us the crucial difference between personality and essence. The process leads us, step by step, to a realization of our higher Self. Our temporal, fragmented little ego selves with many faces that function as our personality—the image we show the world—fade in importance as we come to understand them. And gradually, we become essence-dominated—more unified, more constant in the midst of all our varied experiences. Even though essence is sitting there awaiting our notice, we have the responsibility of creating a realization of it: We must *recognize* it and thereby make it real. In fact, many spiritual leaders have taught that this very task is the purpose of human life. But this won't happen automatically; we have to commit to the work of manifesting essence, for it is our very being.

Transformers offers an expanded version of the addiction process and the road we travel during recovery, and on to *discovery* of the true Self that needs no addiction. This road goes beyond materialism into an understanding of the process of Self-creation. This book is written for you who are seeking a deeper understanding of the human process than you've been able to find in current settings that tend to honor only our ego and its outer, materialistic outlook. It is written to validate the emerging "Transformer consciousness" that is calling now for recognition so it can activate within your minds and hearts.

Some Assumptions to Carry Forward

The philosophy underpinning this work is based on the assumption that *controlling* our addiction and other forms of dysfunction is only a beginning. Once we enter into the exploration of essence, we find that these self-defeating habits can be transformed, and that we can proceed toward never-before-dreamed-of natural highs!

A further assumption is that each of us is evolving according to a unique plan, and everything that happens to us in life has a useful purpose, even our sufferings and mistakes. We travel in two worlds at once, the outer, materialized world and an inner, invisible one. We must understand both before any of the journey begins to make sense. Without an understanding of this inner world, our outer experiences will continue to appear meaningless and unrelated.

And a third assumption underlying this work is that humanity is now entering a new stage of evolution where the task is to shift the focus of consciousness from the outer world to the inner one, from a material existence to a more spiritual, purposeful life. Work in addiction comes to the forefront in this monumental shift, in part because addiction is an obvious, exaggerated case of outer focus, of attaching the personality—for its very life—to something residing outside the Self, often in a bottle or in the form of another person.

We are learning, often quite painfully, that the outer life does not satisfy the inner longings. This very dissatisfaction becomes the motivating force behind this inward shift of consciousness. And as we enter more into the inner world, we discover that the next step in our evolutionary process contains a very large and exciting truth that our inner state of mind determines our outer life, not the other way around.

As we begin working consciously within both the outer and the inner worlds, the first thing we discover is that the Self stands somewhere between the visible and the invisible realities, relating to one through the physical senses and to the other through inner states of being. "I" stands in the middle, attempting to align these two worlds with each other so it can feel the comfort of being whole.

The work of Self-creation frees us from the bondage of addiction. Self-creation is our inherent birthright. And for this reason, it is so compelling that it replaces the need for intense absorption in any outer thing. It turns us inside out so that our attention is shifted in a meaningful, inspired, and life-giving direction—which is what we'd hoped the addictions could provide. The human organism naturally strives toward growth, just as a flower reaches for the sun. Surely we all realize that we get off the mark easily, for the journey is fraught with pitfalls. But even though our essence can become buried under myriad false starts—roles we have been caught up in, habits that have gone on automatic, unexamined belief systems that are holding us in illusion—it refuses to be denied. And it will continue its not-so-gentle nudging until we attend to the urges it is attempting to register upon our brain.

What is crucial at this stage in our evolution is for persons who are aware they are carriers of Transformer consciousness to take the lead. Counselors, ministers, teachers, and leaders in all fields of human endeavor bent on changing, remolding, and scolding are reformers, not Transformers. They are not able to endorse another person's delicate inner natural striving to emerge. Reformers only increase the defenses and energy of self-hatred, or develop more and more of the mask that later must be transcended. And since we can never really change another, you can always tell a reformer when you meet one; he or she will be very tired and feeling unfulfilled!

Self-creation is spawned from a base of Self-love and conscious awareness. Transformers know this and do not deny any portion of our humanness as we seek the expression of our genuine Selfhood. Transformers as catalysts for Self-creation are able to accept what is and to live this is-ness to the highest possible level.

Transformers do not work merely from logic, with our external mode of thinking our way through linear time. They work mainly from a higher intellect called the intuition—a type of knowing that comprehends whole truths based on experience that has now become understood, rather than fragments of truth that have not yet become integrated into wisdom. For all wisdom comes from our own experience, never from studying someone else from afar, or from memorizing things from books. Intuitive knowing is a merging of our experience with the wisdom of understanding, a synthesis of the left brain and the right.[12]

Transformers know there is nothing new under the sun, that all truth must be rediscovered individually, as the quest that gives each of our lives meaning. We know that we don't have to evolve, but if we do choose growth, no one else can do it for us; we are Self-evolving organisms.

Somewhere I heard that truth can never really be taught, but it can be caught! This fits with my experience as a teacher. When people are ready to hear something, they hear it ringing forth loud and clear like cathedral bells on a feast day. The very same truth might have been given out the day before, but it simply passed unnoticed.

Our essence catches truth, based on a reminder of previous experiences that have now become a part of our very being. The outer self (personality), tied to the external world, only memorizes facts based on fragments of data from outer events, which often leads to erroneous interpretations of some portion of our life. But as we deepen into more recognition of the true Self who reaches us from within, all this will begin to change.

As the old analytical and building-block model of reality shudders and resists its inevitable demise, you who are Transformers will need to remember:

▲ **You are standing at the entrance of the new era—and you are its seedbearers.**

You who see the vision as it unfolds, and can accept the challenges, are the ones who are ushering in this dramatic shift where science and mysticism are coming together in a synthesis, and you will often be the target of disdain. But that's okay. You are in very good company. It has always, throughout history, been the case that when something new begins to emerge into an established and predictable reality, fear comes up to meet us everywhere. We are currently in one of those times of "abnormal science,"[13] meaning the majority are still clinging to a scientific view that does not explain reality. It is natural that your new efforts will be mistrusted at first, for there may be no familiar context for people to place them in. So until you have more company, you have to learn to hold the larger picture in your mind and stay focused on your part of the plan.

You will discover that you are in the process of your own rebirth and remembrance of what it all means, and you will feel exhilarated by this awareness. It will get painful at times, however; for anything within you that cannot be contained within the light of the new *must* be transformed. And I promise you, it will! Since personal transformation interacts with institutional transformation, it follows that some of us must undergo this dramatic "shake-up" of our consciousness in order to seed the larger shift.

I cannot say how this book will aid you in your work or in your life. As Transformers, *you* will determine its usefulness. I offer it to you as a part of myself and honor your ability to recognize truth when it is offered and to pass right over the parts that don't compute. Trust your intuition, for it is the mind of your highest Self. And the voice of your soul! So try your best not to resist your personal challenges as you step out a little more beyond your familiar ways.

So be content, for Spirit will guide you, and you'll meet other interesting travelers to keep you company along the way. It's all in the flow, and obviously, your time has come, or you would not have read this far.

A Message

While reflecting on writing *Transformers*, I asked my higher Self to tell me who this book is to reach. I then closed my eyes and waited quietly, and this image came to me:

> *An expansive blue ocean came into view. And then, from the sky a majestic, snow-white ship floated down and silently hovered just above the surface of the water. The ship was made of porcelain, brilliantly white, with an indigo blue deck. On its side were written two words: Mother Ship.*
>
> *As it came to a standstill, a rope ladder dropped over the side. It was small and unimpressive, but quite sturdy. The ladder's six rungs barely reached the surface of the water.*
>
> *Then I noticed people swimming in the ocean, hundreds of them. Most were swimming away from the ship, some playfully, some dreamily, others frantically. There were others farther away, hundreds more, it seemed, who were drowned, or drowning. Then, closer in, several were swimming toward the ship, obviously excited about its arrival and moving in its direction with enthusiasm. Three or four had actually grabbed on to the ladder and were struggling to pull themselves up by their own weight (since no rungs were underneath the water, which would have made it much easier to climb).*
>
> *I was puzzled for a minute when I realized there were only six rungs, since I wanted to write about seven levels of consciousness. But as I watched the first swimmer climb the ladder, I realized it took seven steps to get to the top and over the side. At the seventh step, the traveler disappeared onto the rich blue deck, as though entering another dimension.*

To those of you who find this particular journey meaningful . . . welcome aboard!

BOOK ONE

THE WORLD VIEW

OF THE

TRANSFORMER

A human being has
. . . the spirit of a god,
. . . the soul of a mortal,
. . . the body of an animal.
—MANLY P. HALL

We bring so much energy and enthusiasm to everything we do. But it is our own energy, our own enthusiasm, of which the supply is limited. Why not, instead, draw upon universal energy, which is limitless, allowing it to flow through us, while we remain the channels, the transformers, for this energy? Let us allow this energy to transform us as it flows through us, and through us to transform our world. Why not become Transformers of mankind, rather than self-depleting reformers who criticize and seek to correct? A Transformer creates the new through that which already is, a reformer seeks to destroy that which is in hopes that something better will take its place. The reformer's work is ceaseless, never ending, never satisfied. The work of the Transformer is always complete and perfect within itself; it is always at peace as the energy streams through it out into the world to heal, transform, energize and uplift. Allow yourself to be the Transformer—which you truly are.[1]

—ALEXIS EDWARDS

Introduction: Transformers, Who Are They?

The distinguishing characteristic of Transformers is their de-emphasis of personality. They demote it to the role of a mere instrument for the more important, synthesizing aspect of our nature we call essence, or the true Self. Transformers who are therapists are the alchemists of addiction and neuroses of all kinds, possessing an intuitive understanding of how to transmute the energy constricted in a negative habit pattern into its true nature, a pure, refined quality of the soul, "changing lead into gold."

We don't have to be therapists to be Transformers, though. We can all effect alchemical change on ourselves and on others as parents, teachers, colleagues, people in recovery, people on journeys of discovering the true Self.

Transformers, working from the highest levels of consciousness, teach us to be less identified with the personality, our little, temporal, fragmented "selves with many faces," and more centered in the awareness of this essence, or soul, moving from ego-dominance to essence-dominance. In the future, with the aid of Transformers, we will search out ways to recognize our soul's purpose, which will flood our life with meaning. We will find a language with which to describe the soul. And eventually, we will operationally define the soul. We will learn the techniques for aligning our "instrument," the personality, with our soul's purpose, so that we no longer experience an uncomfortable split between who we are and what we are doing, that familiar feeling of being "off the mark." This work of alignment is the process of Self-creation.

It is a misunderstanding to say that personality is unimportant, however. To read this into what is being written would be to miss the point entirely. It is, after all, through the development of a strong ego that we grow into our fullness as human beings, and it is the vehicle of the personality through which our essential wholeness takes form. Personality is our unique expression in the world, and when refined becomes an individuation of Spirit in action. We are, indeed, a fascinating, mind-boggling invention!

Personality is an instrument, a machine, if you will, consisting of three distinct "bodies" or realities:

1. A physical form that naturally moves and acts on instinct and on orders from our mind. This physical form has its own set of laws that govern it. For instance, it lives in time and space. And also, it has to be acted *upon*; it is not capable of independent action. (Remove my foot, and it will not walk off!) Even our human brains, which we tend to confuse with mind, cannot manufacture thought without the use of an inspirited body. We can assume, then, that our bodies are not the cause of us, for they must be acted upon in order to function. And anything that must be acted upon is an *effect*, caused by something else. This "something else" the Transformer studies is essence, the center of our being.

2. An emotional "body," operating from laws similar to hydrodynamics. If our emotions become blocked, we are like a river whose flow is dammed up, building up untold pressure until some release occurs. Or we go dead inside and stagnate, diseased and toxic to ourselves and others. Transformers know that pent-up emotions are to be released and understood so that this constricted energy can be expressed for the purpose of manifesting our authenticity in the world.

3. A mental life, our unique world of personal thoughts, that is creative by nature and has no limits except those it chooses to construct for itself. Since we exist within a universal mind that is all-knowing and limitless, we can know that

limitation is not a universal law but only exists in the individual use we make of these universal laws.

Personality exists in time and space, it senses and feels, and it thinks—creatively or destructively, for it has free will within the laws of nature that govern it. It is grounded in the material world and at the very same time can also transcend itself and expand outward—back into the past, ahead into the future—wherever it chooses to go—through the use of its mental processes. Amazing! Certainly we must value it immensely, and learn to care for it intricately.

But personality is *not* who we are. It is something we *have*.

And this distinction, Transformers believe, is the key to our evolution!

> I have *a body, but I am not my body.* I have *emotions, but I am not my emotions. And I have thoughts, but I am not my thoughts. I am something much larger and grander than all of these. I am the master of the vehicle. I am pure Essence which has taken a form in order to experience a life in time and space. I am Spirit, both visible and invisible, with individuality, unique meaning and a sacred purpose.*[2]
>
> —*ADAPTED FROM R. ASSAGIOLI*

The purpose of our life is to dis-identify from our partial or false selves and to remember our true nature. As we learn to express ourselves authentically in the world, we fulfill our part in the grand scheme of things. Unless I am my true Self, manifesting truth through me, I really do not exist. Therefore, I am here to shed—oftentimes painfully—the many "not selves" I have created in forming my personality, discovering as I go along which "parts" belong to me and which do not.

When I get stuck and think I am my body, my emotions, or my ideas, I am consumed with ego, which seeks to arrogate unto itself through one of its subvehicles all the power of my being. And my ego can drag me through some very greedy appetites and illusory places. But I must also remember that this little ego has formed over a long period of time and has built up a tremendous amount of energy. I cannot stomp it out, viciously attacking it, because a wounded ego is exceedingly dangerous and only builds itself a stronger fort from whence to get its now multiplied needs met. So I must learn to respect its power, working through its energy, and gradually withdrawing its authority until it learns to be submissive to a more integrated me, my true Self. In other words, I do not wish to kill my ego; I want to tame it and allow it to become a dutiful servant to the master self, my Soul.

In order to become conscious beings, we must die to the dominance of our ego. Christianity and other major religions recognize this truth. Alcoholics Anonymous understands it. And so do the more integrated therapies and philosophies that have taken a long look at human nature. We are talking about the process of surrender. "Lose your life so you may find it." "I have to let go and let God." "I am ready to serve only one Master." "I had to die in order to become reborn." All speak to this process.

Teachers, guides, and therapists of the new era are learning to understand this process of becoming essence-dominated. And they are doing it by choosing to become conscious themselves.

Becoming centered in essence is not merely becoming a better self; it is becoming a *different* self. The lower self has to quit guiding us before the higher Self can get through. Turning our lives over to this higher Self is not giving away our power. Quite the reverse is true: It is *reclaiming* our power, co-creating with the Power that creates all life, the energy behind creation, opting for choices based on truth and goodness.

The Transformer realizes that the process of addiction to anything outside ourselves is ego attachment. When we are addicted, we think that we cannot live without this object (including people), and we believe our ultimate security resides in adding this "thing" unto ourselves. This is false, of course. And so addiction never works. It only takes us off track, looking in the wrong direction for something that can only come from within.

Addiction can serve as our teacher, however. And Transformers realize this as well. Our addictions can lead us to a truth by allowing us to experience enough pain and disillusionment to get the point. Transformers, for this reason, do not attempt to remove pain from themselves, their clients, or people they are in relationship with too readily. For one thing, they know they can't, anyway. The person will suffer until he or she decides to seek another way. The Transformer seldom falls into the trap of being an enabler. Having suffered enough, he or she knows the nature of suffering—its secrets and its power. Transformers relieve *unnecessary* suffering, when possible, but know intuitively when someone needs the experience, negative and self-defeating as it may be.

The energy we have invested in building a strong ego becomes constricted energy as we grow and evolve toward a relaxed and broader perspective. Like an old, too-small garment, ego needs begin to feel confining. As our awareness increases, we realize the ego is designed for another purpose, to actually begin the process of destroying itself for a higher calling. Like the tough acorn that has built itself protectively around the little seed of the oak, ego lets go and becomes absorbed in the act of being essence realized, the true Self. The protective covering bursts open and expands beyond all recognition when this self-transformation process occurs.

Reformers cannot do the work of transformation. They adopt the image of some external ideal and attempt to mold, reshape, or tear us down, trying to make us into something other. Reformers work with what is *not* and usually do not recognize what *is*. Sometimes there may be a place for reforming, but it should never become *the governing principle* for the whole process. Growth occurs by our becoming more and more of who we *are*, not by our trying to be someone we are not.

Transformers work with what *is* about us, not what ought to be by someone else's standards. And by their positive acceptance of us, their total endorsement of our being, they serve as catalysts for lifting us to our highest, most integrated level. They work from above, downward. From the perspective of perfection, they weed out the *im*perfection, focusing on clearing the way for more and more of the authentic masterpiece to shine through.

Transformers look right through themselves and others, with gentle humor, and ask disconcerting questions before which facades and falsehoods crumble, questions like "Who are you?" "What are you doing here?" "Where did you come from?" and "Where are you going?" They love themselves and others freely, but are not attached to any one person's current melodrama. And above all, a fire or magnetism emanates from them, giving off a solid sense of their spiritual certainty.

When you are in the presence of a Transformer, you sense that person is who we all can be: rooted in the never-changing, learning about life from direct perception of truth rather than from others' dogma, fearing nothing and evading no responsibility he or she rightfully owns.

Transformers are tangible proof of the intangible operating in and on the world. They give us a perspective that adds dignity to our human strivings.

And they are with us now! They are growing in number, like a quiet conspiracy steadily working toward humanity's reawakening. We have been hypnotized too long, losing touch with ourselves, getting caught up in our conditions, as though these conditions are who we are. Transformers are here to remind us of our essence, the Self we were intended to be before we lost our way.

The Principles of Self-Creation

You must know the whole before you can know the part and the highest before you can truly understand the lowest. That is the promise of the greater psychology awaiting its hour before which these poor gropings will disappear and come to nothing.

—SRI AUROBINDO

The Universality of Truth

We are creative in the same way as our Maker, only to a lesser degree. Therefore, whatever is true of the whole will be true of each of us, scaled down to our individual level. Every tiny raindrop mirrors perfectly the entire scene that it reflects. Each droplet is a hologram of this immense universe. And this analogy works for people as well. Everything follows a plan based on the nature of the Creative Force. We do not live in a chaotic universe. We can count on it. And whether we like it or not, there are laws governing this creation that affect us—that, in fact, determine our existence. When we abide by these laws, we become their master and they work their magic for us. When we disregard them, we discover (often with great surprise) that our life has become a mess.

27

To be on the road to Self-creation is to discover these laws in action, and is to recognize our ignorance, which has caused the unnecessary suffering we've created in violation of natural law. As long as we are in bodies, we will experience pain. But suffering, no. For suffering is holding on to pain, not knowing how to release it. Our Creator never intended us to suffer needlessly.

▲ **All suffering is a result of infringement of universal principles.**

This idea may upset some at first glance. But if we will realize that the universe is for us and not against us, if only we get in tune with it, we may find this a message of consolation. It opens up the possibility of hope that there really is a purpose in everything.

> There is a reason, there is a rhyme.
> There is a season, there is a time.
> There is a purpose, there is a plan.
> And one day together we'll heal in
>   the wisdom and we'll understand.[1]
>
> —*BOBBY BRIDGER*

Nowhere in the process of creation is there a necessity for addiction or suffering. We were never intended to become hooked on *anything* but the process of our own creation! The antidote for any kind of suffering or addiction is Self-creation. Nothing else is necessary. Discovering the Self brings with it an understanding of the laws that create it. And our search for this universal truth of who we really are is our deepest urge.

Sri Aurobindo said, "Life does not die because it gets worn out; it dies because it has not found itself." Most addicts and miserable people are keenly aware of this constant inner discomfort; the search for that elusive something they are missing, but never quite find, is the basis for their loneliness and addictions. They are looking for their life. Few are worn out. Most of them are filled with boundless energy—so much so, they don't know what to do with it. The unhappy people are going *toward* something, not *away* from it. Not always motivated by fears from the past, the addict and/or habitual sufferer is more often searching for meaning, purpose, and self-definition! And when he or she finds this, the past, no matter how tumultuous, becomes redefined and diminishes to its proper size—simply the necessary tests to get where he or she is.

Transformers work with this *pro*active view of human beings, rather than a *re*active one. They guide people toward their unrealized potential, their proper place in life, not seeking answers from the past so much as discoveries from the future. They work with the future now.

Within this framework of living within the law, which is immutable, and with love, which is spontaneous, the Transformer needs only one definition of addiction:

▲ **Addiction = Attachment = Nongrowth**

In this chapter we will discuss the laws of the Self and the laws of the process of Self-creation that have evolved from Transformers' direct experience of working with people needing help.

If people will work with these laws, they will discover that, indeed, they are guiding lights for the dynamic work of Self-creation—in themselves and in others.

The Mind as Creator

What I see without is a reflection of what I have first seen within my own mind. I always project into the world the thoughts, feelings and attitudes which preoccupy me. I can see the world differently by changing my mind about what I want to see.[2]

—GERALD JAMPOLSKY

We live in a world that is infinitely responsive to what we make it. Without our input, the world is neutral, meaningless, a blank canvas. You and I paint the canvas according to the image in our mind, colored by our feelings. We give it its meaning. This is why two people can have exactly the same experience and respond to it so differently. We are creators! And creators *act*. We are not robots, who can only react. Unless, of course, we are operating in the world like sleepwalkers, in which case we will be robots, and we will not be creative.

All unconscious actions turn out to be robotlike reactions to life, perfectly predictable, following our program by rote. Addictions and attachments spawn predictable, mechanistic, unconscious acts, programmed from habit, founded on a stress reaction that happened in the past. At some point in our development, an inner alarm went off, warning us that something could not be handled. And in response, we turned to something predictable—a bottle of alcohol, a prescription for Valium, or some other obsession, to give us our solution. Now perhaps several years later, we've forgotten what the original danger was; we are simply unconsciously following our habit like a basset hound follows his nose.

But creators are artists. And artists create originals! When I am creating, my canvas will respond accurately to whatever I choose to put on it. And I can constantly continue to choose, moment by moment, what I want to put into my world. If I opt for a negative experience, I descend into a universe that says, "Okay, a negative experience it will be." And instantly, the negative forces surrounding this particular event become my reality. My consciousness, for this moment in time, is residing in a world that I created, where all negativity about this particular subject hangs out. Until I choose to shift out of this place, my negativity builds upon itself, attracting more just like it, and I can become overwhelmed. If I opt for a positive experience, I ascend into another universe that immediately cooperates, and instantly, forces begin moving to manifest a positive result. And as the positive gains momentum, I find myself feeling wonderful, delighted by the beautiful world about me.

On a more abstract level, this same principle holds: I also have a choice about whether to know myself or not. The work of Self-knowledge is a very high work. Socrates saw it as the three most important words in the human language: "Man, know thyself." If I choose not to know myself, perceiving my life as meaningless and turning my back on the search for truth, I begin to die. My Self does not evolve. The universe will immediately cooperate and help me die. Everything I experience will indeed lack meaning, will become deathlike. On the other hand, if I choose to know myself and am willing to struggle to find this very special kind of knowledge, I am given more help than I could have dreamed possible. Self-knowledge is suddenly everywhere I look. And my world becomes transformed. I find that I have stumbled onto the path that leads to enlightenment. My teachers appear to guide me, and I feel exhilarated and compelled to follow!

When we choose this path of Self-knowledge, we begin to discover we are in an inner state of harmony where our actions begin corresponding to a deeper truth within us. It is as though everything flows naturally and easily. Even what had seemed impossible before fades into nonexistence, and a new possibility takes its place. And we know we are on the path, our path.

When the inner and outer are disharmonious, we emit a

certain vibration that automatically reverberates in our lives, connecting up with other vibrations of the same type. This produces a general jamming, which disturbs everything in the outer life, making it all seem wrong. We know we are off our path. Or, we could be resisting something we need to grow through that is on our path and painful to look at.

Through Self-knowledge we realize our life does not unwind from the outside inward, as we had always thought, but from the inside outward. When we make this transition in our thinking, our world becomes a miracle. There is a rigorous correlation between our inner state of being and our outer circumstances. For the first time we *feel* what it is to create—even if only for a moment. This feeling is exhilarating to the Self.

When we opt for the choice of knowing ourselves, we become an individual. We leave the masses who are choosing nongrowth for the sake of safety. And we will be condemned by many. It takes a great deal of courage to become a Self. Most people are content to remain within the conforming masses. If we choose to leave the crowd, we will find ourselves beyond the clear-out bounds of society's norms, where the laws are created for the masses who do not think for themselves. When we start thinking for ourselves, developing an individuality, we become lonely, for we don't fit in anymore. We have no choice but to move into the vast wilderness beyond the boundaries of mass consciousness. Now we know *we* are co-creating our life with a Higher Power. And we are responsible for our own creations, not society, not the outer world. Now we must become fearless and sane. Our thinking has changed, and we are different.

▲ Transformation does not occur from changes in the world outside us; *we* create the miracle . . . from within!

Even so noble an act as turning our lives over to a Higher Power will be a meaningless gesture unless we connect this dynamic energy force to something within ourselves. "I surrender" is an inner act of letting go, a willed action of getting out of the way so that truth can come in. The "me" who surrenders is a little ego-dominated me who thought she had to run the show. Now the "I" who manifests my God-nature in the world, my true Self, can take over. I follow the dictates of the higher Self, who receives its power directly from the Source where all truth resides.

As my true Self emerges and takes charge, I discover this is my essence, the one I lost touch with during my process of ego development. I realize that I no longer have to be caught in the web of mechanical living, because now I have experienced a higher possibility. Using ideas that are bigger than me, my mind has become the Creator that has led me to the truth of my being. I realize my connection with the Source of all knowledge, the Higher Power. As long as I thought I needed something outside myself to be complete, my world complied with this belief and made addiction and suffering my truth. Now I know better. The Creator is not just outside me, but inside as well. This energy is a dynamic, transforming power *within me*, not just a remote God-out-there-somewhere.

And in cooperation with this high energy, I co-create my life. My act of surrender was doing my part. And *when I do my part*, based on the truth, the Higher Power co-pilots my life.

The Higher Power can reach my true Self. It will not heed the little me that was caught up in the crowd of society, for it is off the mark. There is no alignment with truth there. When I have the courage to be real, I can surrender, and then the Divine can take over. Addiction to something outside myself is no longer my truth. My addiction is gone, for it has lost its power. I am no longer allowing it to be my god.

As these new seeds of transformation take root in my

mind, to say I must control an addiction becomes an irrelevant concept. If I no longer live in a place where the addiction exists, what is to be controlled? Controlling implies pushing something away from me, conquering it, holding on. When I control, the addiction still has power over me, because I still have to concentrate on it, feeding it energy. I am saying, yes, you still matter to me greatly. You are still my master.

When the true Self takes its rightful command, addictions can be let go of, simply dropped and walked away from. I will turn and focus my attention in another direction, on another way of being, literally moving to another place. The same energy that was used in holding myself away from a powerful addiction is now freed up to be directed to its rightful place: discovering the nature of the real need the addiction was masking.

As I begin to Self-create, I realize that something very natural to my being was sitting there all along, awaiting expression, pushing to emerge. This is an important key, that this natural something was there all along, a little spark of my true Self ready to learn about itself through expression in the outer world, ready to actualize. We are never adding new qualities to ourselves if they are part of our true Self; they are merely awaiting their turn to be recognized and made real. But because I blocked the emergence of this part of my Self, out of fear, I got stuck in an addiction instead. And then I thought addiction was my truth. If I *think* it is my truth, it will *become* my truth.

▲ **When we decide to let go of the addiction, by the act of surrender to the Higher Power—an action willed by the true Self—we draw from within ourselves that quality of the true Self that the addiction was masking. Now we are ready to manifest it.**

THE ACT OF SURRENDER, A WILLED ACTION

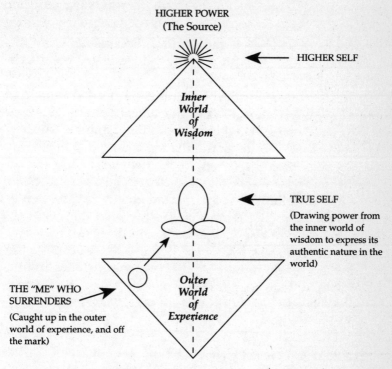

HIGHER POWER
(The Source)

HIGHER SELF

Inner World of Wisdom

TRUE SELF

(Drawing power from the inner world of wisdom to express its authentic nature in the world)

THE "ME" WHO SURRENDERS

(Caught up in the outer world of experience, and off the mark)

Outer World of Experience

What aspect of the Self was trying to emerge when life seemed so painful that I chose an addiction instead of the natural process of becoming? When was that moment? Was I afraid to think? To feel? To *be*? And if so, what? At some point it happened. And I deluded myself into believing that something out there could give me what I needed. I turned outward instead of inward and lost touch with my higher Self in the process.

When transformation occurs, the energy vector swings from the outer world (the addiction) to the inner world (the quality in me seeking expression). I discover my addiction was my teacher, designed to show me what was trying to emerge. Maybe I thought I needed pills to calm my nerves. I learn instead that I'm only nervous when I'm not myself, trying to be someone I'm not! As my true Self, I can calm my nerves by becoming centered in realistic thoughts and positive actions, a good diet, and healthy coping skills. And the more I practice these positive things, the calmer I get. I have courage. I can handle stress.

Or, as a woman, maybe I thought I needed a man to define me. So I drank to cure my loneliness and sense of rejection. I learn instead that my beautiful, feminine true Self was sitting there all along awaiting the chance just to be.

Maybe I thought I had to be defined by society as important. And so I became addicted to busyness to cover my sense of failure. I learn instead that I am inherently important, uniquely designed to do my own thing so perfectly that no one else in the world can do it like me. And society does not exist, except as I define it. Now I can see the answers are inside myself. And my strength comes from a larger source, that Higher Power of which I am a valuable, irreplaceable part. And the universe says, "Yes. It is so."

▲ **Transformation is not trying to be another way,
pushing for the answer. It is *being* the answer. Be *now*
who you want to be, even if you think you can't.**

This is the secret, the key so many have missed.

As Yoda said to Luke Skywalker: "Try, no! We do or we don't do. There is no try."

The Laws of the Self

Human beings are inherently designed to merge the "angel" and the "fallen angel" within, the primordial conflict be-

tween innocence and experience that has plagued humankind since the beginning of time. It is human nature to crave
that familiar sense of fading back into that undifferentiated
"empty fullness" of the ineffable Eternal Parent who wraps
her cloak of comforting wholeness around us in a state of
nondualistic, infinite bliss. Paradoxically, it is also our nature
to discriminate, to separate off from the masses and enter
fully into an experience of individuation, seeking our own
creative expression. To get beyond duality and avoid feeling
pulled apart by these opposing drives, we can learn to be in
both places at once—unified and unique. This skill of expanded focus requires a penetrating understanding of the
Self and its world.

Studying the meaning of the words *individuate* and *differentiate* provides a clue to the paradox: To individuate means
to exist as an indivisible whole, to be undivided. To differentiate means to divide, to be recognized as different. Some
aspects of life serve to unite us, while others divide. And
both types of expression seem to be necessary for our advancement.

Transformers, who work with the superconscious mind
as well as the subconscious, have found that it is the soul
that individuates. The soul is concerned with our process of
Self-creation, knowing we must each develop one small measure of the God-expression, yet never losing sight of our own
indivisibleness. And it is the ego that differentiates. The ego
is concerned with building something special to be noticed
and rewarded by the societal world. Within the concept of
individuation resides the reality of an enfolding/unfolding
universe, one where events are drawn up from the undifferentiated whole into explicated occurrences. When our ego
completes an event, absorbing its lesson and integrating
another fragment of itself, the event fades back into the
wholeness of life as something now completed and made
known. Once a thing has been explicated by any one of us,
the next time is easier for someone else.

OPPOSITES RESOLVE

Transformation of the psyche (individuation) involves the resolution of opposites. Emerging from a womblike state of undifferentiated potential, we first fall into the polarity of being/nonbeing, and ultimately descend into our daily existence with duality arranging itself into numerous pairs of opposites that require our eventual and essential resolution. Splits like life/death, good/evil, effective/ineffective, conformist/nonconformist, desire/desirelessness, active/passive, smart/dumb, and so on reflect this existence.

Transformers pay homage to a person's journey into Self, for they know that the experience of the human psyche is the truth that we seek. That truth does not reside out there in bookstores, in gurus, in programs of self-control, or even in spiritual paths. They also know that this experience of the Self can never be known through societal mass-produced dogmas or concepts (even these). Rules for the masses have their place in group living for the unthinking populace, but not in the transformation of the individual psyche, whose integrity is internally consistent with what is good for the whole. Transformers know from the heart that we can never mistake formula for wisdom.

In understanding the process of individuation more deeply, two thoughts prevail:

1. *Life is never static.* (Least of all the inner life!) All of us are seekers, consciously or unawakened, forging our way through the densely populated unconscious array of potential experiences, in the process of our eternal becoming.

2. *To name is not to know; to experience is to know.* Because we are ever becoming, the Transformer is leery of the "isms" and the "ics" of Western science. We must be willing to sacrifice, at any moment, our tightly held beliefs based upon theories that peg and categorize from external world views. In the words of Goethe's *Faust*: "It is wisdom's

final say that freedom and life belong to that man who must reconquer them each day." Psychology has substituted labels for knowing; the Church has substituted blind faith for knowing. Either discipline can become a societal trap for the journeying Self.

Naming from within our own process as indicators of Self-discovery can be helpful, so long as each label is viewed as not static, but emergent. For example, if my observer self (a part of my true Self) notices a pattern of behavior in me, by stepping aside and objectifying, it can free me from its control. "Oh, that's just my Mafia Mom self needing to overreact just now to feel her power with her children." Or "Southern Belle self just sent a manipulative thought through my brain to see if she could appear helpless and adorable." Getting distance from these pseudo selves frees me from their unconscious possession of my mouth, eyes, ears, and actions, and I can choose to redirect the energy.

▲ **The quality of each experience, as we draw it forth and live it, becomes the substance of our wisdom.**

Transformers deal constantly with the duality between Western psychology's need to label and pigeonhole the psyche's conditions, and the formless flowing of the more Taoist stance that life is happening in the intervals between the forms, words, and concepts. A Transformer's experience with clients and other seekers has taught him or her that the individuation process we undergo to become whole is always just beyond our conceptual grasp. Yet, there are certain axioms about the Self that have emerged from experience that we can utilize as guiding principles.

Here are some significant ones from Carl Jung's thinking as described by Stephen Hoeller.[3]

1. There is an indwelling spiritual component of the Self behind our body/mind that is an organic part of the human psyche. This Self (*pneuma*) is experienced as the urge toward wholeness, and has been left out of Western psychological thought until now with the advent of transpersonal psychology.

2. This *pneuma* carries on an active dialogue with our personality self, even though we have the free will to tune it out or distort its messages through our active, outer-directed left brain.

3. *Pneuma* has its way of speaking to us through symbols. Its signatures are everywhere in our daily lives, actively participating in our unfoldment through dreams, visions, altered states of consciousness, and synchronistic events, those acausal coincidences alive with meaning if we will but stop and take note.

4. These spiritual dispatches reveal deep patterns and conditions that can be traced both forward and backward into time as pointers to our true spiritual direction, keeping us on the mark as we travel through our conditions toward completion of our individualized purpose.

5. Prior to establishing conscious contact with *pneuma*, our lives are dictated by blind habits, beliefs, and addictions, often leading to conflict or downright foolhardiness. Unaware of its roots in the unconscious of humanity's collective history, the self blindly sets out to recreate a semblance of its wholeness through unconscious, egoistic projections and falls into the familiar trap of thinking it alone is determining its events. It errs even further in believing the unconscious or deeper aspects of human motivation are unreal imaginations or fantasies, valuing the outer life to the exclusion of the inner. Our life is perceived as caused by external circumstances, when, indeed, the causative levels remain hidden within the deeper strata of the unconscious.

6. This alienation of the ego from its deeper Self, with its companion feelings of isolation, forlornness, and homesickness, must be fully experienced before it can be trans-

formed. "Not out, but through!" becomes the psyche's wild cry as it learns it must experience its own dramatic bout with darkness, the negative side of its nature, before it can complete itself. Why? Because if we just pursue the light, we become lopsided and lacking in substance, denying the shadow of our own nature and projecting upon others what we perceive as evil. Hatred, bigotry, war, and other forms of unacceptable thought and behavior have their psychodynamic roots in this phenomenon of projection. The negativity within us, being only one side of our nature, can hold its power only by remaining in the dark. Once accepted, the compulsion to act from these incomplete dark elements within subsides and becomes balanced by each one's positive opposite quality. We return to our wholeness.

7. The goal of spiritual growth is an integrated completion of the Self, not a moralistic perfection. When completed, the Self resembles a being with qualities religion attributes to "God." Qualities such as love, wisdom, active intelligence, holiness (wholeness, health) all become manifested through us. "Ye are Gods" is not a statement of sacrilege but one of fact. This is not to say that *all* of God's work is intrapsychically expressed through us; but it does give credence to the transcendental experiences of humankind that have been noted throughout the ages.

To make the unconscious conscious is the real work of humanity, its divine dance. And if we do it in the right spirit, we will neither be caught by the implicit or the explicit, but will instead hold each with a precious acknowledgment that ensues from maintaining an attitude of expanded focus.

The process of individuation is the inherent tendency of the psyche to remain conscious and not give up its light of understanding by falling prematurely back into the undifferentiated void and dissolving into nothingness. The most important tool we have for this process of Self-creation is the controversial quality of *desire*. Throughout history there has raged a battle between the East and the West, wherein the one views desirelessness as the highest good, while the other appears caught up in a world of gratifications and achievement. When we attempt to resolve this dualism by spiritual dogma, we screech to a halt short of resolution. On the one hand we feel that desirelessness is phony; and on the other, we feel desire is evil and unavoidable.

Carl Jung provided a way to synthesize this apparent duality by defining desire as a combination of pleasure along with the urge to individuate. With this definition, desire translates into a commitment to the experience of the forces of life as-it-is, a path of consciously committed action, the path of the heart. Jung warned that if we attempt to give up desire prematurely, we can perish from "psychic pernicious anemia" and become a "psychic corpse," lacking the motivation necessary to individuate.

Transformers view descent into the earth's raw, transformative forces of vitality and tribulation as the link with heaven's mission for us. Without the two coming together in an honored juxtaposition of acceptance, we will remain unmade, irrelevant, and in a great deal of confusion.

> If you bring forth what is within you, what you bring forth will save you. If you do not bring forth what is within you, what you do not bring forth will destroy you.[4]
> —THE GOSPEL OF ST. THOMAS: LOGION 45

Now, with the Transformer's spirit, check this out with your own experience and you will know the truth.

The Law of Transcendence
(Or the Paradox of Change)

We see now that change does not occur when we try to become someone we are not, but instead when we become more of who we are. This paradox has its roots in the principle of transcendence, which says, "I can move to a higher (more loving) level only when I have accepted fully where I am now." If we try to stop ourselves from being what we are now, or pretend to be beyond some issue we've not worked through, the energy becomes supercharged into that very characteristic we are attempting to change or deny. And since more and more energy is going into the undesired aspect, we only manifest more of what we're trying to get rid of.

If I am spending a lot of my here-and-now feeling that "I've just got to quit such and such," then my vital energy is going into this particular aspect of myself I don't like, feeding it more and more. Consequently, that energy is not free to go anywhere else. Now we can see why addictions cannot be controlled (as I grit my teeth and squeeze); they must be *transformed*, freeing up this constricted energy to flow in another direction.

If we examine this principle for a moment, we realize that statements we make to ourselves or others that are designed to reform them, trying to force them to be someone they aren't, do not work. They only contribute to the problem. "You'd better quit that behavior," or "Why don't you shape up and be more like your brother?" are not helpful statements, because they are based on a violation of the natural Law of Transcendence. They are confusing. They take us farther *away* from ourselves instead of more *into* ourselves.

Transformers use statements, instead, that sound more like this: "I'm aware this pain is happening in your life. What do you think could be the lesson in this for you?" Or "What new quality in you is trying to emerge?" Or "Of course, the positive side to this is . . ." This kind of attitude accepts people where they are and helps them discover the meaning in their suffering. It is an attitude that says we are all growing, and we all get stuck in different places for different reasons, depending on where we are in our own process of growth. We do not grow at the same rate, nor do we grow evenly. I might be highly advanced in my ability to order my life, but very immature in matters concerning patience. Someone else might be patient and forgiving, while their life is in total disarray from a lack of order and precision. It is not for us to judge where someone else is growing or not growing. Life will show us, and we will all receive the "tests" that we need in order to advance.

Transformers just naturally feel it is okay for their clients, students, children, colleagues to be who they are. Transformers are willing to be there to offer assistance to those who wish to open and become free of limitations—including themselves. In other words, a Transformer is naturally nonjudgmental.

When people feel this self-acceptance transferred from their counselor or teacher to themselves, they are free to move on to the next level—more integrated, more loving. Until this "miracle of self-love" happens, they are stuck right where they are. Transformers facilitate this beautiful act of self-acceptance.

The Law of Polarity

We began in Oneness, because

> *God is human.*
> *The Creator is the Created.*

Like water and ice, which appear different but are really the same, the dualities we experience are really two phases of a single process. But once we became created, we hypnotized ourselves into seeing things according to human laws (duality), rather than according to God's laws (Oneness). So, for every negative action, emotion, or thought, there is an opposite of equal force that is positive, sitting quietly in the background, for that moment *unexpressed*. And though we divide things into positive and negative in order to experience them, these polar opposites can never really be separated or they would lose their definition.

On this level of existence we tend to see everything as polar opposites. It is somehow important to us to split things into parts so we can work out our conflicts. How can I know pride if humility does not exist? How can I ever feel powerful if I have not known feelings of powerlessness? One will be figure; the other background. And our tendency is to focus on the one that is currently figure. We still don't see the whole.

As we learn more about human growth, we discover this is natural, because we are progressing from partial truths to integrated wholes. But, in truth, all is working under the influence of One Purpose.

▲ **Conditions that seem opposed to our highest good are merely chances to test out the truth principle we are currently being exposed to in order to expand our consciousness.**

While we are caught up in a fragment of reality, it is through experiencing opposites that we learn. But once we understand the nature of the dualistic human factor, such as pride/humility, we transcend into something entirely different (say, self-acceptance). We are then living in a higher dimension, and the pride/humility split is no longer relevant for us. It no longer draws on any of our energy. Work-on-ourselves often becomes just a matter of deciding which end of the continuum we are going to pay attention to.

Ancient Buddhist psychology (Abhidharma) worked with these wholesome/unwholesome mental qualities very pragmatically. Factors leading to mental illness were seen as having an opposite wholesome side of exactly the same strength. Buddhist psychologists diagnose people by whatever negative factor they see in operation within the personality and prescribe as an antidote the positive, opposite factor. Building the positive side produces balance. The tension goes out of the negative quality.

Take greed, for example. If that's where we're stuck, we must first (often with the help of someone else) acknowledge the greedy element. We become aware of it, see it in operation, and claim it *without judgment*. Then we can move toward this opposite characteristic, which would be nonattachment (not *having* to have something) or generosity. As a person begins concentrating energy on nonattachment or generosity, greed energy lessens, the negative quality is transcended.

In addiction counseling, some of the dichotomies we work with are these:

> *compulsivity/nondoing, false viewpoint/clarity of vision, powerlessness/will, greed/nonattachment, passion/compassion, envy/impartiality, agitation/composure, depression/expression, egoism/confidence, indecisiveness/direction, delusion/insight, extravagance/simplicity.*

Delusion and insight cannot reside in the same space. Once clarity of vision is gained, false viewing is impossible. When impartiality (loving things equally) becomes your reality, envy is no longer an issue. Can you see how this works? Polar opposites are transcended to their original source, the point of Oneness from whence they came.

It will seem to us that we no longer contain energy in the particular "split" we felt about a certain thing. We will just *be* whatever it is we are when this split is no longer a reality. I won't have to *try* to be insightful, I just *am* insightful. I don't have to force myself to make decisions, I am a confident decision-maker, with a sense of direction in my life. No energy is expended battling this particular dualistic concept. Once we have risen above a certain difficulty in our nature, the polarity is no longer experienced, and we are functioning at a higher level of integration.

OUR TWO NATURES

And the polarity continues outward, pervading our very sense of selfhood:

With the intuition comes a special joy . . . a sort of recognition, as though we were always two, a brother of the light who lives in the light and a brother of shadows, ourself, who lives down below and repeats gropingly, in the shadow, knocking himself about everywhere, the gestures of the brother of the light, the movement, the knowledge, the great adventure of the brother of light, but it is all paltry down below, scraggy, clumsy; then suddenly there is a coincidence . . . we are one. We are one in a point of light. For once there is no difference and this is joy. And when we shall be one at all points, this will be the Life Divine.

—SATPREM

We feel drawn in both directions, by a lower nature and a higher one, toward an outer world of experience and an inner world of wisdom. Sometimes we are in one, sometimes the other, as though we are indeed living in two worlds, as two distinctly different natures. And then those rare moments occur when the outside matches the inside, when it all comes together and we feel whole.

So, who am I? Which nature actually represents my true Self? In seeking my identity, what do I look for? And how is my outside world supposed to fit with my inner sense of things? We are, indeed, a developing self, seeking integration of the two worlds, the outer and the inner, as though the Self is sitting in between the two, attempting to align the input from each reality. We are a mixture of the energies from the lower nature and the higher one. The lower nature pulls us into the worldly life, while the higher nature urges us toward attainment of our highest, most integrated human qualities, such as truth, goodness, and beauty.

In the outer world, the personality experiences events designed to teach it how to live life consciously. In the inner world we experience states of being, or psychological, mental, and spiritual space. Here we attribute meaning to our outer experience, and this leads to wisdom.

In studying ourselves in depth, we discover that, in truth, we are indeed one unified Self, but unfortunately, we do not often experience this unity. In the outer world of experience we actually function as many little partial selves, reacting this way and that to our environment. Sometimes these partial selves are even in conflict with one another. My perfectionist self pulls me toward order and duty; my spontaneous self urges me to flow this way and that. Or, my quiet, meditative self nudges me toward inaction, while my frantic self drives me out of the house charging off in all directions. Without Self-knowledge, we are victims of these little selves, pulling us here and there, reacting to whatever comes into view. With Self-knowledge, we find we are on a path of discovery.

We can formulate our life based on the truth of our experience. And this leads to integration. Or, if we fail to learn the truth from our experience, by computing our findings on a falsehood, we move, instead, toward disintegration. Or we stagnate. The most common way we misperceive our experience is by giving away our power to another who tells us how it *ought* to be. Until we reach a point in our development where we can observe what we are doing *as we are doing it*, we are hopelessly spinning around in a world we do not understand, repeating the same old patterns and tapes over and over again. This is nongrowth (or neurosis). And when this becomes too painful, we often opt for an addiction. We clutch at something "out there" to make us feel better.

This battle between truth and untruth, the higher nature and the lower, is life's game. It is the work of becoming conscious. It's a rough game, especially when we don't know the rules. So learning about ourselves and our life, and the connection we have with universal truth, is a life and death matter for all of us. And this matter of identity, this question of which me is in charge, turns out to be the cornerstone to Self-creation.

Fortunately, we have a helper within us for this process of becoming conscious. There is an umpire for the game of life, a self who can be impartial and point out what's happening in the process, to enable us to get a hold of it. It is an observing self, who gives us the option of acting rather than reacting. It is a portion of our true Self that is centered in reality, for it is our soul's agent in time and space. The soul, living in the transpersonal dimension, cannot enjoy itself without some way to experience events. Consequently, it projects down into life the observer self so that it can creatively manifest, in the image of its Maker, Spirit. Without an observer, there can be no *experienced* experience.

Observer self is here to point out the truth (soul level) of each situation we encounter, talking in soul language, doing its job of culling out the soul events, or the significant reality, of each situation we participate in. If we wish to evolve, we must listen to our observer self. It will keep us on our true course.

This aspect of the true Self is not caught up in melodramas and predicaments. It can see right through them and can choose to act consciously in any given situation. Our true Self is designed to actualize our perfection in the world. In order to transform addictions, we must learn to differentiate between the true Self and the little partial selves that are running around reacting to everything. The true Self draws its energy from the superconscious mind, the inner world of wisdom, our blueprint and our future. The little partial selves draw their energies from the subconscious mind, our past programming based on illusion and fear. We will learn more about these superconscious and subconscious energies later on.

It will be helpful at this point to refer to Appendix 2, "A Model of Human Nature," page 284. You will see here a model of the selves and how each one does its work in evolving our nature out of chaos toward integration.

The partial selves are the representatives of our lower nature. They are determined solely by a process of external cues and responses to life, like little robots. When one of these little selves takes over our organism and masquerades as the true Self, we are stuck in mechanical reactions and don't evolve, as there is nothing about these responses that helps develop individuality. They are merely carbon copies of pieces of many other people responding to the same cues in like manner in a particular set of cultural norms. "Aunt Sally always did it this way. That's why I do it." They operate solely in the outer world of experience, without understanding. They are concerned with getting their needs met, drawing from the subconscious, which is governed by the ego. When our needs are being met at any given moment, we feel contentment. But only until some other unmet need stirs, and then we feel dissatisfied again.

These little partial selves are my lower self (a term I will use for convenience from now on to identify a partial self caught up in the outer world of experience). And here is what I'm like when my lower self takes over: I get up in the morning and the sun is shining, so I feel good. Or, it is gloomy and dark outside, so I feel bad. I go in to cook breakfast and discover we are out of eggs, so I feel bad. I wanted eggs! Then, in searching around, I discover some muffins my daughter has made, so I feel good. Then my little boy comes in and says, "Mother, I'm mad at you 'cause you won't let me have company tonight." So I feel guilty and bad. Next, my older son comes in, kisses me on the cheek and says, "Hi, Mom, I love you." So I feel good. I think about my day and nothing excites me, so I feel bad. Then the phone rings, and it's a friend inviting me to lunch, so I feel good. I walk in and sit down at my desk and notice the huge utility bill for the previous month, and I feel depressed. Then I rebalance my checkbook, and I discover I have more money than I thought I had, so I feel a lift. And on and on throughout my day.

And where, pray tell, am *I* in all this? *Who* am I? I am merely going through my day responding to whatever my outside world happens to drop in my lap. This is the robot me, my lower self, fragmented, filled with conflicting needs and preferences, living according to unexamined rules and dictates of societal structure, in a world I do not yet comprehend. And since my society is based on contradictions, I have many of these little selves, part of me here, part of me there, one who can love being a certain way to please so and so, and another who can be its very opposite, to please such and such. At this level, I am being tugged apart. And that hurts.

It is this sort of pain that finally leads us to a higher level of functioning where Self-knowledge begins to seep in, because, quite frankly, we just get worn out. As I grow and learn, and begin to seek this knowledge of myself and my world, I discover I have another possibility, another me who can think for herself and escape the tortuous world of contradictions, who can rise above it. This is my true Self who can direct my life creatively, gaining its perspective from its observing function, which stepped aside for a while to get an objective picture of my reality. My true Self is becoming conscious! She is residing in the battleground between my two conflicting natures, my ego and my soul.

And my true Self does get knocked out of the driver's seat from time to time, especially when my self-esteem is low, or I've experienced something painful and debilitating. She really has a hard time being heard sometimes, because she is often so utterly covered up by the web of externals and the noise of my lower self, babbling on ad infinitum.

But the true Self has an advantage: She is the expression of my soul! She is the integration of the knowledge and experience, both inner and outer, I've assimilated, equilibrated, and *completely* understood. She is a reflection of my pure beingness. Without her, my higher Self would have no vehicle for expression in the world, no concrete form. Its energy would exist only in a world beyond the physical plane, where experience is an irrelevant concept.

> *I am from everlasting the seed of eternal life. I am the intelligence of the intelligent. I am the beauty of the beautiful. . . .*
> —THE BHAGAVAD GITA

I'M NOT IN THIS ALONE

When I am operating from the true Self, I am the me that is unique, the one who has her own natural thoughts, feelings, and ideas that come from being absolutely in touch with my own individuality. *No one else is exactly this, only me!* This is the me that is eternal, because this me is truth. I am the intelligence of the intelligent and the beauty of the beautiful, the authentic actions of truth, eternally. But eternal life does not come about by chance, nor does it happen without tremendous effort. The eternal Self has to be nurtured into existence. In other words, if I don't do me, I don't get done. Self-creation is our human destiny, really, the only purpose in life. We are here to recognize and realize our God-nature. This is the earth experience. But we operate within a law of free will. We do not have to evolve. We can choose inaction, nongrowth, ignorance, death, addiction. We have the right, you know, for we are not, after all, puppets!

For those who choose to grow, however, we discover we are not alone. We are all here to assist each other in this incredible work of Self-creation; even those who choose not to evolve are often our teachers.

▲ **No one comes onto my pathway by accident.**

We come and go into each other's lives for a purpose. And the purpose is to point the way toward truth. Consciously experiencing untruth can even lead to truth!

We cannot always know what another's mission is, or where others are on their path; we do not have total understanding. But we can trust the process. We can become conscious of causes and effects operating in our lives. We can begin to help ourselves and each other discover these patterns and consequences that occur by the choices or nonchoices we make. These causes, effects, talents, likes, dislikes, yearnings, aversions—all of it—lead us to Self-knowledge, to Self-creation. We are here as guides, students, teachers, and companions for each other. Someone once said that truth is God communicating with Himself. When I have the courage to allow my true Self to emerge, I am performing the work that is uniquely mine, *being my Self*.

As we learn to observe the Law of Polarity operating in our lives, we begin to recognize an important fact: Our robot selves are also valuable little instruments for our advancement, working to produce order and comfort for us. It is good to keep these little selves well oiled and polished, in excellent working order, because they are our way of connecting with our environment.

The lower self has a sacred function: to remind us of our needs and warn us when we're overstepping our boundaries. It also cleans up the house, puts gas in the car, and fills the empty pantry. But it is *not* who we are! And it *will* meet our needs at whatever cost. So we must allow the real Self to guide these little selves, not the other way around. The lower self is ruled by ego. The true Self observes fairly and chooses actions based on truth. The higher Self is the whole, the archetype, while the lower self is the fragments.

Higher Self urges us toward our completion. For this transpersonal Self, manifested as the true Self, "It is the future which draws, not the past which pushes," says Sri Aurobindo. It takes the experiences from our past as grist for

the mill, and applies meaning and purpose, love and understanding to these experiences, incorporates this meaning,
and moves forward toward completion. It *never* hangs on to
the past.

The true Self feels irresistibly drawn by its own destiny-
in-the-making. It possesses the courage to act instead of
react, even though it may be against popular opinion at
times. It delights in authentic expression, realizing its creative powers as a portion of the larger energy source that
powers all of creation, the energy some call cosmic consciousness and some call God. Self-creation is a microcosmic action
within the gigantic process of all creation. When we are Self-
creating, we are aligned with the Higher Power.

Beyond Polarity

In studying self-actualizing people, Abraham Maslow
found that healthy people transcend dichotomies. They get
beyond a world view that sees everything in opposites. Work
and play merge; the most sexual person becomes the most
spiritual, the most innocent, childlike person becomes the
most mature, etc. No longer are they consumed with the
conflict that expresses itself as either/or. Back in behind it all,
they are in touch with their source, or root-consciousness,
the higher Self, not of this world at all, motivating us from a
place beyond the personal. This is truly our permanence, the
Original Cause of our being, the One who is with us always.

Even though our selves-in-the-world disappear when we
sleep, meditate, are in a coma or a faint, this higher Self is
always present to bring us back again to whatever reality we
need to be in. From another dimension, it reaches down,
making itself felt in our life. This Self is above our experiencing, and unaffected by it. It is not bothered by physical
ailments, emotional swayings, or the busy flow of our mental
life.

The true Self is the higher Self's "projection" in the field of personality. It is our synthesizing center. When we are centered, we are a pure reflection of this wondrous transpersonal Self, like a perfectly calm lake with no ripples.

> *Weapons cannot hurt the Self and fire can never burn him. Untouched is he by drenching waters, untouched is he by parching winds. Beyond the power of sword and fire, beyond the power of waters and winds, the Self is everlasting . . . never changing . . . ever One.* Know that he is, *and cease from sorrow.*
>
> —THE BHAGAVAD GITA

The Law of Love
(Expansion or Contraction)

And now, the most important law of all, for it is the law of God:

> *You live that you may learn to love. You love that you may learn to live. No other lesson is required of Man.*[5]
>
> —MIRDAD

"All is love, and all is law" is another paradoxical ancient maxim. Love is Spirit expressing itself; law (truth) is the *way* love is expressed. Love is spontaneous, ruled by the law of free will: We can give it or withhold it, it's up to us. The laws of the universe are set and immutable. But only the spontaneous expression of these laws, the *decision* to express them, can bring them into practical use in our everyday lives. Once we understand this, the laws become ours to express, lovingly. Infinite Spirit (love) expresses through immutable law. Love is spontaneous; law is impersonal. This resolves the paradox about life's seeming to be made up of spontaneous actions on the one hand, but controlled and fixed on the other. Both statements are true.

▲ **Love points the way for us to express our human
nature; law makes these ways possible.**

But what *is* love? I cannot think of a word more often
misused or misunderstood than the word *love*. Everything
from simple preferences to grand acts of passion become
subsumed under its heading, when, in fact, love is not even
a subject/object matter. Love is a state of being. Love is not a
virtue, but a necessity—more essential than food, light, or
air. For until we are love, we do not possess a Self. All love
begins with love of Self, because the Self is God, and God is
love. There is nothing but love; but we have not discovered
that yet. We are still bothered by love, pained by it. And as
long as this is the case, we haven't found love, for we have
not found our Self. In loving anyone, or anything, we are
truly loving our Self. When we cannot love a person or a
thing, we are not loving a part of our Self. Total Self-love is
universal love, love of all, love *for* all . . . where nothing is
deprived of our lovingness.

Love clears the perception so that truth can be seen.
Some have said that love is blind, because it can see no fault
in its beloved. Would we could always be that loving. For
that is truth: There *is* no fault in our beloved! Whatever fault
we find in another is always just a fault of our own. We are
meant to love all that is earthy, because all of the earth is in
us. And we are to love heaven, too, because all of heaven is
in us.

"Love is the only dimension that ever needs changing," writes Thaddeus Golas.[6] At any moment I have a gauge
that tells me whether or not I am loving and to what degree.
This knowledge is contained in my physical body. Contraction is the move I make toward unlove. Expansion, like space,
is total openness, total love. Whenever I am in a state of
expansion, I am permeable. I do not resist anything; there-

fore, I am able to flow absolutely, and everything and everyone can become a part of me and I a part of them. Contraction is fear. It is addiction. It is insecurity, anger, paranoia. I know when I feel it because it makes me very tired. Holding in like that is exhausting, especially when I feel it is crucial to do so.

Working on loving is a nice kind of work. It means as I go down the street, walk into a room, sit at my desk, whatever, I can ask myself: How much am I loving right now? Why am I loving so much? What is making it possible for me to feel this way? Or, uh oh, I'm feeling contracted and unloving. I really cannot stand her! I wish she would go away! What's going on now? How am I stopping myself from being able to love this particular person at this particular moment? My work-on-myself becomes an exercise in awareness about the continuum of love, *my* continuum of love.

When I am loving, I love everything, and when I am unloving, I cannot love anything or anyone. This is how it works. *Love needs no subjects or objects.* Learning to love means learning to tap into that part of me that loves and can invite others into that space with me. Unlove means I leave others outside, and I am therefore isolated. Love is our natural state of being; unlove is an unnatural state.

What are the conditions that make love easy, and what are the conditions that seem to make it impossible? No matter what, it's okay. That is where you are just now. So try to love yourself as much as you can from whatever state you find yourself in at the time. This is the beginning of love. Love yourself as much as you can.

This is always where you are to start—*exactly where you are!* This is total honesty, the truth, the only way you can be fully present and centered in the here and now. And you *must* begin with yourself. Why? Because you will only be able to love others to the extent that you can love yourself; there is no boundary line between you and others. In love, we are all one. In unlove, we are all separate. Love yourself as much as you can, and you will see that you are loving others as much as you can. And love takes in everything else, even unlove. So, pretty soon you are loving even the unloving.

But learning to love is very difficult, because of all the obstacles we've constructed within our personality that get in its way. And in order to become loving, everything within our personality structure that is incompatible with love must be transformed. Because love and unlove cannot share the same space. This is the work-on-ourselves that takes a lifetime. And we never arrive, for we are always just beginning. There isn't even any place to go. It's all in the journey. Here it is—right now.

Summary

So here are the three major principles of Self-creation—Transcendence, Polarity, and Love, or complete acceptance of what is.

Whether you find yourself a seeker of help or one who is sought out by another, I hope the knowledge of these laws will help you. Because it is all the same dance. It is merely a question of whether you are leading or following at any given moment. The truth is, all of us, all of the time, are doing both. I conceptualize it as a human chain: There you are, leading others you're a little ahead of and being drawn by some who are ahead of you. This is the human chain of love, which we become a part of as we begin following our true path, the way of Self-creation.

And now the ancient saying, "When the student is ready, the teacher appears," becomes a thundering reality to you. You will discover that everything and everyone on your path is a potential teacher, and always has been (if we had been awake to see it). But we can wake up now. It is never too late; we are always just beginning.

The Transformer facilitates this transformation from reaction to action, from being tossed about by the "winds of fate" to living a life of meaning and direction. We help others feel their *own* potency (not ours) and discover their *own* unique purpose in life (not our idea of it).

When modern psychology began to study healthy people, much that had gone unnoticed about human nature came to light. One of the biggest discoveries has been that when people become passive, unhealth tends to feed upon itself. Creative energy, originating from the higher Self, tends to be self-renewing, producing its own chain of growth-producing events and patterns in a person's life. In the neurotic (or unhealthy) person, this creativity is perverted. Energy goes into self-protective or self-defeating directions; or is stymied altogether, handling inner fears and imaginings; or attempts to assuage a passion or a desire. And we don't notice these behaviors because they are unconscious, therefore not available for critical analysis or reality-testing. Unless this perverted trend is reversed and a feeling of potency and intentionality awakens our creativity, a chain reaction of powerlessness, self-hatred, and passivity sets in. This description of how unhealth develops is the story of addiction.

▲ **We can recognize an addiction by its lack of life-giving qualities. It drains us of our prime energy, the energy to Self-create.**

Addiction, therefore, becomes the block to Self-creation, because it is passivity. It keeps us stuck in the past, going over and over the same old tape, even though it does not work. The key to growth, then, lies in reversing this passivity, this nongrowth choice, into *intentionality* toward a creative act that utilizes one's creative energy pool to move toward something chosen and healthy. Like a muscle that atrophies when not used, creative energy goes slack and needs a big push to get back in shape if it hasn't been used for a while.

Addiction, then, can be viewed as the inverted form of our natural human creativity.[7] The evolutionary drive toward health inherent in humans cannot be ignored or violated, as it is our core human quality. So, in that sense, it is undeniable. Illuminating our individual way of truth is the purpose of the higher Self; *following* the way, is the work of the true Self, operating in the world of outer experience.

And now Aurobindo's statement, "Life does not die because it gets worn out; it dies because it has not found itself," can be more fully realized. To be true people-healers, we become Transformers, drawing people forth toward our and their potential reality. We carry the vision of a life lived in active freedom, that fascinating, courageous, so-very-human act of Self-creation, the *real* turn-on most addicts will die for, or without.

2

Becoming:
A Description of the Lower Self

Of all the fables in the world, we ourselves are the most fantastic.

—MANLY P. HALL

This multileveled human being in the process of Self-evolution is indeed a complex creation! It is no wonder we stay so confused. Especially since most of us believe we are acting as one unified Self! Until we can understand "our many selves" and the manner in which they function in the world, we are like a person standing on a plank while trying to lift it: We cannot get any distance from ourselves in order to see what's happening.

Consciously choosing to enter into the process of becoming *is* our evolutionary task—our deepest existential urge. And this urge translates into our felt experience as tension. We are painfully aware of the gap between what we are now and what we know we can be. And we know no one can evolve for us! We must do it ourselves, and we fear that we cannot.

So let's take a deeper look now at what actually happens to the Self as we proceed through the outer world of experience—life—toward integration of the personality, the cornerstone of Self-creation.

61

By our very nature, we are a mixture of the many aspects of the Self, each with its own way of assisting us toward Self-creation. We are here to express ourselves in the world *where we live*. We have been given a concrete, actual form of expression (our bodies) that need not be denied. Remember the Law of Transcendence: We don't get to "heaven" by trying to be something we are not, but by accepting *fully* who we are.

Our materialized personality is our instrument for bringing the higher energies into direct manifestation in the world of relationship, without which we would be formless and ineffective, like a puff of wind with no substance. Even if I am experiencing pain, I am learning to understand it more completely. And as I do, a great wave of love and appreciation sweeps over me. I realize for even a moment the absolute beauty and perfection of this physical being in which I am encased.

And further, I realize that my ego is a very loyal friend. Its sole desire is to take care of me. But now that I understand the nature of my selves—the partial ones, my true Self, and a Higher Power—I see that my ego must be guided from energies higher than my personal reality. For unchecked, we know it is liable to do *anything* to get our needs met, including self-defeating, neurotic, or addictive behaviors.

▼ **In personality we are many; in essence we are One.**

When in doubt about what my ego is doing to/for me, I can always go higher and within, to that place of wholeness that knows truth. The ego gets caught in fragments of my reality, seeing the particular portion it is caught up in as the whole truth. Consequently, my ego can deceive me greatly about my total reality. For example, my daughter may get angry with me and move out of the house. I might interpret this action through the lens of hurt feelings and conclude that she doesn't love me anymore. When seen from a more comprehensive level of reality, in the entire context within which this event occurred, it becomes apparent that she needed this anger to gain the momentum to break her dependency on a mother she was too identified with. In order to achieve the natural developmental task of individuation, she utilized anger for a higher purpose. The experience of an angry interchange was a temporary state, a fragment of reality. The process of individuation was the truth. If we become identified with the anger, we might sever a relationship. If we remain steady and identify with the truth, the relationship flows on gracefully to the next stage.

Ego, the master of my personality's needs in the outer world, operates along three planes of reality: a physical/instinctual plane, a sensual/emotional plane, and a mental plane. Principles operate at each level that determine its natural course.

The first level is the physical/instinctual, where we learn *order*. When we order our lives, we learn right action, which produces confidence and self-mastery.

The second level of consciousness is sensual/emotional in tone, where we learn about *pleasure* and *devotion*. It is "the place" where we learn to connect with feeling in relationship with others. Here, we learn right feeling.

The third level is a mental environment, where we learn through *comparison/analysis* how to study about Life and the Self in relation to life. Here is the training ground for right thinking.

▼ When the natural drive at each level of consciousness
is allowed to express itself, we move gracefully and
with ease toward personality integration. If these
natural urges are thwarted, stagnation or disease
sets in.

The three types of energy converge upon each other, building in a hierarchical manner so that each greatly affects the other two. This evolutionary process is how the personality structure becomes human. Without its monarch, the mind, which develops at level three, this hierarchical construct has passions, but no reason; emotion but no intellect; desires but no will. In other words, this lower self can act as a dangerous animal if not constrained by a responsible intellect capable of recalling the past and being cognizant of a future.

This personality construction is best expressed by a triangle—the only pattern where three lines converge.

LOWER SELF
(POTENTIALLY, THE VEHICLE FOR THE TRUE SELF)

As we evolve, our physical/instinctual and sensual/emotional experiences form our mental life, so that these become a hierarchy from the densest to the most spacious (unformed) types of energy.

MOTIVATING FORCES OF THE LOWER SELF

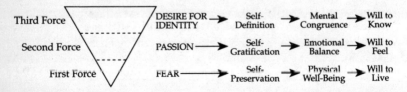

While in the stages of personality development, from birth to maturity, we operate in the lower self. We are dependent on the world outside to define us and give us what we need to survive. Consequently, the outer world of experience is, at first, our only perceived reality.

As we evolve toward integration, we move through three distinct levels of consciousness, each functioning as a total universe for the spiritual developmental task we are to complete at each level.

▼

FIRST FORCE:

The Will to Live

(The Fear Response)

COGNITION: **Self-Preservation**
QUALITY: **Order (Physical/Instinctual)**
BASIC URGE: **Fear**
PITFALL: **Isolation**
INTEGRATION: **Right Action**

This is the primal energy force with which we begin life, our most basic need. The little baby comes into the world completely dependent upon its environment for its very life. Its first task is to discover that it is safe to be here. And from this secure feeling emerges our first solid affirmation: the will to live. As it reaches for its mother, the child is given what it needs. And its needs are quite simple at this point: nourishment, nurturance, and comfort. It has the capacity to draw all this from only one source: mother. Utterly basic.

So basic, in fact, that if gratified long enough for trust to develop, the little person tires of this simplicity and healthily expands to another level of consciousness. Now it knows it is safe and has therefore laid the foundation for choosing to live. The child will now move with confidence toward the larger world of sensual and emotional experiences.

All our lives we will experience first force as a physical way of functioning. Being identified with our physical nature teaches us to listen to our own body. Our body is our little animal. And, as with a cherished pet, we must treat it well, nurture it, feed it properly, and make certain its needs are met. For, without a clean and healthy body, we cannot do the arduous task of Self-creation that occurs throughout personal evolution. We could not bear the strain. Consequently, we must develop the sensitivity to recognize our body's true needs, while at the same time maintaining a certain amount of discipline in life so that the true Self remains the master of the body's appetites.

SECOND FORCE:
The Will to Feel
(The Passion Response)

COGNITION: Self-Gratification

QUALITY: Pleasure/Devotion
(Sensual/Emotional)

BASIC URGE: Passion

PITFALL: Duality

INTEGRATION: Right Feeling

The child is now ready to learn about pleasure and pain, excitement and boredom, passion and contentment. Now there is a whole spectrum of emotional life to explore and assimilate. As the youngster begins to separate itself from others, it enters the world of opposites, moving toward what is pleasurable and seeking in a healthy fashion to avoid pain. Now the child can function in the outer world—life—and if this urge toward gratification of the senses is allowed expression in a realistic and positive manner, it becomes the will to feel, preparing it for a normal and lively adolescence.

The person will have learned to trust the messages of his or her sensual nature. If uninterrupted by ignorant and neurotic others, the person absorbs each experience on its own merit, correctly interpreting what life is teaching as truth. The person then moves toward more healthy development—liking pleasure, disliking pain—and becomes confident in knowing how to get needs met appropriately. He or she knows how to live in the now, unencumbered by weighty fears from the past or anxiety about the future.

But we must remember that second force is our emotional body and thrives on passion or any kind of feeling state. Suffering interests it as much as joy. *Force* and *intensity* of feeling are what it seeks. Its *nature* is to feel. It likes for you to be angry, to get your feelings hurt, to lust and be greedy, as much as it likes ecstasy and excitement. It is truly as interested in hatred as it is in love. It likes violence. It is the self that is curiously fascinated by spilled blood and guts at the scene of a horrendous accident or in a horror film. And it seeks constant change. It is naturally restless. Consequently, we must learn very early in life to become the master, not the servant, of our emotional nature.

▼

THIRD FORCE:

The Will to Know

(The Identity-Seeking Response)

COGNITION: **Self-Definition**

QUALITY: **Analysis/Comparison (Concrete Mind)**

BASIC URGE: **Identity-Seeking**

PITFALL: **Fragmentation**

INTEGRATION: **Right Thought**

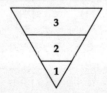

At this stage of development we are fully in our adolescence, figuratively speaking, and preparing for the responsibilities of adulthood. We are now becoming identified with our mental life, having completed much of our emotional development. At the forefront of our emerging consciousness, ideas about who we are come into focus. We are seeking a realistic, satisfactory concept of ourselves. Here is where we begin adopting roles and attitudes we feel good about or drawn to. Conversely, we seek to avoid roles or self-images that would make us feel bad. This is the level where our values are formulated, based on what we've learned experientially through pleasure, pain, and comparison and analysis as we've lived our personal lives.

We have learned to live in certain ways that feel right to us. When something does not feel right, we experience guilt, shame, or some other discomfort. We are preoccupied at this level of consciousness with how others see us. By now we are quite formed from the learning we have acquired outside ourselves. We want our inner sense of identity to be congruent with how others see us.

If my natural growth is uninterrupted, I will confidently operate from attitudes and roles based on values that I trust and believe in. I think of myself as a good girl, a pleasant person, a peacemaker, attractive, a good student, a leader, a good Christian, a hard worker, loyal, practical, or whatever other images I hold that fit my ideal. If, for some reason, I try on a role that violates my self-image, I immediately feel discomfort and seek to remedy the situation, either inwardly (by changing my values to fit the role) or outwardly (by changing my role).

This level of consciousness provides us the training ground for self-definition. It is where our personality learns to express our true Self in the world—how to discriminate between roles that really fit us and those that do not. If I make it through this level naturally, I develop the will to know. A curiosity is spawned concerning the deeper levels of truth about life and the Self. Because this is a mental level of functioning, unbounded by concrete reality, it becomes the point of entry to an expanded way of being in the world that enables the creative imagination to work and transcendence to become a possibility. If we continue to evolve beyond this point, from learning to discriminate well between fragments of truth and comprehensive truth, we will take a leap in consciousness.

But here again is a warning: If we become addicted to our intellect, fully convinced that our *ideas* are reality, we will be stuck at the mental level of functioning and fall prey to a mind that loves to keep us set apart. We will be caught up in the desire for status.

At the third level our intellect calculates purely for the ego, even on spiritual quests and in meditation. We need to remember that we have our little mind to use as an instrument, but we are *not* this mind. We are larger and grander than this wee intellect can ever fathom. It is up to us to learn to discriminate between the countless things our little ego mind wants, versus the one big thing our higher Self wants for us, which is the expression and fulfillment of our own true and unique purpose.

The Development of Personality: A Summary Statement

So now we have built our vehicle, the self designed to function in the daily world of outward involvement with people and things. I have described how this process unfolds and the forces that move us when there is a minimum of distortion or interruption. And I have also touched on how we can become so caught up in the outside world that we lose our sense of Selfhood, in which case the lower self takes over and masquerades as the true Self.

The most important message I would like to express about this development of the personality is this: Each stage we have described so far is *necessary* and intrinsically *good*. We cannot move to the higher levels of human functioning if we do not develop first an integrated personality, composed of three essential characteristics: physical well-being, balanced emotions, mental clarity. Essence is dependent upon personality for its expression in the world. Paradoxically, the higher must attach itself to the lower for its very existence.

I heard a story one time about a farmer who was busily tilling a rich plot of soil when a stranger appeared and expressed amazement at the beauty of the farmer's land. "This is truly God's country!" exclaimed the stranger in his praise. To which the farmer curtly replied, "Well! You should have seen what a mess it was when God had it all by himself!"

The lower, the earthy, must do its work properly. We all know what happens to people with sick bodies or emotional and mental illnesses. They are preoccupied with their disturbances, their lives a wreck. Physical illness keeps us stuck in a physical level of consciousness, preoccupied with our symptoms. Emotional imbalance leads to chaos or a mental institution. And lack of mental congruence causes one to be confused and ineffective in life.

▼ **The ego will continually draw us backward, toward the level where the unmet need exists, until the need is met.**

In other words, the energy the person requires for Self-creation is constricted and focused in the lower self, which always looks to the *outer world* for its solutions.

We all know from our own experience that it is impossible to make it through these three stages perfectly. So the act of Self-creation need not be dependent upon *perfection* of the personality. If this were the case, none of us could ever do it. Each of us, in our own life story, has received from our personal environment a particular set of neurotic situations and painful relationships we've been required to deal with.

Most of our parents, God bless their souls, have pockets of complete mental delusion they draw from in forming standards that do not fit with human nature, or crippling experiences of their own that have had enormous negative effects on them and, consequently, on us. Not to mention aunts, uncles, grandmas, schoolteachers, preachers, bosses, friends, and heroes who have influenced us according to values that had little or nothing to do with our well-being.

When we were kids, most of the grown-ups in our lives operated from the maxim "Children are to be molded and corrected" rather than "Kids are beautiful creatures designed to realize their own uniqueness." Consequently, we *had* to develop a false personality in order to survive. And this is the genesis of the multiple little partial selves that make up the lower self. As little children we had no alternative in seeking ways to avoid neurotic people who felt in charge of us. But it is *in this very battle* between truth and false personality that each particular child learns the lessons it needs from life that will give it spiritual staying power for later living the inner life. In other words, nothing happens by accident.

Ultimately, however, we are not intended to be victims of *anything*—even our parents. It is *as* we recognize our defenses and coping styles that we learn later on what we fear, who we are, and where we're stuck. These are the negatives that define the positive side of the pole for us on our journey into Self-creation.

▼ **Victimhood is a myth that only leads to powerlessness.**

The world is ruled by laws that operate naturally and perfectly for our own good. Through my experiences, a neutral universe offers me a way to strengthen my character or my love in some manner that may not be as yet evident to me. As mentioned earlier, our greatest strengths are born out of the substance of our greatest weaknesses. If we've had a certain difficulty in life (a chronic physical ailment, poverty, a drunken parent, teachers who were hard on us, etc.), especially if the difficulties fall into a pattern, we can know these are our own personalized obstacle courses designed expressly to prod us along in our growth and to teach us the laws of the universe.

The most important tasks in our process of becoming are to make sense of our past—by reliving the negative parts *without judgment* and forgiving ourselves and others for any harm that we perceived. Portions of the past that still bother us represent the content of the subconscious mind, remnants of experience we have not assimilated properly, still holding us away from the knowledge these experiences were designed to give us.

The segments of our past that are no longer alive to us, we have *become*. They are now part of our true Self, having been instrumental building blocks necessary to our unique creation. The experiences we assimilate are understood and let go of; they are the underpinnings for intuitive knowledge, which is a higher form of gathering information than memorizing facts about the outer world.

The past has come before, to show us where we are going; the future is there to draw us toward our eventual completion. In the act of Self-creation, we are to respect our past, draw from it what lessons we need—cleaning up any unfinished business, and discovering the patterns and the meaning in our suffering and joys. If there is physical, emotional, or mental work left to do, we evoke our will to complete the tasks, whatever they may be, and then . . . we move on.

▼ Being stuck in the past is just another form illusion
can take. (Evil is "live" spelled backward.) Complete,
with honesty, whatever is bothering you, and then . . .
stop looking back.

3

How Addiction Unfolds in the Personality

We all certainly know what addiction feels like. The "clutched" feeling in the gut when an addiction cannot be gratified . . . the feelings of sheer terror experienced when a perceived threat looms into our consciousness saying, "Maybe you can't have this anymore." The dictionary definition of addiction is "the compulsive need for something habit-forming." I don't know a better prototype of this phenomenon than alcoholism. In studying the alcoholic, we can see the entire process of addiction unfold in the personality.

Experts cannot agree on a single definition of alcoholism. Some call it a disease; some say it's a symptom of a psychological problem; many say it's a problem in living; some call it an allergy. It's been labeled a moral weakness, a statement of immature personality, a character disorder, a neurosis. Some say it doesn't even exist, that alcoholism is merely a description of someone who drinks too much, and if the person will simply drink less, the problem will go away.

In my opinion, all definitions contain some truth. Like the blind investigators studying the elephant, it depends on which part of the animal you are examining. But a common denominator in all the definitions is that the investigators are studying the lower self who is addicted. Alcoholism is being studied in the light of and defined by the effect on the physical body or the outer life of the person.

Comprehensive definitions of this kind are workable and lead many alcoholics into treatment. Alcoholism, according to most modern-day experts, results in family, social, legal, financial, physical, mental, and occupational breakdown. In educational and treatment settings these terrible truths are spelled out. Often, these experts allude to the word *spiritual* but do not elaborate. The spiritual is the *unseen* dimension, the causative level.

Even though the spiritual resides in an invisible world, it is, in fact, the very ground of our being, our true reality, the higher Self. And it can take form. To round out our awareness of the problem, let's take a journey into this hidden dimension, this Self living in a vehicle contaminated by addiction.

Alcoholism is a spiritual predicament. It is the inner side of the beast that contains the causative factors of addiction. By some set of circumstances, it has found its way into its host, and is now a part of the personality structure—an alien substance intruding cruelly, imposing a terrible stress on the person. Addiction is not a part of the true Self!

So what is the host to do with this alien creature? It can rebel against it: "Why me, Lord?" It can lose faith in life: "Well, if this is how it is, I'm not going to try anymore." It can deny its existence, hoping the pain will just go away: "I'm fine, really, I am." Or it can suffer nobly: "This is just how I am; I'll just have to live with it."

But nothing can change the fact that the addiction is there.

The spiritual predicament is the felt gap between the personality distortion and the perfection our soul is seeking to formulate in the world through us. The presence of the addiction presents us with an opportunity for growth. It has arrived to force us to look at ourselves, specifically at those strengths and natural qualities of our essence the addiction is masking. Addiction is more than a concept; it cannot be contained within a definition. It is a miscreation of the soul's intention.

The Origin of Addiction

Our sense by its incapacity has invented darkness. In truth there is nothing but Light, only it is a power of light either above or below our poor human vision's limited range.
—SRI AUROBINDO

We've wound up in a world of duality because the light plunged into its own shadow. Negativity became an aspect of our experience.

If we can understand this truth, we will see how all our addictions originate from this first duality, the invention of darkness mentioned by the sage. But is the negative "bad"? Addiction is not evil; it is merely a narrowness of vision, perceiving a false vision of ourselves and our world . . . thinking we are someone we're not, doing things we don't even have to do. Addiction is darkness . . . a way of not being.

Aurobindo tells us that the positive does not abolish the negative any more than the top of something annuls the bottom!

Our negative human-made addictions exist in relation to their positive spiritual companions. They complete and explain each other. Each by itself cannot *really* be understood. Until I know the positive quality (a portion of my essence) I'm withholding by hanging on to my addiction, I cannot possibly understand my addiction. I must go for the one truth behind this apparent duality if I am to know freedom. *Who* am I? *What* am I seeking? What part of me am I withholding/expressing?

The lower self (our addicted selves) can only operate when forces one, two, or three are experienced *without* energy from any of the higher levels. Since this is only one half of reality, the material side, and we are operating as though it is the *only* reality, we are caught in a web of illusion, incapable of realizing the larger picture. *We need this thing or person for our survival,* we feel. *There is no other reality!*

When the lower self and the higher Self operate together, transformation can occur. We have a chance to break out of our limited world view. The two working together create a synergistic effect . . . another whole reality. We accomplish a feat we had deemed impossible. We discover we *are* that very person we had longed to be but had almost given up on.

But remember, the top does not annul the bottom. We transform the bottom by climbing from it, *through* the addiction. The addiction is the very stuff our transformation is made of. Because we've been hooked on relationships, we now know relationship. Because we gave our power away to a substance, we understand our own unique potency. Because we died to our old addicted ways, we now can live without fear. We did not choose to live like sheep who never strayed; we risked. We got our feet wet. We entered into life—got stuck, got into trouble.

Now we've learned. Our newfound goodness is not built upon naïveté. Our obedience does not come from the weakness of never having had the courage to try. Our knowledge comes from an overflowing of strength that has become floodlike in its forcefulness. There is now life in our understanding of addiction because we've been there.

▼ **The highest part of us can only exist when there is energy to move it, and this energy is the overflowing from the lower levels of our experiencing.**

We are hierarchical creatures: Only when our bodily needs are met can the energy move to the next highest level of functioning. Our higher knowledge is *rooted* in our knowledge of the lower. People may think they're saints because they have never committed a sin. But if they have never been tempted and never committed any error, there is no energy for turning inward to seek a higher way. Most saints and sages would tell you they have traveled the road you have traveled and have experienced the failures and mistakes just as you have. The only difference between them and you is they are further along on their journey, having completed, or nearly completed, the life. They *know* and are living from their being. We are *learning*, for we are still becoming.

When we make the transition from ego-dominance to essence-dominance, the force of the higher Self descends and takes up the whole nature, part by part, and does what needs to be done with it, rejecting what must be rejected and transforming what needs to be transformed. This is the act of Self-creation.

At this point in our growth, there is an illusion we must guard against—another pitfall. When the higher Self begins to overshadow our meager personality, our tendency is to throw out the lower self. But the two *must* work together. This is our unique destiny, the human condition. For the first time in the entire process of evolution, we are to spiritualize the material right down to the very bones. We enter fully into the stuff of life and *make it holy (whole)*, to raise it to its highest good.

There is an absolute goodness in the very heart of the things of the earth. We have been too deluded to see this, having bought into so many myths about "the evils of the flesh." The Spirit in us has not yet finished discovering itself. We are in transition. The higher Self is still looking for all its expressions of consciousness.

Your weaknesses are woven into the very stuff that makes you *you*. You've *needed* those experiences in your past that you've labeled "wrong" or "bad." They have provided the tension in your life that now makes it possible for you to Self-create. Your weaknesses and your strengths are one.

Now can you forgive yourself? *We simply are who we are at the moment.* This is not a license for irresponsible behavior; it is a statement of fact.

Our task is to continue to be seekers of truth in order to become *seers* of truth, tossed between our search for heaven on the one hand and a rich earthly experience on the other. What we're saying is, "Yes, that's exactly where we are and where we need to be." We can acknowledge this without guilt, without blame. We are doing the work of being human. Our only failure has been to set our two natures against each other . . . heaven there, earth here, one good, the other evil. *This* is the original sin, the separation, the error *demanding* correction. We are to unite the two and realize one is the other, to discover the infinite within the finite, the holy amidst the profane. Each weakness in us is a call to strength—our addiction, the dark side of our truth.

And perhaps this is our final destination: to experience the joy of having been *all that is*, has been, or will be, right here where we are . . . in a world of experiencing. We are not trying to leave life, but to expand it. To know it all.

The Transformer's View of Addiction

Following are the working definitions a Transformer uses for addiction.

Addiction = nongrowth. It is a way of staying stuck in the past, repeating like a robot the same outworn modes of operation that do not work. Habits are desires objectified, repeated by unconscious action. We cannot maintain an addiction consciously. We have to put ourselves to sleep in order to act out an addiction. Conscious awareness, moment by moment, fully in the here and now, transforms addiction.

Addiction = attachment. When we are attached to something or someone, we have forgotten who we are. We feel we cannot be whole without this something. We experience pain and suffering whenever our attachment threatens to leave us. Attachment is the cause of suffering. Addiction is the cause of suffering. Nonattachment does not mean noncaring; it is non*needing*, nonobsessing. Nonattachment removes emotional investment so that one can truly see clearly and therefore care appropriately for the other's sake. Paradoxically, attachment is nonloving.

Addiction = postponement. Repetition is hypnosis. We did it yesterday, we are doing it today. Tomorrow will be the same. Repeating, repeating. And this is how addictions grow. The more we repeat, the deeper we carve the groove, the more the affliction is worked into the fiber of our being. We know we want to do something else with our life, but always we feel . . . tomorrow. Then I'll be ready. Tomorrow I will be stronger. Tomorrow I will have gained more knowledge; I will have more energy. I will be out of the current crisis. *But tomorrow never comes.* And transformation happens now. It is this moment. Because nothing has to be *done* for transformation to occur—no looking to the future, no desiring an outcome, no goal.

Transformation is simply an awakening out of a dream state, a realization that happens in the mind. It is an instant realization that we lack nothing at all. We just open our eyes and see. And the seeing transforms!

Addictions must be entered into fully before they can be transformed, because they must be recognized . . . understood. Mindfulness is required. (See Exercise #3, page 257.) They must be experienced fully, recognized for what they are, understood, accepted . . . then the energy goes out of them. Going into the silence (Exercise #10, page 271) is a way of becoming mindful.

Education about the Self is the initial process in addiction counseling. People must be reeducated about who they really are in order to transform their debilitating addictions. Tuning into the Self is the second phase. Then, quite naturally, people will be ready to work through fears and resistances that block this true Self from its rightful domain as master of the personality. As these fears and resistances are understood and accepted, and the true Self takes hold, the addiction loses its power. When we operate from our true Self, a natural high occurs, because the true Self lives in the now, alive in everlasting renewal.

We are receiving stations, designed to respond to orders from our higher Self. There are only three positions we can wind up in: tuned in, off the channel, or receiving with static interference. Static comes from fear or illusion (resistance). Transforming addictions means *tuning in*.

Understanding the nature of addiction is understanding the nature of desire. A desire can never be fulfilled. This is its nature, to be constantly wanting. And the more we seek to fulfill it, the more we feed the desire, creating more and more of it. When we understand this, we can drop the future, the wanting more and more. We can be content. We can live in the now.

Addiction as Blocked Creative Energy

▼ **Addiction is nongrowth, a way of being stuck in the past. If a natural urge has been thwarted, addiction can set in. Therefore, addiction can be viewed as blocked creative energy.**

To free up constricted energy is the Transformer's task. Transformers need to know how to identify and work with each level of blockage within their own personalities and the personalities of the people they're working with—the physical, emotional, and the mental levels. But we must remember, the personality is never really that simply dissected; all levels will be involved, but one primary block will stand out with its own particular set of characteristics.

Even while stuck at a certain level of consciousness, we will still exhibit signs of that quality of *force* operating in our actions. However, this quality—self-preservation, self-gratification, or self-definition—will seek expression through perceptual distortion. In other words, the person will attempt to gratify these natural urges in unnatural or self-defeating ways.

BLOCKED FIRST FORCE: THE URGE TOWARD SELF-PRESERVATION DISTORTED

A person stuck at this level of functioning will behave in a fearful, childish manner, for this is a very unidimensional level of consciousness—motivated by the simplistic urge for self-preservation. The basic sense of security that grounds us for living in this world is either haphazardly formed and randomly reinforced or missing. Fear is the quality of the force that feeds this mode of existing in life, driving the individual incessantly toward meeting this unmet basic need for safety and well-being.

When this initial stage of development is blocked, the world is perceived as an unsafe place, and the person feels alone and unprotected. Since natural ways of meeting these needs are not predictably available for the person, he or she will find unnatural ways to cope, become incessantly attached to any surrogate person or object that answers to the now distorted need. The child might feel panicked outside a safe room, without a familiar blanket and pillow. Or, the child might appear horrified when a stranger tries to relate to him or her.

The older person might eat compulsively in order to feel "full" (completed); or pop a pill or load up with booze when anticipating an event perceived as threatening. He or she might take on a neurotic, needy love partner to make him or her feel needed. Or he or she might engage in ritualistic and compulsive behavior, compelled to repeat over and over the same limited safe patterns, day to day. Some of these patterns are even useless. But they fill up the time and preoccupy the person so that he or she does not have to think or feel. Most of this person's thoughts will be fear thoughts, and many of his or her emotions will be anxiety-based.

The will to live, the spiritual development task at this level, is sporadic and shaky, perhaps even nonexistent. Instead, the person has become deathly afraid of life, unable to experience newness or expansion without untold anxiety. There are worlds out there to explore, but not by this one. This person can't imagine getting off familiar ground. And please do not introduce such a person to new philosophies or religions. This person's whole understanding of the universe is predicated on a limited point of view, usually unexamined (but safe) belief systems constructed in a stereotypic manner. "All foreigners are dangerous." "Only baptized Christians go to heaven." "Only people who work hard are valuable," etc.

Mistrust and fear operate in all this person's relationships. No matter how loving and consistent someone else is in his or her life, this person does not experience this love because he or she cannot believe in it. The entire world is seen through the lens of hopelessness and mistrust. Paranoia. Fight or flight are his or her chief defenses, depending upon temperament. Some people are hostile and aggressive at this level of dysfunction, while some are passive and withdrawn. All feel isolated, perceiving themselves as separate and apart from everything and everyone, truly alien and alone.

If and when such people have met enough of these basic security needs, they will begin to expand life to new patterns of living, new relationships, or new energy in old relationships. They will exhibit a sense of self-mastery in life and will be able to give it direction. They will have discovered their own sense of potency. Cheerfulness and a bit of a sense of humor will appear, replacing the old paranoid view. They will show an interest in living that is exciting for the counselor and other Transformers in their lives to observe. (Counselors, you don't have to worry about informing your clients of this advancement beyond the first level; the clients will tell *you* . . . by their very desire for newness.)

If this level cannot be transcended, for whatever reason—maybe the damage has been too severe—the person is stuck in a fundamental, almost totally instinctive view of life that functions on a subhuman plane of consciousness, incapable of moving to a more integrated level. His or her potential is stagnated and death becomes a secret wish.

Some might choose to die slowly, through some chemical addiction or some other self-defeating pattern. Some might simply withdraw, continuing to merely exist, passively or bitterly, without a real zest for life. Some will choose death through suicide or a violent accident. If the will to live is thoroughly thwarted, neither the therapist nor anyone else can prevent the ending of this life.

BLOCKED SECOND FORCE: THE URGE TOWARD SELF-GRATIFICATION DISTORTED

If this natural stage of development is denied or contaminated too greatly by unaware parent figures or unnatural situations, the child learns to mistrust its interpretation of sensual and experiential data. The natural yearning for self-gratification becomes repressed or runs rampant. Either extreme causes untold emotional misery for the budding individual. Passion is the quality of the force that feeds this level of functioning in human personality. The basic needs are now physical plus emotional. The emotions take the focus now.

When this feeling stage of development is thwarted, the person does not know how to deal with emotions. Feelings are perceived as scary, bad, or unnecessary. And since our emotional life is a vital part of our humanness, we will have to do something unnatural to replace the core need for emotional expression that is going unmet. Expression of love and compassion, rightful anger, grief, joy, excitement, and the other ways of feeling naturally human are replaced by pleasure-seeking, living dangerously, creating melodrama and hysteria. Or we take the opposite tack: denied feelings, constricted natural reactions to life situations, and repressed, stale, stereotypic, and rigid responses to life.

People blocked at the second level of consciousness are confused about what their senses are telling them. They are out of touch with their feelings. When, as a child, they felt sad, mommy told them they didn't. When something felt good, daddy said, "Shame on you, you are just imagining it." When pleasure was derived from something against the parents' moral code (which usually included anything sexual or aggressive), the child was punished. Now, the grown-up children cannot judge for themselves what they are feeling or *if* they should feel it.

People stuck at this level of human functioning have not developed the will to feel. Their feelings become alienated, remain undifferentiated or forgotten, repressed or projected. The affective life will not be based on reality and will build a fraudulent self-concept and a false picture of the world. Herein lies the seedbed for hysteria, manic-depressive psychosis, depression, anxiety reactions, and other forms of misdirected or unbalanced emotions. Violent rages often occur in people whose emotions are stymied. The pressure builds until something touches them deeply enough, then out it comes in inappropriate ways.

When little children are *naturally* passing through this stage, we can see innate curiosity and a healthy desire for pleasure modeled for us. For instance, if you observe little children carefully, you will see that they go after a new object with all five physical senses, exploring each fully. They will taste it, smell it, look at it, feel it, and listen to the sound it makes. Once the object is thoroughly examined (known), children spontaneously toss it aside and completely lose interest in it. This is the natural unfolding of human curiosity that leads later to Self-knowledge and knowledge of the world. The child teaches us that we are designed to be learners, seekers of truth who literally gobble up our universe. Once we've assimilated a portion of it, and know it fully, we move on to something new. Onward and upward. This is the paradigm for expanded awareness in all its simplicity.

We begin by exploring our outside world, the home in which we find ourselves after being born into the larger reality outside the womb. Then, as we become grounded in our experience, we turn inward to explore the inner world, the psycho-spiritual realm that leads to total Self-realization. Gratification of our sensual/emotional needs and feeling passionately involved with life become the groundwork for relationship to others and feeling at one with our world. Feeling is good. Passion is strong feeling; it is connecting; it is the cornerstone of a higher order of feeling called compassion. Sensual gratification grounds us in our feeling nature and later becomes transmuted into aspirations to serve humankind as a whole. The energy vector shifts from taking pleasure to giving pleasure, from selfishness to selflessness.

When people begin evidencing balanced emotions, control over useless or excessive appetites, and a desire to do something other than seek their own gratification, they move beyond this feeling way of being connected to the world and expand to the next level of integration, the mental level, or feeling wisely.

If this natural feeling stage is not allowed free and appropriate expression, people remain stuck in a level of being that is either fraught with too much emotional chaos or too little emotional response. Or they live on a pendulum, swinging between depression and excitation. For those of you wanting more information on this failure of proper emotional development, a study of Freud, Sullivan, Horney, or Jung will augment your knowledge in this area.[1]

In working in the field of addiction, I find that most alcoholics suffer greatly from a misunderstanding of their emotions. Many experts say alcoholism is an emotional/affective disease. (In ancient philosophy, the element of water symbolically stands for the emotions. In astrology, Neptune rules water; consequently, esoteric astrologers refer to alcoholism as a "Neptune conflict.")

When we cannot trust our feelings to guide us appropriately in life, or believe feelings are so dangerous they must be denied, so much confusion and pain result that it becomes necessary to block feelings. Severe mood swings and all-or-nothing thinking result. The emotional either/ors place us in a world of conflictual dualism. It's either terrible or it's perfect. I am either all good or all bad. Either God or the devil is masterminding me.

You can see why many will choose a chemical addiction at this level of dysfunction: Booze or pills can either put us into denied feelings or take us out of feeling anything, whichever is needed. Many addicts are seeking the highs or the lows of chemically induced states of consciousness for excitement, because they are totally identified with their feelings.

They do not discriminate what they feel; if pleasure is not possible, then pain will do. Intensity is the goal of unbalanced emotions.

BLOCKED THIRD FORCE: THE URGE TOWARD SELF-DEFINITION DISTORTED

If we get off track at this stage of our development, we lose our sense of identity, becoming encased in the lower self. As you probably realize by now, the lower self is nothing but an intricate mass of physical, emotional, and mental habits, held together by a few ruling passions and desires, associations it has made from knowledge of the outer world. Turning to the outside world to find our identity is how we lose ourselves, not find ourselves. We are again caught in illusion, for the true Self is within.

Third force is a mental stage of development, but it is still driven by the emotions. The motivating force in our lives becomes a desire for status and a drive to please others—

seeking awards from society, or emotional dependence on people who approve of us or make us look good. The mind's image of ourselves is in operation here. If we do not receive this needed endorsement from the people whose opinions matter to us, we suffer a sense of low self-esteem or loss of identity. If we cannot succeed at gaining society's approval due to poor choices, constant failures, or missed opportunities, we become neurotically addicted to something that will substitute for this good self-feeling. We might seek status in a subculture we can fit into. Or we might compulsively collect status symbols, even when we cannot afford them—new cars, houses, fancy clothes, boats, bragging about important people we know, exaggerating titles we've held, building stories about ourselves that give us a certain image in the eyes of others. And when any of these is taken from us, we feel humiliated, even shattered, for our story has become who we are.

If we are finding our identity completely from things outside of ourself, we are living quite precariously, vulnerable to all kinds of conditions, for we have no control over these things or these people. The will to know, which is our essential developmental task at this mental level of consciousness, becomes warped. Instead of going inward to know ourselves, we become an expert or fanatic in some tiny little reality we can master—the best bridge player in the club (with absolutely no sense of humor about the game), the perfect housekeeper, the expert at the races on Saturdays, Mr. Alcoholics Anonymous, etc. Authoritarianism, dogmatism, fanaticism, myopic thinking, constricted ideals are ways the mind can become stuck at this level in order to meet the self-definition demands of the ego.

And, of course, if all else fails, we can become chemically dependent. Our concrete mind, designed to bring us Self-knowledge, which is the entrée into higher consciousness, has run amuck, gravitating compulsively toward more and more knowledge about the *outer* world, still susceptible to emotional imbalance. We are living in the ignorance of incomplete experiences and half-truths. Therefore, we are powerless to master life, because to see falsely is to live falsely. . . .

> *As if by enchantment, they see the False as the True.*
> —*MAITRI UPANISHAD*

Strife Consciousness: The Environment of Addiction and Neurosis

If my personality has formed according to principles based on the truth of human nature, I will have a unifying center for my identity that can function in the world with little conflict between my inner feelings and my outer life. I will have developed a healthy attitude toward myself and will consequently desire knowledge about the depths of the self. This will attract the energy of my higher Self, and I will be on my way toward more integrated levels of functioning.

If, however, I have *mis*created my reality, based on a fraudulent view of my self and my world, I will be ruled by my lower self, a false personality who functions as though it is my true Self.

The former leads to enlightenment; the latter to stagnation or disintegration. Now we can see that the biggest enemy of Self-creation is the lower self attempting to operate without the light of its counterpart, the higher Self, the ego running rampant with no master.

At this point let's review the nature of this lower self, the principles that govern ego-dominance, so we can better recognize this tricky little transitory "being" that loves to take us over.

*The lower self draws its data from the outer world of experience, believing it is the **only** reality.* Consequently, it thrives on half-truths. Its director is the ego. The ego *will* get our needs met . . . one way or another.

The lower self draws its conclusions from the subcon-

scious mind, programs based on the past, when we were less than conscious. It only sees fragments of truth. It is emotionally attached to life, based on fear, passion, or desire for status or ownership. It only functions on the first three levels of consciousness, in a world of deficiency and addiction.

The lower self cannot rise above itself. The lower self is totally into its experiences. Consequently, there is no self who can rise out of it and see what is happening. It says, "My experiences *are* who I am." It feels determined completely by its experiences. This is the genesis of victimhood.

The lower self's three keynotes are limitation, sensation, and egoism. It cannot love; it can only "use." Its energy feels forced instead of flowing. "I've *got* to be it; I've *got* to do it; I've *got* to make it."

The lower self keeps us locked into a sense of separateness and isolation. It is a robot self, *re*acting to life rather than acting creatively through choice. It has many faces, for it copies varieties of personalities. Its behaviors are acquired, not intrinsic to the true Self.

By keeping our attention focused outward, the lower self blocks our inner development. It is ruled by feelings of scarcity: "There isn't enough for everyone. I must struggle to have my share."

▼ **The lower self operates in the world of strife consciousness.**

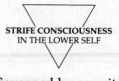

Harmony Consciousness:
Turning the Inside Out

In order to see how we redirect our energies away from strife consciousness, identifying with the outer world of experience, toward harmony consciousness, identifying with the higher Self, we need to study Appendix 2 on page 284, which shows how the human being journeys through the levels of consciousness seeking its wholeness. This is known as the process of becoming.

Whenever we feel we are dominated by our lower self in a particular situation, we can raise our vibration to a level where strife does not exist. If we seek the truth beyond the apparent duality, we will find ourselves living in a world of harmony rather than strife.

STRIFE CONSCIOUSNESS
IN THE LOWER SELF

HARMONY CONSCIOUSNESS
IN THE HIGHER SELF

1. Governed by scarcity consciousness.
2. Motivated by the need for self-control.

1. Governed by abundance consciousness.
2. Motivated by the need for Self-expression.

STRIFE CONSCIOUSNESS
IN THE LOWER SELF

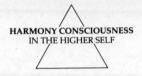

HARMONY CONSCIOUSNESS
IN THE HIGHER SELF

STRIFE CONSCIOUSNESS	HARMONY CONSCIOUSNESS
3. Perceives falsely.	3. Perceives truth.
4. Sees fragments and separates.	4. Sees through all states and conditions to the overall pattern and unifies.
5. Utilizes the senses as receptors for taking in desires.	5. Utilizes the senses as outlets for illumination.
6. Views the body as the truth about who we are.	6. Views the body as a symbol, the vehicle (or instrument) of our soul.
7. Recognizes limitation and gives it power. (Focuses on the condition.)	7. Recognizes limitation and ignores it. (Focuses on the perfection behind the condition.)
8. Gets caught up in melodramas, sees them as truth.	8. Rises above melodramas and asks, "What would I do if I were in perfect spiritual harmony just now?" and *acts* accordingly.
9. Feeling state: anxiety, striving.	9. Feeling state: contentment, joy.
10. Believes we must correct mistakes.	10. Knows to abide by universal truth, which automatically corrects mistakes.
11. Believes things are inherited and inevitable. (Does not realize that thought is creative.)	11. Knows we will attract to ourselves everything we believe in. (Thought is creative.)

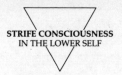

STRIFE CONSCIOUSNESS
IN THE LOWER SELF

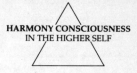

HARMONY CONSCIOUSNESS
IN THE HIGHER SELF

12. Exalts the material world. (Humans come from experience through which they travel.)

12. Exalts the soul. (Humans come from the One Source.)

13. Believes human nature must be reformed.

13. Knows human nature is already perfect. We only need to realize who we are.

14. Believes the important thing in life is material success.

14. Knows the important thing is to learn truth.

15. Lives governed by fears of the past and future.

15. Lives governed by the present.

16. Is attached to rewards of work.

16. Surrenders reward of work to a Higher Purpose.

♦ **If I die to the dictates of my ego and surrender to the higher Self, the Self I really am, I will be reborn into truth.**

This seed thought represents a type of conscious shock that can hit us in our intellect at the third level of consciousness, which leads to rebirth into a transcendent state. Please note, this thought is describing a rebirth, not a better and better way to live the old life. If you will notice in Appendix 2, the two triangles, describing the outer world of experience and the inner world of wisdom, are discontinuous.

We must *die* to the old way before the new life is possible. Everything we thought we were, we aren't; and everything we thought we weren't, we are. To see future possibilities as they exist in the inner world, not yet materialized—or, for that matter, to conceptualize *anything* new—requires a leap of imagination. It requires a certain working of the mind's ability to create images and ideas based on what we sense might be possible. It involves reaching up to a place that hasn't yet happened in time and space. This is the true translation of the word *faith*, from the Greek word *pistis*, which means literally "another kind of thinking."

Really, what's happening is a kind of remembering, a recalling something from a distant past, from a collective awareness residing way back in the recesses of our minds. Since something can never come from nothing, we must realize that on some level we already know our future. Or to put it another way, the future is already contained within the present moment. We are on the way to becoming the person we were always intended to be, like following a blueprint to its finished product. It is as though we've already dreamed the dream; and now, we are privileged to be able to experience it.

The Observer Self: ## Our Agent of Consciousness

As we learn to move into the fourth level of consciousness, we learn to separate the part of our mind that is constantly active from our quiet mind, which is both a silent witness and a dynamic director of our energy. We realize we have been the victims of our active mind, like a laborer in a thought factory, or of our emotions, which continually mistake the force of the sentiments for the force of the truth.

When we can experience this quieter mind, we discover we are in a state of observing ourselves in action, affording us a chance to decide creatively what to do in a given situation. As stated in Chapter 1, the observer self can see what is going on without the distortion of the analytical mind or the static interference of emotional reaction.

To see, we must stop being in the middle of the picture!
—SATPREM

The observer self is the *key* to transformation, for it enables consciousness to work. It has been explored in many philosophical systems, sometimes called the *fair witness*, the *watcher self*, or the *observer*, One transpersonal theorist defines it as:

That which is capable of observing the flow of what is—without interfering with it, commenting on it, or in any way manipulating it . . . it simply observes the stream of events both inside and outside the mind/body in a detached fashion, since it is not exclusively identified with either. . . . Once he realizes each can be perceived, he simultaneously realizes that they cannot be his real self.[1]
[Emphasis mine]

—KEN WILBER

When we operate from the observer self, we experience the various levels of naked reality without the mental and emotional veneer we've covered them with by the limitations of our lower self. We see without judgment. Things can no longer be perceived as good or bad, black or white. We see them in terms of exactitude or inexactitude, hitting or missing the mark.

The observer self is the nonjudgmental energy of acceptance. It prepares us to love ourselves by placing us in the right frame of mind. This is where mind and heart converge. It is more expansive than the intellect. The observer does more than change our ideas about things. It changes our level of consciousness. If we only change ideas, we are still spinning around on the same wavelength, executing one more pirouette in the same mental space. To change our consciousness is to change *where* we live inside, to expand our state of being.

This is no small feat for those of us who are used to feeling and intellectualizing our way through life. As this beautiful type of fourth force first begins to work in us, we will enter a state of self-remembering. At first we will remember ourselves (who we truly are) only now and then, as though we interrupt our daily routine to recall this amazing truth. ("This is not me! This is merely something I am doing.")

Then we will go through a stage of disciplining ourselves to remember who we are, forcing ourselves to work harder at not forgetting. This stage will still feel frustrating, and we will fall into judging ourselves for being forgetful.

Then one day we will realize the dynamism of this effort nudging us right in the midst of other activities. We will remember more and more often.

And then the remembrance gradually becomes part of our conscious nature, living in the background, like a little muffled voice. All we have to do is withdraw from the outside world a bit. And there it is—an inviolable, peaceful retreat, a place of pure seeing.

FOURTH FORCE:
Awakening
(The Accepting Response)

COGNITION: **Harmony Through Conflict**

QUALITY: **Harmonizing Higher with Lower Nature**

BASIC URGE: **Accepting, Harmonizing**

PITFALL: **Attachment to Conflict**

INTEGRATION: **Self-Creation**

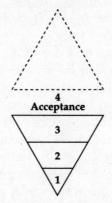

Look again at Appendix 2, page 284. In the space between the two triangles lies the bridge to higher knowledge, the fourth level of consciousness, where the Transformer works. Here in this space lives "I," the true Self.

At this level of awareness, for the first time I am able to rise above myself and see what I am doing as I am doing it. I am awakening! And I am beginning to love myself. I have the vantage point of the observer self, the one who can look *up* at my potential and harness this magnificent energy, as it looks *down* at what I am doing in the world and decides what choices to make and on whose terms. I am learning to accept myself *as I am* and life *as it is*. Free, at last, of the constant constraints of my limited ego, I can do my being, acting creatively in the world, rather than reacting mechanistically to cues from my environment.

My ego is more solid now, intensifying its efforts to keep the lower self in the driver's seat. It will work on me to make sure I don't leave any unmet need floating loose, unattended. But my higher Self is also a reality at this level of functioning. I can decide whether or not my ego is to lead, or whether it will be subservient to the me who can see what's really going on from a more integrated viewpoint. So my ego can now become my instrument. I no longer see the ego as my enemy. I am entering a world of self-acceptance.

It is with fourth force that we practice nonattachment, the art of letting go and letting God. Letting go is an active force that wills our ego to release its perpetual judging and accept things exactly as they are. Both "the good" and "the bad" have become part of *the plan* for me. Fourth force can love me unconditionally because it sees my real nature down underneath all its defenses, ego needs, and half-truths that until now have been ruling me. The process of self-creation integrates through fourth-level consciousness.

I am amazed at some of the feelings I now have about myself. I feel forgiveness. I feel calm and centered. I can feel okay about myself, even in the midst of a melodrama. I am operating from my heart, but with intelligence, the beginnings of love. Jesus' saying, "As a man thinketh, *in his heart*, so is he," becomes a thundering reality to me now. This force really does feel like thinking with the heart. It is not a naïve, mushy love that allows others to walk all over it. It has dignity and discrimination. It has understanding. It seeks, above all else, to harmonize the two natures I possess. It will even sometimes seek out conflict in order to resolve a situation on a higher level.

This level of consciousness is the battleground where all

of life is fought consciously. The lower self is still able to take charge because it is a creature of habit. We are still in the process of unlearning a set of imperatives we inherited from earlier periods of our development. And sometimes a need at level one, two, or three will dominate our personhood. Until we become aware of it, it has us under its spell. But the observer self at level four is always available to awaken us. In fact, with practice, we discover we can tap into this resource anytime we choose.

Now that fourth force is awakened in us, we are always willing to see the truth unless a lower need overwhelms us. In this case, we find that we must go ahead and just be where we are, in our lower self, running on ego power again. But it won't work for long, because now we can forgive ourselves, which brings us back into our hearts. Now we have discovered a more honest way to live. And the heart's truth always feels better in the long run. You can count on it. Now I can forgive myself for the mistakes I've made, the wrong paths I've taken, and the time I've wasted. I can see more clearly how it was all needed.

Fourth force is the energy the Transformer uses to work from a caring position, from the heart. Here we can accept ourselves and others as we and they are, without the distortion of our own ego's arrogance and defenses. Fourth force can just sit there, being aware, and allowing the others to be in their space—seeing, loving, and hoping to share truth in a way they can receive the benefit. This kind of relating is not goal-oriented, nor does it have to prove anything. It is comfortable just being there, understanding and accepting.

Fourth force is the mere beginning of love, and it can sometimes draw to itself its opposite. Remember, we often learn by contrasts. At this level I am working on being loving and learning to use my creative imagination to open myself up to new ways of being. It is natural that I will sometimes not love, and sometimes find myself in an unimaginative, robotlike state of consciousness where, again, nothing new seems possible. The difference, however, is that now I have the capacity to pull myself up by my own bootstraps and come out of this unenlightened position. I am not yet enlightened, but I am working with transforming energy for the first time in my life.

From here I can see with a cleared-out perspective what I *need* instead of only what I *want*. And I can also see *you*— the other—for the first time, as subject of your own life, rather than just an object in mine. I can love you even if you do not return the love. I can allow you the freedom to be yourself, even when your choices go against my own needs. At this level, I am in the process of transcending subject/object love. Though I still have passion and emotional energy that comes from second force, I also draw to myself compassion and the ability to focus on another.

Level four is an *eros/agape* mixture of love, sometimes called *caritas*, meaning charity. It is a combination of the very human, passionate love that is pleasure-directed and the Christ-consciousness love associated with self-giving, spontaneously offered without calculating the cost or gain to the giver.

But even this level can create an addiction. When experiencing the conflictual side of seeking harmony, we can get hooked on the excitement of the ups and downs of conflict, and bring ourselves down. I've known some people who come from the heart so excessively that they lack the balancing energy of will in their lives, sometimes indiscriminately choosing a feeling way of living over appropriateness or logic. Then level four devolves into level two, and an addiction to melodrama can ensue. We turn our life upside down with too much change, attempting too many intimate relationships, and, in general, making our life a mess.

Since here we are attracting situations that are teaching us to open our heart, we will have lessons to learn in forgiveness and discrimination in the various kinds of loving. Having fallen into the pit of indiscriminate love, we can become polarized in love/hate, good/bad, expansion/constriction, and have problems with intimacy/isolation. Any use of drugs that accentuate the senses can be very detrimental at this level of consciousness, for it will exaggerate the conflict.

As this level becomes more cultivated and refined, we will learn to discriminate with our heart. An ability to love wisely will be noticeable in our relationships. We'll know when to love, how to love, and when to let go. We are now manifesting a healthy will to balance the softer love energy.

From this heart-felt level of consciousness we will notice our ability to forgive others who do not share our particular value system. This is another form of acceptance. The quality of open-mindedness manifests in our personality. Imbalances in the physical, emotional, or mental levels no longer cause such blurred vision. We are getting clear. We are becoming responsible adults. We are letting go of childish attitudes, beginning to take our lives seriously—with nonattachment and a healthy sense of humor, with caring and concern. Self-sacrifice is no longer a negative word.

The confidence of knowing how to meet our own needs makes a need less demanding. This confidence stems from a newfound use of the creative imagination that operates at level four. Up until now, our imagination ran wild with us, exaggerating errors of the past, bemoaning perceived mistakes and abuses, or fantasizing about unattainable illusions. Or it would carry us off into the future, catastrophizing about what might happen *if* this or that. Now, through fourth force, we use our imagination creatively and constructively in the *now*, discovering ways to transcend or resolve situations with a unique response. The imagination becomes brilliant and distinctive, because it no longer merely copies the crowd. Now it can do its own thing, drawing from the higher centers where the unique response to the soul's urge can usher forth. This is the level where beauty emerges. The artist sees the higher while utilizing the lower.

The superconscious energy is now available to create images beyond where we have already been. This kind of energy *transcends dichotomies*. A new realization occurs: Two heretofore perceived opposites can reside in the same space.

It does not have to be one or the other. I can be childlike *and* mature; sexual *and* spiritual; playful *and* a serious worker; committed *and* free, and on and on. The two become one, transcended to a higher level where the dichotomy becomes irrelevant. This knowledge aids people who feel torn apart by either/or thinking, believing they must make a drastic choice between two unwanted extremes.

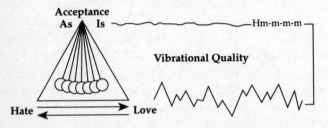

Creative imagination works in the *now*, drawing energy from the superconscious mind, offering us brand new creative solutions to life's dilemmas. Destructive imagination works in the past and the future, motivated by programs from the subconscious mind, and its message is usually one of hopelessness. At level four we begin to harmonize the energies of the imagination and activate its tremendous power to transform our lives. (As one way to activate the creative imagination, see Appendix 1, p. 251 for the uses of guided imagery.)

This is the level where Transformers work. They draw from the very highest principles about life and human nature and then, in a therapy room, in a practical manner, they create their own unique response.

Harmonizing the Higher and the Lower

Let me reiterate that levels one, two, and three are *discontinuous* with levels five, six, and seven. Fourth force provides the bridge. Acceptance—surrendering the need to control, judge, or manipulate life—is the key to transformation. After level three is reached and third force is operating in our lives, the personality is getting into harmony with itself. The three lower bodies are aligning to function like a well-oiled machine. So, simply because we are beginning to love and understand ourselves, we naturally begin to work at level four, the acceptance response, unless we get stuck in addiction.

But love and acceptance are not enough if we want transcendence. We can become trapped in a well-integrated personality. We can be the best professional in our field, the best citizen on the block, the most successful business executive in town. But we will not live a transcended life, unless we begin to think anew.

If you've ever talked to an intelligent, highly functioning person with absolutely no knowledge of or interest in the life of the spirit, you will know exactly what I mean. Higher knowledge is not a "reality" to these people. Talk of God, destiny, a Higher Power, and the like are considered too private, cop-outs, or irrelevant. Living the practical life is enough. It is all they are seeking; spiritual things don't pay the bills. Things must have a utilitarian purpose. God and poetry are meaningless. These materialistic people are not concerned with being, only with doing. The concrete world is their only reality. Everything must be literal. But unfortunately, *literal* understanding cannot make contact with higher understanding. To access higher knowledge requires a leap into the creative imagination and a willingness to accept the more subtle subjective realities as real.

This tends to be the difference between the Western and the Eastern view of the world, the Western being more concerned with the outer life, accomplishing tasks for a practical, rewarding, and productive existence. The Western viewpoint rarely concerns itself with matters pertaining to the inner reality. While on the other hand, the Eastern approach views the inner life as reality and the external worlds as *maya* or illusion. There is no Western word for *maya*. The closest analogy is the idea of a mirage. Maya is the kind of reality where you see something at a distance and reach for it, but when you arrive there, "it" is gone, only to be seen again at a distance. This is the Eastern view of outer reality. The ancient Tibetans called the seductive external distractions *maya, glamour,* and *illusion,* occurring on physical, emotional, and mental levels of development.[2]

Love, compassion, clarity of vision, harmony, creativity, oneness with nature, spiritual quests—these are the facts of the life of the transpersonal. Mastering inner truths, expanding consciousness, seeking ways to serve humankind are the goals the transcender seeks.

This is the world view Transformers prefer. But though they tend to transcend daily life and the material world, living creatively with little need for external consistencies or rules, they also live in the world lawfully, honestly, and with a sense of responsibility. They do not view transcendence as a license to escape responsibility. They embody, in fact, Maslow's definition of the self-actualizer who transcends. They are more altruistic, more responsible, and *more* concerned about humanity than the ordinary person who is not actualizing.

Many people addicted to substances or processes, such as drugs or relationships, are transcenders, seeking to live ordinary life extraordinarily. Much of their problem is that they are trying to live in a world made up largely of nontranscenders, and are seeking help from nontranscending people-helpers—left-brain–dominated psychologists, social workers, etc., who have been trained exclusively in the scientific mode so prevalent in Western thought. Transformers can live in both worlds, the right brain and the left, transcending the dichotomy between East and West. They know how to be *in* the world, and not *of* it simultaneously. They make excellent therapists for the chemically addicted client.

Lower Needs Meet Their Divine Complements

Now that we have thoroughly explored how we are intended to develop, and how fourth force comes into play, let's look ahead to see how the higher triangle, when activated, creates transformation in our lives. This is an overview. Chapter 5 looks at each of the higher forces in detail. And Chapter 6 fully describes a model for transcendence.

As the lower self completes its task of experiencing and meeting various needs, learning to function in the world, a very subtle event occurs, all at once or gradually. Personality becomes more passive, while essence quickens, becoming active. This reversal has been observed by many and has numerous names, such as the metanoia experience, conversion, the divine marriage, enlightenment, or being overshadowed by the soul. Jesus said, "Lose your life and you will find it."

Fourth force is functioning, and now, as if by magic, the higher centers descend into the personality sphere. In this harmony state, the physical body, the emotions, and the mental life begin to align. The higher triangle becomes activated and creates transformation. What began as two discontinuous triangles now becomes merged into a symbol we all recognize:

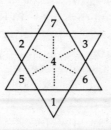

Level seven has overshadowed level one with its dynamic and complementary qualities—unity, discrimination, courage, divine will, and self-mastery. Insecurity, at level one, is synonymous with feeling alone, cut off from the world, frightened of annihilation by others outside ourself. The courage to *be* is insecurity transcended (which is what love and will merged together bring). We cannot fear annihilation if we are aware of being at one with everything, guided by the divine Self. Insecurity, in fact, becomes an irrelevant concept. Fear is transformed into the courage to act as one's true Self. Love of God, which is synonymous with love of Self, is the unifying force that now dominates the person.

Level two is our sensual playground, the place where we rightfully learn to connect with our world through knowledge of the five physical senses and the personality's emotional life. At level two, we are completely identified with our physical senses, believing our feelings are all that we are. These needs and fears become transcended through awareness of our soul nature. Knowledge from the intuition tells us we are souls traveling through a lifetime of experiencing, which takes the sting out of ungratified physical pleasures. How can I fear lack of physical gratification when I realize that I am a beautiful soul evolving through a lifetime, eternal and forever perfect in all ways? When I realize I can *choose* sensual pleasure, but do not have to have it, a sense of freedom and peace washes over me, and I am content. As level six descends upon level two with its complementary force, love and wisdom unite. Passion is transformed into compassion. And self-gratification transmutes into a desire to serve others. We are now totally in love with life. Through fourth force we have become fulfilled and now spill over with a love we yearn to share.

As fifth force pours into level three, the mind is transformed. Bits and pieces of Self-knowledge, acquired through the roles we've played and the Self-concepts we've adopted from our experience, become knowledge of the whole. Comprehension replaces discrete units of fragmented knowledge. We realize who we really are, rather than mechanically functioning like others thought we should be. We begin to express our true nature in the world, not someone else's idea of it. Dispassion enables us to see objective reality rather than our distorted sense of it. Action replaces reaction, and we become creators of the God-self, transcribing accurately our little part in the divine plan. The will to know has become an intensely focused love of truth.

We all must pass through level four. We cannot transcend to a higher level until we fully accept where we are now. This seems to be an inviolable principle of life: Total acceptance of what *is*, is necessary for the work of Self-creation. This is the law of transcendence made operational within human personality.

As you can see from the model, one and seven, two and six, three and five are the three polar opposites we work through. Each pole adds up to the number eight. The number that, when turned on its side (∞), is the mathematical symbol for infinity, a marriage of spirit and matter. This stands for the divine balance achieved as a result of working through life's teachings to gain substance and spiritual staying power. And each set of "opposites" passes through level four in order to blend the two energies on each pole, making each number eight a twelve—1–4–7; 2–4–6; 3–4–5. Twelve is the completion number in the Bible—twelve disciples, twelve tribes of Israel, etc. Other ancient teachings also refer to the number twelve as symbolizing completion.

We are never on *just* levels one, two, or three. For example, when we are stuck in a level two addiction and seeking to transform it, we are automatically working on the two/six polarity. The Law of Polarity is in operation here: We learn things by experiencing their opposite. This is why we must never ask for something unless we are sure we are ready for it. When I ask my higher Self to give me patience, for instance, I will activate all "patience tests" I need to teach me this quality. I will become invaded by rude people and given seemingly intolerable situations to master. I will be more aware than ever of how very *impatient* I am. If I ask to become loving, I will be shown in glaring Technicolor the unloving side of my nature.

Events that happen in the outer world are totally irrelevant and insignificant unless the higher Self is participating in some fashion.

There are only two types of events the evolving soul seeks: (1) *Tests*. Situations and difficulties that we learn from—events that create the sand for our oyster, designed to give us spiritual staying power or to work through a *karmic balancing*.[3] (2) *Expressions of the true Self.* Ways to become authentic—doing things in the world that are a true expression of our natural gifts and are part of our purpose in life, and by so being, help us aid humankind. Anything else we do in life is ultimately insignificant.

The soul delights in its work of Self-creation. You will find enthusiastic cooperation from your higher Self when you commit yourself to the work of significant advancement of the Self. Transformers can aid themselves and others in keeping to the task of Self-creation by guiding people away from time wasted in irrelevant pursuits that would not interest the soul.

The following model provides an illustration of how the lower energies are transformed by the higher, based on a merging of Eastern and Western thought. You will note that the pattern of the energy flows from the bottom three levels to the top three, forming a menorah, the seven-pronged candelabrum of Judaism—which graphically illustrates the fact that the seeming polarities are *one energy*, two ends of the same arm.

When the drives of the lower self are brought under the jurisdiction of the higher Self, the transformed energy brings about its evolutionary reward: Our inherent, divine ability to *know* and to *be* is realized. Effortlessly, we *are* love.

As long as our energies are constricted in the lower self, driven by the ego, we cannot purely manifest our true nature. Our lives are contaminated by misperceptions and unnecessary fears. Below I have outlined the Eastern concept of the *chakras*, energy centers that exist along the body's main axis, to help us see where these energies become trapped in the physical body, blocking our pure expression. These centers

ENERGY MODELS OF SELF CREATION

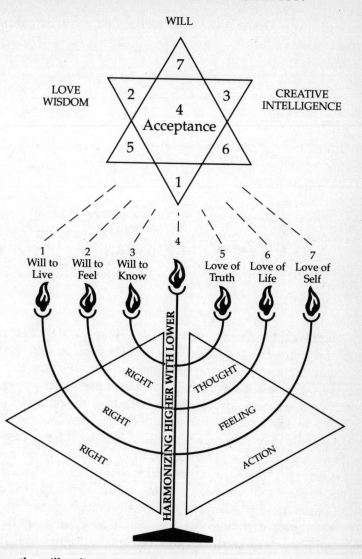

When the will to live is activated through right action, the will to feel through right feeling, and the will to know through right thought, then by the process of acceptance (fourth force), we master the attributes of authenticity, nonattachment (the merging of love/wisdom), and receptivity to divine will. The result is the advancement of the individual to a level of mastery of the physical world. He or she is now One with his higher nature.

ENERGY CENTERS IN THE BODY

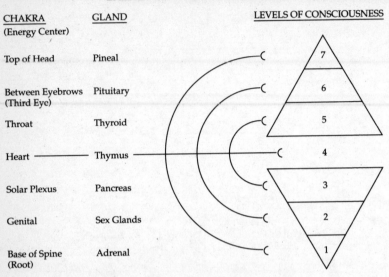

CHAKRA (Energy Center)	GLAND	LEVELS OF CONSCIOUSNESS
Top of Head	Pineal	7
Between Eyebrows (Third Eye)	Pituitary	6
Throat	Thyroid	5
Heart	Thymus	4
Solar Plexus	Pancreas	3
Genital	Sex Glands	2
Base of Spine (Root)	Adrenal	1

correlate with the seven levels of consciousness we are studying, and can serve as a diagnostic tool for ascertaining where a person's energy is being dissipated. All energy is one. It merely expresses itself through the various centers depending upon the organism's perceived needs of the moment.

The word *chakra* means "wheel" in Sanskrit, and is conceptualized as a spinning wheel. When a wheel spins, its outer perimeter moves the fastest, through more space, with more diversity than the center. This outer rim corresponds to our greater material self, moving about frantically in time and space. As we go inward toward the center of the wheel, we experience a slowing of movement to a quiet stillness, which is the very center of our being, the higher Self, the center of consciousness.[4]

Symbolically, within each of these dynamic chakras we can see a correlation of our personal physical world, our emotional energies, and how our mind and spirit function. For example, the solar plexus is the place where we feel hurt feelings, and assertiveness, or physically experience digestive problems or the proper assimilation of food. The moving focus of each center reflects very concisely our basic needs and our basic nature, cutting across the dimensions of physical, psychological, mental, and spiritual.

Each of these centers represents the point where a nucleus of nerves come together to perform their most important functions. Likewise, each gland is represented as the major control for each center:

> *Modern medical research has established that the endocrine glands serve as strategic points of interaction between physiological, emotional and psychological functioning.*[5]
> —SWAMI RAMA, RUDOLPH BALLENTINE, SWAMI AJAYA

Based on the law of correspondence, as expressed by the ancient hermetic maxim, "As above, so below," the physical body is a microcosm of the gigantic macrocosm of which we are all a part:

> *These centers (called "chakras") have been rediscovered and described in many different cultures. Identical locations are noted in such cultures as far away and unrelated to India as that of the Hopi Indians in America. . . .*[6]

As the menorah shows us, we are required to go through life in the physical body to learn how to be whole. When we get stuck in a negative place, we are simply being tested. Now perhaps we can see why we must never put ourselves down when we see ourselves operating on the negative side of a quality, such as tolerance/intolerance. We must acknowledge our deficiency without judgment and remove our attention from the error, placing it instead in the direction of the positive quality that is its desired opposite, through right action, right feeling, and right thought. If we become unloving and unforgiving toward ourselves, we get stuck in hateful and disapproving responses, which then draw hatefulness and judgment into our world by the bushels. It's better to forgive ourselves. In this way, we keep our inner world clear for the positive energies of truth, love, and divine will to manifest in the congenial soil we have prepared for them. A strong and active will and a desire for a pure heart are our best protection against unwanted negative qualities. And more, these higher urges that emanate from our wholeness are the forces that create the Self, so it can manifest in this reality through us.

Being: A Description of the Higher Self

In our model (see Appendix 2, p. 284), we now move into the formless world of being, the archetypal energy that is our human essence, the perfection beyond becoming. Traditionally we think of this dimension as the spiritual world, as opposed to the material. We have considered it to defy analysis. Scientists say this area cannot be empirically defined, as it is part of a subjective, amorphous universe that may or may not exist. But the law of correspondence aids us here: "As below, so above." By realizing the material self is a reflection of the greater macrocosm, we find we can indeed define the higher regions of humanness. The spiritual world does not have to remain an uninterpreted mystery. This universe is the mirror image of the one below. Our materialized world devoid of human-made distortions, turns out to be its mirrored image:

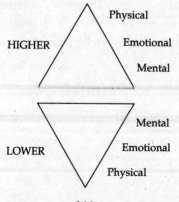

The higher mental, emotional, and physical areas represent three distinct functions of being, each having its unique part to play in the transmutation of the energies constricted within the lower self, in the process of Self-creation.

These higher functions manifest through us when our lower chakras are open and clear. We are then in a spontaneous state of just being ourselves. We experience these functions as energetic forces, basic urges that flow into our daily living unimpeded by the limited intellect. These qualities are cognitions of a higher order, which ultimately refine the intuition. They are the building blocks of Self-creation, or the ability to "art" ourselves.

This formless higher world is where meaning resides—beyond time—already in existence before the creation of anything. This level is *not* becoming, *not* passing away; it is being—the primal Cause of our existence. This is the true Reality. But we must "see" in a new way to recognize it.

> *There can suddenly be opened within the heart or in the mind a realm of experience that is not the external world . . . and we are then bathed* in the light of Meaning.[1]
>
> —*MAURICE NICOLL*

Discovering the meaning and spiritual purpose of our experiences is the reawakening, the transformation, we all seek. Meaning is another word for God. It is *curative* in nature, for it gives our Self its sense of wholeness. It can be experienced mentally, emotionally, or physically, depending upon which of the following three levels or streams of consciousness we tap into.

FIFTH FORCE:

The Love of Truth

(The Creative Response)

COGNITION: **Creative Intelligence (Higher Mind)**

QUALITY: **Creative Imagination**

BASIC URGE: **Self-Creative Expression**

PITFALL: **Abstraction**

INTEGRATION: **The Intellect**

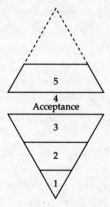

This is the level of higher mind concerned with greater reality than the personal ego's projection of what is real. Energy originating at the fifth level separates the wheat from the chaff, weeding out false viewing, and bringing us clarity of vision as it is learned by the organism. By use of the higher mental functions, abstract knowledge, comprehension, insight, and the creative imagination activate. Here, we begin to Self-create, having tapped into the gift of the higher mind—the creative imagination. We've begun the process of integrating the ego's intellect with the higher intuitive function of the soul by learning to work with the soul's ability to image. Remember the truism: We can only have what we can imagine.

Fifth force contemplates, then expresses itself in two modes, an active one of Self-creative expression, and a passive one of comprehending the whole truth of situations and events. Here, the *will to know* the outer world at level three shifts inward to seek Self-knowledge. It is the level where we begin to do our being, rather than taking on roles and identities that are false. An intrinsic value system has now emerged, drawing its approval from the higher Self, no longer needing so much endorsement from the outside world. What we value is now being manifested in the world as observable fact. No longer are we controlled by an external "should" system. Our "shoulds" are internal now, natural urges coming from deep inside us, expressions of our essence. We begin to express our unique purpose in life, utilizing our bodies, emotions, and mental faculties in service to the higher Self.

It takes no energy to do our being; in fact, it energizes us. *Stress occurs from the tension of trying and pretending*. At this level we begin flowing effortlessly toward the activities that are intrinsically right for us. We are following our grain. When we are doing the work of the God-self, we will find ourselves to be at the place where we are the most comfortable and at home. The struggle for most of us has been in letting go of the images and expressions that do not fit, or the ones we've outgrown, and learning to trust our innate ability to recognize, image, and bring forth the emerging real Self.

In esoteric teachings, level five is seen as the home of the White Magician, because this type of energy can wield the power of the mind to actualize thought in the material world. Molding thought-forms that direct matter toward manifestation exemplifies creativity in action at the fifth level of consciousness. This level is where true understanding occurs. Its maxim: The truth shall make us free. From here, we see beyond the fragmented knowledge of level three to the larger whole behind it all. We can see where and how each part fits together, grasping the purpose behind each "part" and how and why these particular events are manifesting right now in time and space.

Level five consciousness can recognize the significant in insignificant things, and the wonder in the commonplace. It comprehends the lesson life is teaching us when we experience something unpleasant, honoring the profit gained from any difficulty when taken in the right spirit. It affirms the unity in nature, seeing that "all is miracle." Through its subjective experiencing, it imagines a desired future and sets about expressing it.

When functioning at this level of consciousness, we can see all things with impartiality. We can gain as much enlightenment from ironing a skirt as we can contemplating a sacred symbol or attending a holy ceremony. Emerson was utilizing the fifth force when he said, "All things are friendly and sacred, all events profitable, all days holy, all men divine; for the eye is fastened on the life and slights the circumstance."

To develop this level of consciousness, we must learn to imagine and master acuity of mind. We listen to the world—both the inner and outer realities—and discover:

▲ **The subjective meanings we give the events in our lives become the first stage of a future manifestation.**

Through this type of cognition, we manifest truth in our daily routines, becoming models of individualizing human beings, and we learn to behave with integrity. This sets us apart from the masses of people who are refusing to take responsibility for their true natures, which are co-creative and divine.

There is a danger to be pointed out here, however: We can become so global and broad-minded in our approach to life that we lose the sense of concentration or discrimination necessary for the act of creating. We can fall into the pitfall of abstraction and live "from the head up," while our spiritual values will become irrelevant in the crucible of daily living. Or we can shut off our feelings and come from a dry intellect, believing we are being spiritually insightful.

This quality of mind has its physical counterpart in the throat center (chakra), where we learn to give and receive from life, taking in the truth of our being, and expressing it by having the courage to "sound our note."

▲
▼

SIXTH FORCE:

The Love of Life

(The Compassionate Response)

COGNITION: **Inspiration**

QUALITY: **Love/Wisdom (Higher Emotions)**

BASIC URGE: **Compassion/Aspiration to Serve**

PITFALL: **Overidentification with Humanity's Suffering**

INTEGRATION: **The Appetites and Emotions**

```
        ╱╲
       ╱   ╲
      ╱  6   ╲
     ╱─────────╲
    ╱     5     ╲
   ╱─────────────╲
         4
     Acceptance
   ╲─────────────╱
    ╲     3     ╱
     ╲─────────╱
      ╲   2   ╱
       ╲─────╱
        ╲ 1 ╱
         ╲╱
```

This drive manifests itself as a high love for all beings and aspires to serve the whole, for as it looks within, it sees the nature of the human condition and the work we are to do for the divine plan of evolution. When tapping into this rich energy source, we comprehend with compassion, and we become ignited by the fires of inspiration; we yearn to serve. This is a feeling state of consciousness that formulates in such areas of human endeavor as philosophy, psychology, religion, teaching, and healing. It is the marriage of love and wisdom, which must always be merged, for love executed unwisely becomes indiscretion, and wisdom administered devoid of love becomes blind and sometimes even cruel. At this level of our unfolding, the *will to feel* that dominated us at level two is purified and refined.

This is the opening of the "third eye" of which the mystics speak, its physical counterpart residing between the eyebrows. We cannot always explain how we know what we know at this level of consciousness, because we are sensing beyond logic. But neither are our inspirations devoid of logic: They are a synthesis of the truths we've ingested from interacting with life's processes, which, if digested and honed, become our talents and skills. The artistic, the musical, the poetic are activated from within and then embodied as living expressions of Spirit that come directly from our Source.

When we are on fire with the life force, we naturally begin serving life and others by just being ourselves. Just as the ego's chief desire is to serve the personality, the soul's deepest urge is to serve the whole by participating not on the sidelines of life, but joining in fully and uniquely, doing our own dance. As creative movement teacher and evocateur Gabrielle Roth once proclaimed to a group of us: "If you don't do your dance, it doesn't get done." The expression of our native talents, skills, visions, and dreams are the gifts we bring to the kingdom. And these expressions are richly seasoned by the depth of the suffering and tensions we've had to undergo in order to gain substance. This substance, then, is used by Spirit as grist for the mill in the making of the artist within.

Sixth force expresses empathetically, meeting others and ourselves right where we are in the moment, really listening and hearing with the magnetic energy of the soul. It operates from the law of attraction and repulsion, meaning we are drawn to others, or repelled by others, to the point that something creative is felt. This is the Christ-consciousness love known as *agape*. No longer trapped by the human passions that can become so possessive and limited, this level of consciousness is a passion for the whole.

If we become overidentified with humanity's sufferings, however, this feeling of high aspiration can take on too much of others' substance and become heavy; our service then bogs down in the conditions of living, and no longer inspired, we lose spiritual force. So we must make certain that we process our feelings when we feel unduly burdened, and own what parts we've become attached to or have allowed to take us down. Perhaps we'll discover some psychological unfinished business left over from a past personal hurt, or an issue we've denied and allowed to sink into unconsciousness.

Sixth force balances the lower nature's ego-centered appetites, emotionalisms, and desires, which reside at level two. Here, we meditate, and see the world more clearly. And often, we can see right where humanity is stuck or stumbling—and sometimes we weep, or sigh. At the sixth level of consciousness we access the archetype of the World Server, and are taught from within our right place in service to the whole.

SEVENTH FORCE:

The Love of God (Self)

(The Unifying Response)

COGNITION: Intuition
QUALITY: Spiritual Love/Will
BASIC URGE: Unity Consciousness
PITFALL: Indiscriminate Use of Will
INTEGRATION: The Human Will

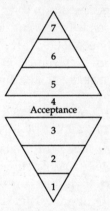

This is the home of the highest kind of cognition, the intuition—where the human will aligns with the will of God and manifests spiritual purpose in the world of outer events. From here, we can intuit not only our personal truth, but how we are fully equipped to serve humanity.

There are four ways of receiving knowledge from the intuition. The highest way is called *illumination*, which is revelation of the sacred in all things. Or, we can experience an *inner hearing*—a voice that says, "Go, do thus and so." And we know we must do it. A third way is to sense a *contact* with someone or something that evidences a relationship or liaison with the higher Self, an emissary from the transpersonal realms. And fourth, we can find ourselves *taking an action* that we had not intended with our logical mind, but suddenly feel must be done. All of these are ways of being in touch with higher knowledge. It is important to realize that the intuition is *never* wrong. It is the voice of your soul. It can be transcribed inaccurately, however, because we are not totally purged of all the ego's misperceptions about life and love. So there are important guidelines to follow when learning to trust the intuition in order to avoid mistakes that can occur if the ego takes over and interprets the message through the distortions of personal desire:

1. Uncontaminated intuition brings a feeling of inner calm and certainty, a sense of resolution that holds no doubt. There might be pain, because sometimes the revelation will mean letting go of some cherished attachment. But underneath the pain will be a sense of rightness that is unchanging, no matter what mood we are in.

2. The truth of the intuitive flash will synthesize other important things in your life. In other words, it will not violate or confuse any other truth that already exists for you.

3. Intuition will feel like *flowing* rather than *forcing*. It will not require effort to follow through on what was received; doors will easily open, rather than close, as you carry forward the message.

4. There is a sense of quiet humility with true intuition. It does not boast or brag. It has nothing to defend against and nothing to defend. It just feels like the natural next right step. No drama. No extremes. It has an is-ness that cannot be denied. And though the ego may go through ups and downs about impending changes or actions, this quiet knowing continually returns and settles into your center.

5. Intuition often comes in the form of symbolic knowledge from the inner side of life, which requires us to go beyond a literal interpretation. For instance, it may show you

an imminent physical death in a dream, when really what is happening is a kind of ego death.

6. Never act upon intuition without giving it the test of logic. Intuition does not live in time, so sometimes its messages come and the timing is off. It is better to wait and see if the message holds for a while, rather than acting impulsively. Test it out. See if doors open as you proceed. If each step seems effortless and natural, keep moving toward the goal. If you begin to feel that you are "pushing the river," this could mean the voice of a partial self is masquerading as your intuition, and the message is off the mark.

Seventh force expresses the quality of true being—the new "body"—its urge, to manifest the soul perfectly on earth. Physically, it opens at the "crown chakra," or the top of the head. Because of its unitive quality, it is referred to as a "place"—heaven, nirvana, paradise. Here there is no conflict; all is One, in perfect harmony, with perfect knowing. We get glimpses of this level of consciousness in our highest moments, but they are usually very fleeting. They are those magic moments when a pure truth, pure beauty, or pure love emerges and is expressed through us. These are the "peak experiences" spoken of by Abraham Maslow.

Certain drugs have taken people here; but seldom, if ever, do these experiences integrate, unless the person is willing to undergo the purification and daily practice necessary to maintain a true commitment to this exacting spiritual state. An integrated personality is a prerequisite for the proper use of this spiritual will. Drug abusers or imbalanced people who crave this kind of high in addictive ways do not possess an intact personality. Maya, glamour, and illusion will cloud the vision and give its host a distorted or fantasied impression mixed with ego desire or harmful extremes. Such people misuse will and power in the world, and if adept in the esoteric arts, they become Black Magicians and dangerous manipulators of spiritual principles.

Disintegration can occur if we find ourself at this level

before the organism is purified enough to handle the energy. Seventh force enables us to know for a fact that we are the full and final arbiters of our own destiny. Many are still not ready to face this fact, still caught up in the need to blame themselves or others for the "mistakes" they have made. Or they seek distractions that keep them from feeling the guilt of unmet requirements of a true spiritual advancement. Until blame, shame, guilt, and victimhood are transcended, it is unsafe for us to rise to the level of full understanding, where total and complete responsibility for our lives is demanded.

Seventh force is characterized by the courage to persist and by the absolute, unswerving awareness of our destiny. This is the energy that purifies and matures the *will to be* that is spawned at level one. Seventh force and the power of intuition put us directly in touch with the very goal which was our original intentionality, the purpose of our life. Like a luminous pressure, it "pushes the world and each thing in the world toward its own perfection through all the masks of imperfection" (Satprem). When our highest intuitive faculties are accessed and utilized for the good of humanity, we have become an individuated Personality, now able to reflect God's will through our natural ways of being. We have come home; we are now an embodiment of spirit.

Summary

The levels of consciousness residing within the domain of the higher Self are three distinctly usable transpersonal forces. As we can see, we truly *are* these three amazing types of energy that emanate from our soul-consciousness, perfectly designed to serve as specific Transformers for energy constricted in the three lower levels. The three below serve as a mirrored reflection of the three above: three in the world, and three beyond the concrete world. The ego's will to live, to feel, and to have an identity become the love of truth, life, and ultimately, God. When the two are merged, we are able to be in this world, but not of it. We have transcended our need to be attached to outcomes, and can just relax and be. All our willful effort to grow and expand is fully rewarded in effortlessness.

It is exciting to realize that the key to this entire operation lies in learning to use the powers already contained within us. Transformers merely invite us to be who we are; nothing has to be added to the Self, only released.

A Model of Transcendence

Transformers know that personality and essence are two distinctly different energies and that recognizing this difference is the *key* to understanding human nature. They break through the veil of partial truths that most of the helping professions are caught up in.

To summarize what we've learned so far, the main point is to realize that we are fourfold beings. The causative level of our behavior in the world is the spiritual dimension, our unique impulse to live a life of significance, a life that enacts our primordial purpose. Disease can occur at any level along the way when we get off the mark. Transformers check to see where they have gotten off track—on which level the pain is manifesting—and intervene at that level. They know the level of intervention will be the *symptom* level, and understand the cause will be in a higher (deeper) place.

For example, a physical treatment, such as a massage, will not cure an emotional illness, such as imbalance caused by a temper fit. It will only temporarily relieve the stress. Emotional help *can* cure a physical problem, however, since the emotional level is closer to the cause than the physical. We have to remember that we are hierarchical beings, with the physical being the most dense and the spiritual the most refined. Emotions are closer to the body, and ideas and beliefs are closer to the spiritual.

To continue our example, an emotional treatment cannot cure a mental insanity. For example, emotional calmness that comes from the technique of meditation will help to formulate clear, sane thoughts. But if an insane thought persists, even though the person meditates daily, the emotional stability will disintegrate every time the insane idea gets activated. Working to clear up the insane idea *will* heal the emotions, which in turn will heal the physical.

Transformers emphasize clearing up irrational thinking, releasing pent-up emotions that were built up from these thoughts, and guiding themselves and others to new action in the world based on truth and harmlessness. Because Transformers operate *consciously* within the Law of Cause and Effect, they know that any action, speech, or thought that brings harm to another individual will rebound upon its sender. Therefore, they train themselves and the people they work with to *act rightly* in life—to live according to a realistic value system and to treat others with an attitude of harmlessness.[1]

Working on the physical level of an addiction, using such techniques as detoxification and Antabuse, will not help an addict in the long run unless the emotional, mental, and spiritual aspects of his or her nature are accessed and healed. Energy constricted in the physical body will manifest as physical problems, just as energy constricted in the emotional body will manifest as imbalanced emotions *and*, possibly, a physical imbalance as well. At the mental level, constricted energy manifests as rigid, stereotyped, or unclear thoughts, which in turn can set off an emotional reaction. And behind it all, the spiritual Self has been denied its authentic expression. This is the process of how we go off track. So now, in order to understand the work of the Transformer, we must look deeper at the human being as an energy system and explore how constricted energies are released and redirected.

Energy: The Unexplored Factor in Addiction

Transformers, working from the fourth level of consciousness, are fully accepting of their own or another's current predicament, regardless of its nature. Transformers work within the law of transcendence, which says:

▲ **We cannot rise to a higher level until we accept fully where we are now.**

When someone is manifesting a natural urge negatively, the first task will be to redirect these misused energies. In order to do this work, the Transformer must have a precise understanding of how the three lower energies are specifically transmuted through the activation of the three higher energies.

THE ALCHEMY OF THE HEART

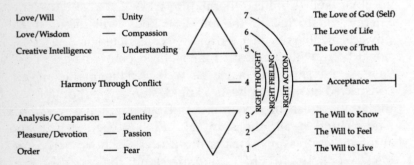

Love/Will	— Unity	7	The Love of God (Self)
Love/Wisdom	— Compassion	6	The Love of Life
Creative Intelligence	— Understanding	5	The Love of Truth
Harmony Through Conflict		4	Acceptance
Analysis/Comparison	— Identity	3	The Will to Know
Pleasure/Devotion	— Passion	2	The Will to Feel
Order	— Fear	1	The Will to Live

RIGHT THOUGHT / RIGHT FEELING / RIGHT ACTION

Level one deficiency transcends through seventh force. Both levels are "physical," the form or structure of the organism—ordinary being and transcendent being. Level two transcends through sixth force, a feeling/emotional state of being. Level three transcends through fifth force, a conceptual (mental) state of being.

Level four is the Transformer, the work of the heart. Fourth force is activated when third force is operating fully within the personality. In other words, until we learn to use our minds in a new way, extricating ourselves from mass-thoughts not based in experience, there is no vantage point from whence we can perceive the "conscious shock" that awakens us to the need to get beyond ego. If we cannot think anew, we will be content to become a better and better person, but we will not be a *new* person.

Fourth force is actually four energies: the personality energies of the physical, emotional, and mental levels combined with heart energy, the energy of acceptance. Fourth force becomes both the battleground and the bridge where experience and being meet for the first time. Its symbol is the cross, which equates with suffering. For this reason it is called "the plane of harmony through conflict," because it means being in the world and learning not to be *of* it. This is the path of the heart, the alchemical work that transforms our lives.

We live in a universe whose nature is duality. And through our experience of duality, we learn. When we became *created* from *uncreated* energy, we experienced our first dualism, inventing a state of consciousness based on experiencing opposites. Consequently, we work on a pole of dualistic energy like a pendulum swinging from the lower to the higher and back again. Both the higher *and* the lower are okay as long as the ego stays in its rightful place and does the job it is designed to do. But one without the other is never really sufficient.

Let's look again at the model used by Transformers in their work with addiction. (Refer to Appendix 2, page 284.)

For example, as we learn to transcend a need for passion to a state of compassion, level two energy is overlaid by the energy of level six. Emotional imbalance fades away, no longer the dominant force. Feeling guilty for natural sensual pleasures dissolves so that we are free to enjoy sensual awareness with our total being rather than just a fragment of ourselves. At level two, some people might have to put themselves in a seductive, manipulative subpersonality to relate to their lovemate. Then, once they accept themselves as sexual beings, they will find they can relax and enjoy their sensual self naturally and easily. The therapeutic task here will be resolving the struggle between the sensual/spiritual split within the person. People sometimes fear spiritualizing their sexual nature, believing it will mean having to give up pleasure. What really happens is the pleasures experienced at level two become intensified because they are now spiritualized with total meaning and a sense of sacred purpose.

▲ **When we realize a total concept of something *as we are experiencing it*, we are for that moment perfect.**

A moment such as this creates a state of bliss. The heart and mind have merged. A split no longer exists between the higher and lower.

Levels one and seven work together. At level one we feel isolated, filled with dread and fear of the outside world. At level seven, the organism knows it is a part of the whole, within which it lives and moves and has its being. It simply cannot conceive a thought of isolation. We shift from feeling mortal to a sense of immortality.

The one/seven pole is practical work. The individual or the therapist works with the struggle between powerlessness and personal potency. The highest and the lowest must merge to make a new structure, a structure based on the truth about our natural identity. Doing this work, people learn that they are the creators of their experiences, not victims of anything out there. They feel a sense of self-direction they've never before experienced. At the personality level, this is called taking full responsibility for our life.

When levels one and seven merge, we know we are an integrated, individualized human being. We can choose to use our energy for the manifestation of goodness, truth, and beauty. Taking responsibility for our lives is right living—means using our spiritual will, being directed by our soul's purpose. This is not to be confused with the ego's willpower, which only seeks personal gratification. This is the integration of human and divine will.

Likewise, levels two and six form a polarity, both containing the energy of our feeling nature. The lower emotional level can swing from pleasure to pain and back again. It can get manic or depressive, or it can become hysterical. It searches for the highs in life by identifying with objects and people that give it a kick. Many chemically addicted people are stuck at this level. "If I don't feel high, I don't feel alive."

Going from drug to drug is really no different in principle than going from person to person or object to object looking for that exhilarated feeling of being alive. So we all know what this stage feels like, even though we may not be chemically addicted. For instance, we might think we always have to have the most perfect and gorgeous mate by our side to make us feel excitement. And when we no longer see that person as perfect and gorgeous, we want to trade for a new model. Houses and cars can be used this way, too—or vacations to new and exciting places, growth groups, or even spiritual paths. We can tell these are becoming an addiction if the energy goes out of them once they've been experienced. Satiation leads to searching for a new group/object/person. Frustration of the need leads to trying to get more and more from the same outside source, until we wind up angry or depressed.

Level two experiences—the pain we encounter while seeking pleasure—are the ways we develop a balance between love and wisdom. Learning to love discriminately, and to develop knowledge based on experience, is wisdom. This kind of love is effortless and never based on neurotic need patterns. It will always be balanced and realistic, producing good for all parties involved.

On levels three and five we do the mental work of conceiving the images, concepts, and beliefs that truly work for us. At this level, we resolve the polarity between status-seeking (or people-pleasing) and expression of the true Self. We become who we are, rather than what we thought we should be. If we are thwarted at this stage, we can be extremely rigid in our thinking. Or we can become an obsessive/compulsive, seeking more and more ego gratification by grasping for status from the outer world of experience. We take on jobs just because the title appeals to us. We marry a person just to have his or her identity. It is the ego's way of trying to play the drama of life, choosing the roles and characters it wants to model from living persons or from heroes it has idolized.

Here, the ego learns to express the purpose of the individual soul. The purpose of life, according to the ancients, is to make our spirit Self-conscious on all levels of reality, to gather life's experiences, one by one, and carry them back to the Source. But many of our experiences become painful predicaments. If we become *identified* with our experiences and forget who we really are, we are lost.

We are *involving* in life so we can *evolve*. Oftentimes, it is through trying and being disappointed with a certain role that we learn to let go of seeking that particular identity. Then, other times, it is through fulfilling a role that we grow beyond the need for it. Levels three and five are the active expression of our mental concepts about our Self. The need for ego-identity transcends to a desire for Self-expression when we work with this energy correctly. Before, our energy was drawn in from an outside source. Now the energy reverses and is directed outward from our center. And the outward search turns inward to the contemplative life. (See

Exercise #10, page 271, for help in achieving this energy shift.)

Persons stuck at this level often talk a lot about the important people they have known, the titles they've had, or the social or professional victories they've won. They need for you to notice these things, because these honors are their definition. Transformers can acknowledge this need in someone else and give to it gladly, for they work at level four consciousness. Counselors still totally ego-dominated will become aggravated with braggarts and often fall into one-upmanship. They won't be able to stand seeing others get the attention they are eliciting, for they, too, are stuck at this level.

Level four consciousness can see level three operating because it can "step aside" and disidentify from it. Then it can point out the mistaken search for the identity from the outside and gently direct the other toward an inner search. Transformers can make this point nonjudgmentally . . . just clear, straightforward, *truthful* energy passing from heart to heart.

THE SPECIAL SIGNIFICANCE OF THIRD FORCE

Self-transformation happens in the mind, and becomes an option for the first time when our will to know turns inward and we begin to say "Who am I?" (third force). Before this time, we are victims of our physical appetites, emotions, moods. Third force is mental. And the intellect contains the ability to release its limitations and think beyond itself, utilizing big mind, at level five. This, of course, is only true if we have built a bridge between our concrete and abstract minds (levels three and five have merged). And as you now can see, this bridge is the open heart.

When emotions think for us, as they do when we're operating at level two, they will only cognate within the limits of the feelings and desires of the moment. This is why we cannot trust an emotional response in decision-making. Haven't you sometimes heard yourself say things like "Well, I hope I never see her again!" in a fit of anger, or "I don't care what they say," when the exact opposite is how you truly feel.

When we act impulsively on emotion we nearly always feel later that we have made a mistake. It is during the clearer mental times that we get a glimmer of the higher or wider truth. We gain this clarity from our experience once we become conscious of what we're doing, through a willingness to observe ourselves objectively: "I've been worrying so much about trying to live up to everyone's ideas about this, I am just now seeing how much I really dislike my job." Or, "I say I want to be a bookkeeper, but when I'm actually doing the work, I hate it." Using third force lets us compare actual experience against our ideas *about* the experience by taking note. This will to know reality-tests and practices thinking new thoughts beyond the desire-nature. By this correct use of our concrete minds, we draw data by comparison and analysis and make logical decisions based on the outer world's experiences.

Third force can also do something even more amazing: It can *shock* you into a new awareness by imbedding a *seed thought* in your mind. Seed thoughts are concepts that contain transformational energy. They jolt our consciousness into a new way of seeing. George Gurdjieff called this process "the conscious shock" that must precede our awakening from a chronic state of sleepwalking. (See the Bibliography for the Nicoll and Speeth books on Gurdjieff's teachings.)

The truth principle contained within a seed thought is a principle residing at a higher (more integrated) level than the person is currently operating on. We can recognize this higher truth when we hear it, even though we've never heard it before, proving that we are really spiritual beings by nature; we are always just being re-minded. In other words, we've always known the truth, and truth will continually descend upon us if we move enough beyond ego-dominance to hear it.

A seed thought, then, is planted in the mind, nurtured, and begins to grow, manifesting the fruits of its nature as we synthesize other ideas that fall into place around this new organizing principle. You can use the seed thoughts printed in bold face in this book as you practice in transforming your mind. But remember what might serve as a seed thought for you might not for me; they are uniquely individualized according to the level of being achieved and the contents of our personal life history. We can distinguish seed thoughts from ordinary thoughts by the amazing jolt of energy they carry—a grand "Aha!"

One of the tasks of Transformers is to supply plenty of seed thoughts for people they encounter. Toss them out and see if they catch hold. And remember, truth can only be caught if the receiver is open and mentally prepared to receive it.

Acceptance, the Bridge

Transcendence through the polarities always requires level four energy. Acceptance of what is—ourselves as we are and life as it is—serves as the bridge to the higher centers. Without this quality we could not love ourselves enough to examine our faults or our true needs, nor would we be able to imagine ourselves as ever being any different from what we've already been. So we never just work with one/seven, two/six, and three/five. Instead our work will be with one/four/seven, two/four/six, and three/four/five.

There is one exception to this, and it pertains to the balancing of our sexual energy: Level two works with levels four, five, our creative expression center, *and* level six, to lift our sexual energy into a spiritual expression. Often we experience this as the voice changing, or sounds emanating from our throat that express a depth of feeling, a mantra, toning, or inspired speaking that we'd not known we were capable of. Then, once these energies are balanced, we no longer require so much sexual gratification from another; we feel more content within ourselves.

But as you read this, remember that we are dealing with a model, not absolute reality. A model serves as a road map, but it will never replace traveling through the territory. As you study these models, your intellect may forget this important distinction and latch on to a theory that tries to replace your actual experience. As Transformers, we realize no model of human nature will ever be absolute or linear in nature. Life is not lived in a straight line. It is experienced more as a dynamic spiral; our energies move up and down and all around, resolving dualities in ways we'll never completely comprehend. We move in and out of our experiences in a cyclic fashion until we have completed them. A particular event will keep recurring in our life until we learn the lesson our soul intends.

While still ego-dominated, we will evidence blocks at all three of the lower levels at once, for they all converge upon each other. But the focus will usually be noticeable on one level. People will appear to be a "one/seven," a "two/six," or a "three/five" type. For example, some people will indicate to us that they are very practical, step-by-step people. They take a one/seven approach to life's issues. With some, you'll note they receive their lessons in life through the emotions, so they speak in the language of feelings and moods—more a two/six response. Others utilize a more concrete mental approach for problem-solving. To reach someone effectively, especially at the beginning of a process, it's good to listen and respond to them in their way of hearing, which establishes a more rapid rapport. But again, this knowledge can sometimes serve as a guide into our own or another's reality, but must not be rigidly adhered to.

Consciousness acts as a searchlight. It focuses the energy in a particular place, putting all our attention there, depending upon what level of consciousness we are operating on at a given time, upon what is interesting us, and where we are putting our intentionality. This, then, becomes our reality; we will tend to see the whole world from that perspective at the time. This is a very important concept for us to realize in our work as people-helpers. It is certainly okay to aid others in transcending their limited viewpoint by offering them a new perspective. But we must get their attention first. And the only way we can do that is to join them in the heart, accepting them right where they are. Then we can work from one level higher and gently pull them upward. But if the level we are working from is too divergent from or foreign to that person's frame of reference, he or she will not hear you.

Someone whose higher centers are opened can see the lower ones at work, but someone who is stuck at a lower level of functioning cannot see the levels above—they simply do not yet exist. Consequently, the person at the more awakened level has more responsibility in the relationship than the other one. This is not an ego trip; it is a fact. The one who can see more of the whole is seeing more clearly; therefore, he or she cannot get away with denying the truth without experiencing some sort of consequence, or karma. And moreover, none of us can pretend to be at a higher level than we are. We simply are at a certain stage along the path of awakening. This is not a game; this is Reality. Level four is where we begin to understand this truth.

Summary

The proper use of creative force Self-creates, enabling the energies of the lower nature to manifest in the world authentically, as an expression of the higher Self's qualities. Misuse of creative force also creates, because mind is creative by nature. When we miscreate, the lower self separates off from the higher Self and operates without the aid of the greater Self's qualities. More and more false personality will now manifest, creating more ego-dominated substance (fog or density) as "reality." Now there will be *more* lower energy to be transformed, so we move backward instead of forward. Whether we are creating or miscreating, we must never forget that we are creative and responsible for our creations.

Creativity follows the universal laws of energy:

1. Energy (emotion) follows thought.
2. When thought and energy come together, something takes form, or "happens."
3. Concrete manifestation requires undivided attention (nondualistic). Thought and feeling must truly become one. "As a man thinketh, in his heart [with feeling], so is he."

In other words, things begin in the subjective realms of thought. The image or perception you "see" in your head matches the exact yearnings and feelings of in-loveness in your heart. And you begin looking for the ways this dream or creation can manifest. When it begins appearing, you follow where it leads you. Your noticing and expressing it is what makes creating such a rich experience. But we all must realize and accept the conflicts or the "rub" of creativity as well. For nothing can get created without the necessary pain or chaos associated with releasing the old while the new takes form.

The proper use of creative force is your birthright as a spiritual being. This is how you co-create your soul's original intentionality, or your part of reality. From *thesis*, through *antithesis*, and on toward *synthesis*, the laws of creativity carry us along until we reach our goal.

As long as the lower self operates as an upside-down triangle, it will misrepresent reality. The energy will cycle within the lower nature and even flow downward toward its densest point. This will literally bring you down. Third force simply *thinks* and then draws conclusions based on sensory/emotional needs and fragmented events. We make decisions based on these partial truths.

This is exactly how all addictions work. We mistake the substance of something concrete for the essence of what we are truly seeking. Looking in the wrong direction, we say to ourselves, if a little bit's good, then more and more and *more* will be better.

> *Do not mistake your bodies for yourself—neither the physical body, nor the astral (emotional), nor the mental. Each of them will pretend to be the Self, in order to gain what it wants, but you must know them all, and know yourself as their master.*
>
> —J. KRISHNAMURTI

The lower self, without the aid of the higher functions, miscreates. Desires become habits, which are nothing in the world but desires objectified and kept in perpetual motion. But let's not forget: In truth, all energy is one. At the base of all our habits, positive or negative, lies the universal desire to express life. This urge, which begins at the spiritual level, is the impulse to Self-create.

If the ego cannot get its needs naturally for safety, pleasure, and good self-definition, it does something funny or unnatural. It will substitute a gratifier, even if this is basically self-destructive in the long run. And the chemical and process addictions are some of these unnatural substitutes for an unmet organismic need. Since an addiction is a substitute, it will never really satisfy. The real need continues to go unmet, its force still felt. It is important to remember that persons in recovery from a debilitating addiction will not be able to maintain a stable sobriety unless the essential need can be met and the constricted energy tied to that particular need can be redirected to hit the mark.

For example, some people may still be stuck at level one with so many basic insecurities that they cannot feel loved by anyone, no matter how much the others profess to love them and even show them their love. Or people may be so imbalanced in their sexual nature they cannot stop the self-defeating behaviors of meaningless promiscuity long enough to gain some healing. Then they may drink or use drugs in order to feel better about their unhappy choices.

If I can get hold of the fact that I need to work on myself and commit to this, however, I will grow rapidly, gaining much insight as I release my pain, fill my cup by meeting my true needs, and discover what's underneath all this fog. Self-awareness and a willingness to own my "stuff" places me on an accelerated path of healing. If I refuse to admit that anything's wrong with me, however, and continue unconsciously searching outwardly for a "fix" and blaming life or others when things don't work out, I will have to grow the slow way: I will have to plod through my life's trials as hard lessons received daily—until at some point, I will hit bottom. Until we can own that we need help, and begin working on the original issues and seeking to meet the real unmet needs we're walking around with, we can never have a satisfying life.

When we learn to take responsibility for our growth and transformation, our experiences no longer have to define us. We learn to use the mind as a magician to imbue our ordinary reality with the essential qualities of wisdom, inspiration, and joy. When we take on this sacred responsibility as conscious participators in our own unfolding destiny, we become seekers on the path of truth. We are no longer victims of the lower self's egoistic drives. But it is through the painful lessons of the ego life that we gain the necessary force to die and become reborn into a life based on truth.

When we opt for this individual responsibility to consciously evolve, we enter into the magnificent work of transforming all of Humanity. And our lives begin to fill with a sense of meaning and spiritual purpose. Our little human wills reach upward toward the ways of the higher Self, and the two join hands in the blending of love and will.

By thy stumblings, the world is perfected.
—SRI AUROBINDO

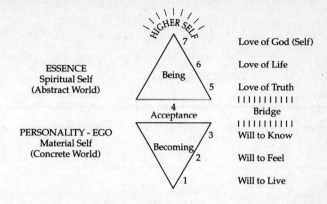

We are like the acorn, striving to become an oak tree. It begins as a raw little seed (essence), unprotected by the tough, hardy acorn shell. This tiny seed—already destined by nature to become a grand oak tree—is doomed if it cannot build around itself a strong shell. The seed represents the raw material we are born with, our essence-potential, containing the God-energy that leads toward perfect completion. The acorn, tough and hardened, is like our personality, the home of our ego, a protective covering for us to use while we are developing in the world. At some point in time—given the right circumstances—the acorn breaks open, shedding its protective boundaries, allowing its essence to pour out from the center, rising up toward the sun, pursuing its destiny. And the finished product does not even vaguely resemble the acorn! Isn't that interesting? And it now produces other seeds, complete with their protective coverings, and so propagates itself.

And this, too, is our story.

BOOK TWO

THE PRACTICAL WORK

OF THE

TRANSFORMER

Living in the present fuses the observer and the observed, harmonizing the mind. Once this is set in motion, the higher functions of evolution take over and start moving on their own account. Look at yourself with clear eyes and the rest will take care of itself.[1]

—*YATRI*

Introduction: The Artists of Self-Creation

Our philosophical mind-set determines everything we do vis-à-vis another. Consequently, this underpinning serves the most fundamental purpose of grounding us in using ourselves as instruments in the life of someone else. The more secure we are in our own philosophical base, and the more clearly we can see reality, the more we emit the quality of *potency*, one of the counselor traits that research has found in high-functioning counselors. Counselors who have potency are people who "walk their talk." They trust in the process of being human. And it shows.

The Transformer's world view works with the highest, most synthesized universal principles, drawing them down from the abstract into the concrete world. The Transformer takes a *pro*active view of humans, which focuses *forward* toward the wholeness that is trying to emerge, rather than backward toward the fragments of past errors. The Transformer works with the future *now*. They use a model of helping that contains four levels, since humans are fourfold beings. This model manifests as four different settings and therapeutic models, which become the appropriate line of work within the context of Transformers' own lives and the lives of those they interact with. (We'll study these levels in Chapter 7.)

Transformers work with three natural laws of energy that determine how human beings utilize their energetic force. It's just now being acknowledged in the field of human sciences that we humans are energy systems. This knowledge is coming in mainly through the area of transpersonal psychology, holistic health, and the new physics. The laws of vibration, energy, color, light, and sound—these will be prominent themes in the therapies of the future.

Transformers are learning to understand the subtler levels of these energies affecting us. The three laws of energy we will study are rooted in hermetic principles—knowledge that was prominent in ancient Egypt and Greece but has been almost lost to us today. These laws are the law of motion, the law of use, and the law of free will. In the next section, these laws will be explained.

Transformers use their knowledge of the superconscious mind, along with knowledge of the subconscious mind, the level where most therapists of the past have focused. The superconscious realm contains the key to transcendence, or the ability to transmute lower-self constricted energy into its higher-Self positive counterpart. For instance, my addiction to something out there was merely the misuse of my precious creative energy searching for an outlet.

Transformers teach us to turn in a new direction, feeding energy into the positive side of the pole, which has been blocked in its expression by our complete and compulsive concentration on the negative. Transformers understand the mechanism of transmutation and bring about transcendence of addictions rather than merely *overcoming* addictions.

Transformers know that what we've thought and fed energy to, consciously and unconsciously, is what we've become.

♦ And because we can change our thinking, we can change our lives. Heaven and hell are nothing but states of consciousness.

In this section we will travel through the spirals of the hierarchical journey through the self-created "hells" we invent as we become attached to things and people outside ourselves to find the answer. And each level of consciousness will contain its positive antidote, the *way through* the addiction.

And finally, the journey beyond addiction will be explored in an extensive interpretation of the twelve-step programs of Alcoholics Anonymous and other addictions. The Transformer is familiar with this twelve-step spiritual path, for it is the universal path we all follow when we move from personal egoistic living, through healthy and resolved relationships, and on into a world of serving others caught in the predicaments of life. It is an organic process.

The Transformer brings us to that inner Reality where we meet our true nature, that place we call our Home. All of these principles and issues will be dealt with in Book Two, to aid Transformers in making explicit their mental and spiritual grounding.

Utilizing the Higher Knowledge

Transformers work from an enlightenment model of human nature. They see us in our perfection and then attend to the blocks and misconceptions that are stopping us from realizing this potential wholeness. They recognize quite easily where we are stuck and choose a method of intervention to match the level where we live.

When translated into the everyday world of someone seeking help, this becomes four different settings, or models of helping, that are hierarchical in nature: physical, emotional, mental, and spiritual.

The Four Models of Helping

When a person is physically ill, we work within the medical or healing model that we know heals the physical body. The person's physical health is below normal. Our goal is to bring the person up to physical wellness.

When people are well physically, they will naturally seek relief on the next level, which is the psychosocial—intrapsychic conflicts (inner difficulties) and interpersonal relationships. The goal, again, is normalcy, or balance.

Once this level is achieved, people seek to rise above their normal level of functioning. They begin to seek the actualization of their potential. Our goal here is to turn people on to their strengths, talents, wishes, and dreams, helping them live life more fully, enhancing what is already healthy and functioning.

When people advance into the Self-actualization level of functioning, as they continue to grow they automatically begin to seek enlightenment, or total conscious awareness of the human being and the universe. Spiritual paths become individualized at this level depending upon the type of individual seeker. There is no *one* path appropriate for everyone at every stage. At this level, ordinary rules tend to vanish. There are no longer norms, comparisons, or even limits. This level of growth has a broad perspective that takes in all other perspectives. In other words, it can utilize the medical, psychosocial, or Self-actualization models of intervention when appropriate; it does not have to pit one against the other, judging one as bad and another good.

Enlightenment means total acceptance with relevance and discrimination of whatever another might need at a particular time in life—seeing clearly how everything relates to everything else. Since this is the highest, most expanded viewpoint, it can look down at the narrower levels and see it all. The following analogy I learned from Swami Ajaya helps us understand enlightenment: Imagine yourself suddenly trapped in a cave, hundreds of feet underground, in absolute darkness—encompassed by a sense of fear and unfamiliarity. Then you discover you have a pack of matches in your pocket, so you strike one and it lights up your immediate surroundings. This affords you the data you need to know that you are okay right where you are standing. But you still don't know what's out there. So, cautiously, you move forward a few feet and you strike another match, now lighting up another fragment of your reality. The light goes out, and you move to another point in the cave and strike a match. Now you "know" three different portions of the cave, but you still don't know the truth of your situation down there. Then, suddenly, someone enters and turns on a light switch. Now, the entire underground cavern is ablaze with light, every nook and cranny illuminated. This is enlightenment.[1]

Transformers tend to approach intervention into the life of another from the enlightenment point of view, even though that person may not be there yet. Language does not lend itself to a full description of working from the enlightenment level. Try to intuit what I am attempting to describe just now. And, remember, a paradox exists here: You don't have to be enlightened to work from the enlightenment model! You have only to be committed to bringing as much light and openness *as possible* in any given situation.

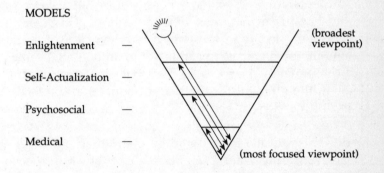

MODELS

Enlightenment —   (broadest viewpoint)

Self-Actualization —

Psychosocial —

Medical —   (most focused viewpoint)

Let me elaborate, to avoid misunderstanding. I am *not* saying that people who work with the medical model are less enlightened than anyone else. Some of the wisest people on this planet are healers, medical doctors, and researchers concerned with the physical body. I *am* saying that when we utilize the enlightenment model, we may very well choose to work within that medical arena for an express purpose. And we will know what that purpose is.

The same is true for all the other levels. However, if people are stuck in the physical/medical model and have never seen beyond this level, they will interpret the entire world through the lens of the medical approach. They will see the physical/medical reality as the *only* reality. Whereas, if they have only advanced to the psychosocial level of work, they will see the medical and psychosocial as the only reality.

The self-actualization level is still limited to personality development. Enlightenment transcends personality, seeing the larger meaning in every situation, taking it all in, but it might choose to focus on any one of the more limited levels *for a specific purpose, for a specific person*.

I think many of us have experienced how this works. Have you ever tried to talk to a closed-minded medical doctor about your fear of taking drugs for a cure of something? She simply cannot "hear" you. She sees a medical answer as the *only* answer possible. Have you ever tried to talk to a social work professor or a psychologist who does not believe in anything but his own model of intervention? This person sees everything in life in terms of a psychological or social problem. Or, have you ever been in a human potential center where the panacea seems to be personal gratification, total honesty-in-the-moment-for-the-sake-of-honesty and total expression of the current ego need? "I am I and you are you and if by chance we meet that's cool; if not, it can't be helped." This attitude is assumed by them to be an enlightened one, but only among people who are stuck in a self-development model of human nature. Every level that looks only at the body, the emotions, or even *the personality as a whole* is still too limited to explain all of our human potential. For we are spiritual beings!

Transformers are attempting to stamp out limitation by learning to let go and accept *everything* as helpful, including the knowledge of how to discriminate what's appropriate for whom and when. And remember:

▲ You do not have to be enlightened to work from the enlightenment model of helping.

The only rule is that we have to be committed to bringing as much light as possible into the here-and-now at any given time, on any given subject. We are committed to seeing the whole and remaining open to newness. And if we will go within and ask our higher Self to give us this expansive point of view, it will be provided.

The Transformer's View of Human Beings as Energy

Because Transformers view the human being as an energy system and addiction as blocked creative energy, they utilize three laws of energy as guidelines for the release of creative potential in humanity.

THE LAW OF MOTION

Life is motion. Even in absolute calm, there is movement. Stillness is movement in repose—in perfect tune with the flowing of a motion-packed universal force.

And since life *is* movement, there is nowhere to stop. We are always *in process*, the process of becoming. The universal energy, of which we are a part, is directional. It takes us upward and inward, heading toward our Source. A natural law of physics, discovered long ago, dictates that everything returns to its source.

So we can count on the knowledge that even our trials and our errors are temporary, taking us where we need to go. Our higher Self will lift our energy constricted in animal-istic, subconscious behavior right on up and into the higher centers that manifest the essential truth of our unique nature. We can transcend our lower self, for that is how we are designed. And when the lower self rebels and gets its way, we can know it is only a temporary victory. The higher Self will ultimately prevail if we continue to choose growth, for this truth is in the master plan that governs the larger Reality.

Transformers work with this knowledge—transmuting the lower drives into their higher qualities. They know that all energy is One. And they can manifest through any of the seven different levels of consciousness. When we understand this, we can use this knowledge as a diagnostic tool. The body will tell us where the energy is flowing—consequently its purpose—or where it is stuck—consequently, its fear.

For example, recently I went through an emotional churning that was created by thinking I was losing a loved one. When I catastrophized about the future without him, I felt the energy in my solar plexus. He has been very important to my ego's sense of confidence, a necessary mentor to me. When I reflected for a moment on his needs and became aware he might need to leave for his own sake, the energy left my third center, and my heart (fourth center) hurt. While I reflected, I was walking along a path in a beautiful park. My consciousness became captivated by a gorgeous blooming tree, and for a moment the glory of nature fell in upon me, juxtaposed against my sadness. I felt the energy go up into my throat (fifth center) as a desired expression of tearful joy and meaning. For a while I saw the whole context of death/rebirth and the natural law of cycles in operation in my life. In that moment, I knew I could let my friend go; I sensed the eternity of our shared love.

Our energy is like the varied colors that flow through a prism. All of it is light. The colors are its distortions, shaded by the multidimensions of desire.

THE LAW OF USE

The ability to co-create life force is the organizing principle of human nature. This act gives us our form. This is what is meant by living as opposed to dying. We have the capacity to constantly create new energies, even to the point of regenerating new cells every seven years of our life. And the moment this activity ceases, our body dies.

The paradoxical human predicament is that we continually manufacture new energy, and then we don't know what to do with it. If this energy just sits in us, unused, it ferments and makes us sick. It must be used. And since most of us have lost touch with the Self-creation it is meant to be used for, we relieve ourselves of it through the seven centers we have studied—the seven levels of consciousness—through fear, passion, or seeking ego status if we still are identified with the lower self. When enlightenment begins dawning, and we are able to utilize our higher centers, we can then harmonize our energies, making our lives creative and inspirational, even blissful. The choice is ours as to how we use or misuse our energy.

The saints and sages teach us that we are channels, drawing energy down from the Source, which contains truth seeds designed for one purpose only—to enlighten us as to our true and rightful nature and purpose. This energy is designed to come in through the tops of our heads and out through our hearts and into the world. And this is how we teach and learn from others. When we are sharing our truths "heart to heart," we are using our energy rightly, efficiently. When we harbor it—through greediness or self-doubt—we feel dissatisfied with ourselves, and we sicken. The energy must be put to its proper purpose.

Transformers concern themselves with their own right uses of energy and with that of those they work with. They learn and teach others this principle of service to their fellow human beings. They know they must never hoard a piece of Self-knowledge, no matter how small.

THE LAW OF FREE WILL

As said before, we cannot move to a higher level until we accept fully where we are *now*. We do not grow by changing into someone we are *not*, but by becoming more and more of who we are.

Yet everyone does not seek growth. And certainly, plenty of us resist Self-knowledge and complete transformation. But all of us resist change some of the time, even ardent seekers of truth. It is an observable fact that we are free to choose growth and change or not. At least, so it appears. But are we really?

Human beings are evolving in a process of conscious evolution. The levels below us (mineral, plant, and animal) evolve with no effort—completely in tune with nature, and with no conscious intention. This does not mean these levels do not have their own kind of consciousness; but it is a consciousness operating *un*consciously.

At the human level we operate with the ability for thought. We have become "Manas, the Thinker," from (*manas*, the Sanskrit word meaning "man.") This thinker in us is the immortal individual, the Spirit-self, clothing itself with personality, but larger, grander than personality. It is the "I" who is evolving, able to observe its process as it passes through its human experiences as it ascends up the ladder of being, a thinking Entity imprisoned in a body.

> *Try to imagine a "spirit," a celestial being, whether we call it by one name or another, divine in its essential nature, yet not pure enough to be one with the ALL, and having, in order to achieve this, to so purify its nature as finally to gain that goal. It can do so only by passing* individually *and* personally, *i.e., spiritually and physically, through every experience and feeling that exists in the manifold or differentiated universe.*[2]
>
> —ANNIE BESANT

We can choose to evolve, or we can choose to remain mindless and asleep. But the tension lies in the essence of each of us to make the choice. Free will is part of our nature, not just a happenstance occurring at random. And since we contain this tension (growth vs. nongrowth) *within the very core of our being*, perhaps we do not really have a choice. I can choose nongrowth, but does this relieve the existential tension within me? No! If even a tiny part of me is awakened, it will observe the unawakened part with concern and seek to force it out of its sleep state. The only way I can feel absolutely no tension is to be totally asleep—totally unconscious. But then, I would be a rock, or unaware of myself. Could it be then that a human being simply must evolve, and *will* at some point in time? We are free to choose when and how we will move forward, but perhaps we are not at all free to choose whether or not we will indeed move.

Transformers work within the law of free will. People can choose their own timing and method of growth, but Transformers know they *must* grow. Transformers keep the tension alive and focused on the growth choice, aware that the self is merely choosing how long to postpone a certain advancement. We *will* evolve—with all the joys, sorrow, and trials this journey entails.

No one can relieve us of the personal responsibility to press forward as an evolving Self. We each must do this for ourselves. We leave the comfort of the many, the society that sleeps, and we venture into the lonely world of the seeker. Transformers see this aloneness as a fact, painfully aware of its truth within themselves. They know, and they feel compassion.

▲ **No one can become conscious for us!**

Specific Life Issues Revisited

Psychology books are replete with information about certain issues that become recurring themes for people and for the counselors who work with them. We will now explore some of these issues, redefined in accordance with the Transformer's theoretical assumptions that are sometimes in direct opposition to the basic tenets of many conventional psychotherapies.

Transformers often find themselves in a "paradigm collision" with the mainstream health professionals. For instance, a Transformer knows that healing always begins in the inner life, and cannot be medicated or "fixed" by an outside expert. In fact, they believe that the power of healing and true authority is always within the one seeking help, and not in the helper. Transformers know there is never an external expert on us, no matter how well trained or intelligent another might be. They see true helpers as people who encourage the natural process of healing and serve as safe and caring guides to discovering this innate wisdom of the organism.

Transformers also know that symptoms are good, not bad, and should be encouraged to come out and show themselves so they can be accessed and healed. They seek to encourage the healing process, and disagree with approaches that repress feelings, or otherwise interfere with what the organism is trying to do on its own.

You will see evidence of this new paradigm thought through the following recurring themes.

RESISTANCE

Force does not become creative until it meets resistance. Light does not become visible until it strikes an object.[3]

—LAMA GOVINDA

Resistance is a gift. And we must learn to respect it. Often the higher Self uses resistance to step down our energy. Sometimes we are trying to move too fast. At times like this, the higher Self will mediate to keep us from blowing a fuse.

Resistance represents the beginning of a change. Something new is trying to emerge from our unconscious. If the resistance is coming from the subconscious, our lower self's unconscious motivations, we might feel fear at seeing this monstrous part of ourselves that has never appeared in the light of day. So we resist, not knowing what will happen if it rears its ugly head. We may need time. Or we may need to be treated gently. It could be we are not ready to make the life changes that will be required once we see this fragment of ourselves clearly.

If the energy is coming from the superconscious, the higher motivations, it means a new quality of perfection is trying to emerge, to be expressed through us. Often, this new quality will also require some life changes we are not prepared to make. What if I do become a leader? What if I let go of my defenses against being psychic? What will happen if my creativity emerges in full force? Many of these higher traits, the glorious aspects of the God-self, can indeed be frightening if they come upon us unprepared.

We can determine the origin of the resistance by eliciting symbols and imagery from our own imagination or from the imagination of the person we're working with. (See Exercise #14, page 277.)

Just for a moment, ask yourself, how do you experience resistance in your life? Perhaps there is a habit, an addiction, you are being asked to let go of, but you resist. What would you be like without this crutch? What is it holding you away from? How do you resist? What behaviors of resistance do you use, what ideas, what feelings? First look at each resistant behavior, feeling, or idea as getting in your way. Now look at each for the *value* that it has for you. Are you surprised? You see, there is a gift there. Resistance can be a teacher; it can point you to where you need to grow.

Ask yourself: In order to allow a new superconscious quality to come into your life, what strengths would you need to develop? What attitude would you need to hold? Are you willing to begin developing them now? Why not? How can you be more consciously aware and cooperative with your higher Self so that your own evolution can advance more evenly and rapidly?

I've learned that resistance gives me the opportunity to contact the part of myself that is scared, hurt, or deluded.

When I choose to experience pain and watch it consciously, it begins to give me its message. I can see what is needed. If I only look at the pain, I do not learn anything. But if I hold both views at once . . . feeling the pain and seeing the *meaning* of the pain . . . both the worldly experience and the higher knowledge . . . I become a channel for truth. I am *standing within* my experience consciously; I am in the process of understanding.

> Let me not beg for the stilling of pain,
> but for the heart to conquer it.
>
> —*RABINDRANATH TAGORE*

PROBLEM-SOLVING

Transformers do not believe they have the answers to others' problems. They know the answer resides within the person. But the answer must come from the true Self. If it is coming from a partial self, it could be simply an emotionally laden reaction to the situation that cannot be relied upon as the whole truth.

When a person seeking help asks you what to do about something, a Transformer response would be: "What does the wisest part of *you* say to do?" or something to that effect. Transformers ask themselves that question about their own lives as well. If we cannot immediately gain the clarification that we seek, we can put ourselves into a state of relaxation and get a message from our higher Self. (See Exercise #1, p. 253.)

In a counseling session, the counselor and the client will discuss the results of this work. Or the counselor may ask the client to go into the silence. (See Exercise #10, p. 271.) Then the person can discover, without any guidance or interruption from the counselor, what truth emerges.

If an answer does not come, or the message is too garbled, ambivalent, or vague to be helpful, a Transformer will work with the client's interference patterns. What is blocking this person's awareness of the answer to his or her problem? Fear, anxiety, or confusion are often a way of keeping the person from having to face the next step that is beyond the solution to this current problem. Perhaps the person is not emotionally ready to face this answer. Or maybe physical illness is weakening his or her ability to cope with the stress of the particular change in life. Trust the resistance and work with it. It will give way if it is supposed to. Trust the process. The only wrong is unwillingess to become conscious. As long as we are conscious of our resistance and willing to take responsibility for it, things can proceed according to the process of Self-creation.

CHANGING ANOTHER

Transformers don't try to change others for a very simple reason: They don't believe anyone needs changing! We're all responsible for our own evolution. The seeds for our unique advancement are already within us. Since transformation occurs from within, Transformers know that to interfere with another's way is to become a toxic agent in another person's life, leading them *away* from themselves rather than toward more truth.

Transformers think in terms of opening rather than of changing. To open means to become more and more of what we are. Our very essence expands as we receive from life the requirements for its unfoldment. Like flowers who know when it's time for blooming, we move toward fuller expansion of our nature in the presence of a Transformer. Transformers encourage and endorse us for being ourselves.

Our opening is blocked only by the fear of going inward to meet our fears face-to-face. When we stand at the portal of our fears, afraid to peek inside, our fears become powerful and demonic. But our fears can only hold their power so long as we won't look at them. Once we do, we discover an emptiness—the void. There is really nothing there at all! Our fears are illusions that exist in our minds. Transformers know that the power of the mind can overcome any fear totally— even the fear of death. Opening is the key to being. We already *are* who we are intended to be. We've just been closed to this realization.

Transformers believe that continuing to work on themselves, seeking higher and higher levels of consciousness, is all they ever need to do. The result is that they become a light unto others, because they reflect the truth. Transformers are like lanterns; their light flows naturally from within, guiding others by their very nature, absolutely without effort. *R*eforming is effortful, tiring, and never really accomplishes anything.

▲ **Transforming is effortless because there is nothing to be done; there is only someone to be.**

MORALITY

Transformers view moral issues as human-created. God is seen as impartial. When we're filled with moral concepts, we become extremely judgmental and condemning. We miss the point of life. Morality belongs to the outer world of experience. Love, wisdom, and acceptance are the truth of the inner world. A moralist becomes a constant vigilante—a sentry of life, not a master of life. Moralists are so busy guarding, judging, and labeling, that they dissipate energy that was designed for Self-creation. And because they suppress their very being, they must condemn yours. Transformers do not see things so much in terms of black and white. Having wrestled with the dualism, they balance the polarity by seeking a higher, more integrated solution. They have come to know that life has to be accepted in its totality.

Transformers adopt the ancient Vedantic saying: "Don't pay much attention to the doing, pay attention to the being. Don't think of what is to be done, just think of who you are." And another, from St. Augustine: "Love God, and do as you will."

Transformers say, *as you are* you are welcome. The problem has never been that others are rejecting you; the problem has *always* been that you are rejecting yourself. You make mistakes in the outer world of experience, *not* because you are bad, but because you don't understand life. There is no improving to do, no place you have to get to. You merely have to learn to look within and realize who you are.

▲ **You have forgotten yourself, and that is your only fault.**

THE HERE AND NOW

Transformers believe the here and now is the eternal moment, the only place where transformation can happen. To be totally in the here and now, one must become goalless, desireless. If we suddenly become aware that we have forgotten time—that we just passed through a space where time vanished—we are in the here and now. And where was desire? Desire always longs for something we do not yet have, so it is always in the future. Or it is stuck in the past, dwelling on some fantasy of what might have been, if only. . . .

Desirelessness is the key to here-and-now living, getting fully into the moment with fascination. It matters not what fascinates us; if our Spirit is involved totally, we are present, filled with life, and being. Our livingness becomes a meditation.

The here and now is the center of the cross—being in the middle of the flow of life:

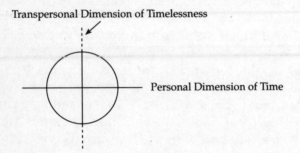

Transpersonal Dimension of Timelessness

Personal Dimension of Time

Life flows past us, experiences come and go, and we are present receiving them, feeling them, allowing them to flow on past. We are right at that place where the personal dimension of past, present, and future *happen*, as the transpersonal dimension enters us "from above," or from the inner side of life.

Christ on the cross is the model of authentic existence—living and being fully Himself, in the eternal now. It is the stance we are all challenged to accept.

The present moment is a chance to meet head-on the tests and trials of our past actions and causes. We can choose to dissolve the stresses and strains we've collected within ourselves by the thoughts, feelings, and actions we've created over the years. To the extent that we can become conscious of these tensions, we can free our constricted consciousness so it can become identified with our true and rightful nature and purpose in life. A wise man told me once: We are here purely for one reason—to dissolve all anger, fear, and repressed resentments we've built up through living our lives, so our light can shine through.

SELF-KNOWLEDGE

Transformers ultimately concern themselves with only one kind of knowledge: knowledge of the Self and the universe It inhabits. They know that this is the one form of knowledge that is transforming. Other types of knowledge teach us to be practical, to live more effectively in the mechanistic world. But Self-knowledge brings leaps of consciousness, synthesizing fragments of truths we already know to a higher octave. This is how higher and higher levels of integration occur.

Transformers live by the maxim: "Know Thyself."

The Self—at one and the same time the Self of all living creatures, and therefore my Self—knows no bounds; so the entire universe is within me, and my Self fills all the universe. Everything that is—I am! In everything I love, I love my Self, for the only things we think we don't love are what we haven't yet come to recognize within ourselves![4]

—*ELISABETH HAICH*

Our business is to turn resolutely away from the limited ego's ignorance and listen to the wisdom that, whatever anyone may say, is sounding within us *at any given moment.*

Seekers of truth must have the sort of courage that holds us firmly in the certainty of our inner aim, even when we are being censured by others in the outer world.

He who hesitates on the brink of the dangerous waters of this knowledge, wishing for assurance of his safety before plunging, will never achieve inner certainty. One cannot learn to swim without swallowing much water.[5]

—*SRI KRISHNA PREM*

Seekers distinguish Self-knowledge from religion per se. Religion can be a path toward Self-knowledge, but not necessarily. For many religions have forgotten that the Self and the soul are synonymous terms.

▲ **Self-knowledge is knowledge of the Spirit and does not belong to any sect or religious group.**

Self-knowledge is the birthright of humankind— whether we choose to claim it or not. Spirit is the very core of our being, and knowledge of this sort provides the road map for the journey into Self we all must make if we are to evolve.

Historically, the priests of the various religious orders have very grudgingly divulged universal truth, preferring the safety of teaching only the standard dogma of their particular framework, presented in a socially approved manner. Teaching the *real* truth about the Self requires moving into wild and dangerous territories, for it gives us the key to our power and the responsibility, rendering us unfit to be a passive follower of any limited orthodoxy. The power of the priesthood is thereby often compromised and, consequently, ineffective.

Records show that the great Christian mystic, Meister Eckhart, was excommunicated for teaching the truth to his people in lay language that they could understand, thereby placing the keys to knowledge directly into their hands.[6] Today, Dominican priest Matthew Fox has also experienced being silenced by the Vatican for speaking of a creative, more feminine and participatory spirituality.[7]

THE TRANSFORMER'S VIEW OF FAMILY

Little babies are born into this world already advanced in certain areas of character and deficient in others. Researchers have noted great variances in babies' talents, likes, dislikes, genius, modes of expression, and needs, which offer the suggestion that we are indeed *not* born equal, if equal means exactly alike. And we were certainly *not* born a blank slate, as Sigmund Freud believed!

Our original family is the context and training ground wherein our basic patterns of thought, feeling, and behavior emerge, can sharpen, or be corrected. A functional family minimizes the weaknesses and builds up the strengths of the children, thereby aiding them in forming a strong, effective ego. A dysfunctional family unintentionally maximizes the weaknesses and fails to build upon strengths, from a lack of awareness of the true needs and potentials of its members. This creates a "karmic predicament" for the individuals to work out. The adult family unit and intimate relationships we choose to form in later years gives us the opportunity to correct the unenlightened attitude and the mistakes made within the original family unit.

If we've learned our lessons, we become agents of transformation for our children, indeed, for our entire family chain. If we do not learn, we continue that particular family's lineage of "neurosis" in a robotlike fashion. And no evolution takes place.

Some of us become "quantum leaps in consciousness" for our family chain. We get into the business of Self-creation and advance so rapidly that we do, in one generation, the work of spiritual growth that usually requires several generations to accomplish. As we learn to be an enlightened member of our personal family, we are elevated to a level of serving the larger family of humanity, in whatever area we've prepared ourselves.

These are some questions Transformers use to help us understand the meaning and spiritual significance of our membership in the families we were born into. Transformers know that on the soul level, we *chose* with care the family we incarnated through. Perhaps the following questions will provide you with some important clues:

1. What skills did you have to build in order to defend against a particular adult in your family unit? And how is that skill now useful to you as an adult in your personal development or in your life's work?

2. What kind of models (negative or positive) did you have in your family that add to your Self-knowledge? How have these models aided you in developing strengths you needed in order to actualize your unique potential?

3. What role did you play in your family that now has meaning for you as an adult in a new way? Were you a leader, a peacemaker, an entertainer? Note how this role helps or hinders you today.

4. Quietly reflect on your original family unit for a few minutes. Now, describe a symbol that, to you, represents the unit. What does this symbol elicit in you? What *meaning* does this symbolic information hold for you today?

5. What enlightenment comes to you if you think of your family as the one you chose on a superconscious level— before you were born? What if you think of your family as giving you exactly what you needed for your soul's advancement? Maybe it wasn't what you *wanted*, but what you needed.

Your reflection upon these questions will provide important clues to your unique purpose in life.

PRIMARY RELATIONSHIPS

Transformers do not view all primary relationships as made in heaven and designed for a lifetime. *Some* are, for sure, but only those that were committed to *consciously*. Many people marry for neurotic, egoistic reasons, having nothing to do with matters of the soul. She was pregnant and needed a father for her baby. He was scared to live alone. She wanted prestige, so she married into a wealthy family with tradition. These kinds of ties are karmic, not cosmic. They contain lessons for the personality to experience that are sometimes learned to completion and transcended. Then the relationship may die a natural, *spiritual* death. (The soul needs for the relationship to die so room can be made for another relationship that is more appropriate for the tasks of the present, or perhaps for you to experience being alone.)

Transformers view all primary relationships as *one* continuation of the *one eternal relationship*. The form may change, but the principle remains one of seeking wholeness.

Transformers look for the purpose behind a relationship. They help people come to terms with the reality of the situation. They do not encourage divorce, nor do they encourage staying together. They merely promote clarity of vision and the courage to act on the principles of love and truth.

THE PARADOX OF THE INTELLECT

Overintellectualization is a danger all counselors and other people-helpers have noted, both in group and in individual work. We need to learn to use our minds to rise above emotional overreacting. And yet, paradoxically, we have all noticed that understanding a problem merely from the cognitive level is rarely helpful.

Here is an insight into this paradox, with, perhaps, a key to transcending it. The intellect does not operate in isolation from the two lower bodies, the emotional and the physical. I can understand something with my mind, but my emotional body and physical body can still contain the negative message I'm trying to overcome. I can *know* I shouldn't feel jealous, and I can rationalize that jealousy is a lower-self emotion that is based on illusion. But my emotional reaction still occurs, and my body hurts. Sometimes we must experience the mental concepts at all levels of being before they will change or heal us.

When knowledge of the negative event is contained in all three bodies, they must all receive the light of consciousness in order to transcend the negative state. And it quite often happens in stages: I might get the intellectual insight on Monday. The following Monday I may feel the energy again, but this time, my intellect and emotion connect simultaneously, and a catharsis occurs. I believe I've conquered the problem after this, only to discover a month later that I am experiencing a nervous stomach when this same situation again presents itself.

So now what? I begin to feel hopeless. Will I *ever* get over this? And the hopelessness begins taking me down into negativity about what a jerk I am! Well, the key here is that I am judging myself, being unloving, therefore *stuck*, based purely on ignorance of what's happening in my consciousness. I have indeed purged the mental and partially the emotional. What's left is lack of awareness at the cellular level of my existence. My cells still have not gotten the message. So a little partial self persists in holding on to a past program, based on memories stuck in my subconscious memory bank. My brain still is not enlightened about the nature and purpose of this particular problem. Since this is a problem with the *un*conscious mind, I will need to use some method that will access the psyche/soma connection and my unconscious mind, to bring about this enlightenment. I might choose breathwork, deep tissue bodywork, psycho-drama, guided imagery with evocative music, or some other expressive therapeutic method. (For example, see Exercise #12, p. 274.)

Though our minds try desperately to run off and leave the emotional/physical difficulties we face in life, it simply won't work. We must enlighten the wholeness of us. Mental, emotional, physical, *all* must be lifted up, spiritualized. In many spiritual or religious philosophies, the body has been viewed as an obstacle, incapable of spiritualization. It's perceived as the heavy part, holding the soul back. This sort of religion attempts to teach us to leave our bodies behind, to turn loose of our gross and lustful animal nature. This splitting off from our bodies and feelings can cause a condition called "spiritual bypass." We try to rise above our unfinished business, as though it will simply disappear if we ignore it.

This philosophy sees the earth as a field of ignorance, and the earth experience as a purging of our animal nature, a place to withdraw from forever. This philosophical attitude, however, violates the message that we are here to spiritualize the worldly. It keeps us in a dualistic consciousness—heaven is good; earth is bad. The highest truth has always been *all is one*. Matter *is* Spirit made concrete. Human *is* God in expression. We are charged with the human responsibility of finding the supreme positive even in the most negative. The high must meet the low, the limits of the past become the ingredients for a future completion. So long as we attempt to leave a part of us behind, unconscious, something remains. And if something remains, it means it must be reworked again and again. We will be doomed to repeat the same patterns in order to have, again, the opportunity to enlighten the remnants that are still in the dark.

Mentally, we all need clarity. We achieve clarity with the third force, the concrete mind, by a process of analytical, critical thought. That in turn activates fourth force, which enables us to view our past, *without judgment*, until we understand it. Then, we draw out the feelings that are stuck with the memory. We assist in the work of catharsis, a purging of the emotional body.

Many therapies teach cathartic techniques. But all effective ones share in common a focusing on the feeling, connecting with it, and getting it out. (See Exercise #9, p. 270, "Focusing on a Feeling.") Now, the body must *express* the pent-up feeling. If it is anger, a striking out, or beating, or yelling must occur. People need permission and tools for this kind of work. If you feel you cannot do it, refer the other person or yourself to a body therapist . . . a Neo-Reichian, Bioenergeticist, Rolfer, a Trager practitioner, or someone trained in breath work, or other methods that access cellular memory. These are merely a few of the experiential approaches to healing available today. If the body still contains the memory, there will be symptoms such as tightness of muscles, rigidity, pain, or illness. Or emotionally, there may be extreme depression, anxiety, or irritability.

We must realize the importance of completing the process from the highest to the very lowest, finally making conscious every little cell in our bodies. Otherwise we fall back again and again on our journey toward wholeness . . . one step forward . . . and two back . . . doomed to repeat. Perhaps the players will change, but the script will be the same old boring melodrama, the shadow without awareness of the light.

In my work, I have found that some people are extremely emotional, with no problem at all in contacting their feelings. And others have excellent use of their mental faculties but little success in getting in touch with feelings. It is good to help overemotional people use their minds, so they will have concepts that synthesize and attribute meaning to their emotions. As a therapist, I ask these clients to face me, eye to eye, while they learn to use their minds to cognate. Sitting directly in front of someone, maintaining eye contact, facilitates thinking. We work with seed thoughts that lift them out of their limited viewpoint. Or with affirmations that reprogram negative, vague, or incomplete thought processes, such as "I already contain within me the seeds of my perfection; I need nothing else." Or we reality-test our ideas and think them through together.

With people who tend to intellectualize their feelings, you can ask them to lie down and close their eyes so they can describe their painful experiences without using their intellect so much. Getting them into a state of relaxed consciousness helps them live for a while very close to their recalled experience, without the interference of your personhood to deal with. In this way they can reach their emotions more easily. They can relive the experience without feeling drawn into communication with you or into intellectualizing their experience. Music and guided imagery work well to avoid overintellectualization. Also, silence. To learn constructive uses of guided imagery, you can study *Psychosynthesis* by Roberto Assagioli, a delightful little book by Shakti Gawain entitled *Creative Visualization*, or my book, *Awakening in Time*. (See Bibliography.)

Please know that these techniques are extremely powerful. It is imperative that we work these on ourselves before we attempt to guide anyone else through an imagery experience. If they are new to you, you may feel a little shy at first in utilizing those techniques that work on the unconscious. Practice on yourself with your friends, and you will discover the power of these techniques for yourself.

Transformers aid themselves and others in descending all the way down—through the densest mental fog, into the emotional churnings, and deep into the subconscious, to the very cellular core of the difficulty. It is as though we seek to avoid the dark half of the truth, when actually, all of it is one thing. Our perpetual torment seems to be that we believe we have this darkness within us, this ugliness we call sin, evil, whatever. But here is how we view it if we are to transform ourselves: The very darkest shadow in us, the one most painful to face, has its exact same degree of corresponding light. We will carry in us the very obstacles that we need in order to *make real* our perfection. Always we will find that the shadow and the light go together. It is our special work to recognize the truth of our dark side in order to know the light. As long as we reject the one for the other, we will continue to fail in our mission of transformation and miss entirely the aim of our existence.

▲ My problem, or my dark side, is a teacher to me—a vital contact with my past that I am to attend to and make conscious. It has surfaced so I can know it.

The Transformer's Healing Function

Transformers act as catalysts for activating and directing the natural process of Self-creation. They perform the sacred function of helping human personality evolve. Transformers have already tapped into the creative powers of the higher Self. With hardly any effort, they seem to know how to give spiritual principles a concrete expression. Physically, emotionally, and mentally, we learn to function on higher and more integrated levels of consciousness until, at some point, our egos become passive and our essence active, and we begin to embody the higher Self. We become *soul-infused personalities*, aligned with our true life's work and creative expression. Transformers are instruments of Self-empowerment.

Misuse of the senses and emotions completely dissipates our ability for peace of mind. It totally exhausts our vital force. Our insecurities at level one turn into greed; love at level two becomes lust or needy love; or identity-seeking at level three becomes power-driven ego trips. Satprem refers to emotionalism as "fog incarnate," for it distorts reality in favor of the sentiment's notions of what is real. These miscreations make us immature human beings—fragmented selves acting in the world as false personalities.

As we become consciously awake, we can only tolerate

so much phoniness and self-deceit. Trying to be someone we are not causes undue stress on our bodies and spirits because it takes so much energy to keep up the pretense. It feels like me against myself—which is exactly what it is. There is a nagging anxiety when we don't know who we are or what we really want. And as long as we are looking outward for approval or gratification from society's rewards, we often panic or feel depressed—because from somewhere deep inside, we've learned that these external gratifications are not really what serves the Self.

Transformers appear in our lives when we make an inward decision to awaken to our true nature and real purpose in life. It's as though a bell rings within us, and we begin to strive toward our highest expression. The ego's personal will looks inward and upward, unconsciously longing for the love and sense of purpose that comes from being in touch with the truth of one's being. Dimly, we begin to sense that we are much bigger than we'd realized and are therefore responsible for much more than we'd ever imagined. We begin to seek whole new levels of functioning, but often without our known consent. Apparently, the higher Self makes decisions that track with our original intentionality beyond our ego's conscious awareness. And though we often feel we've had no choice in the matter, you can bet we've invoked the transformational process, even though it never even registered on our poor little ego's brain.

Invocation is a subtle, energetic process that happens inwardly at certain points in our lives when we begin to outgrow our current attitudes and start to suffocate in stagnant pools of habit, attitudes, or beliefs that no longer give us life. When we invoke a new quality or process, we seek to establish a new thought-pattern at a higher frequency level, which enables us to resonate to a higher vibration. In modern physics this is known as a standing wave pattern, which holds steady in the midst of other lesser vibrations. This invocation, then, will attract to us the people and the experiences that match this new state or quality seeking to unfold through us. Invocation is a function of the law of transcendence. At these pivotal times, we seek to freshen up our outworn doctrines and look once more for spiritual sustenance—a new way of life that befits our deeper nature and carries us to our next right step.

Effort is required to strive for this high goal of personal transformation. The ego learns how to do its part. But this kind of effort is different from outer "have to's" that feel like meaningless duties and obligations. It's an inner drive that is coming from our Source. This drive toward a higher way merges the energies of love and will. Transformers work from level four, making sure the door of the heart (Self-acceptance) remains open so that both the energies from the lower will and the energies of the higher love can join. And gradually, through this process of merging the lower and higher faculties, an intimate relationship between love and will is born. The following diagram will give you the picture:

THE MERGING OF LOVE AND WILL

The Love of God (Self)
The Love of Life
The Love of Truth

UNDERSTANDING
COMPASSION
COURAGE

Self Acceptance

The Will to Know
The Will to Feel
The Will to Live

Being
(Effortless)

Becoming
(Effort)

For so it must be, and help me to do my part.

—A TIBETAN MASTER

Integrating the Partial Selves

Levels one, two, and three, where the fragments of our personality live, are activated by the needs of the ego. When the higher counterpart of one of the lower centers is operating, the partial selves are under the supervision of the true Self and will not get out of control. When we become polarized, however, in level one, two, or three, we feel "victimized" by a little subpersonality. We've become its victim because we have gone unconscious and allowed it to take over. A fear, passion, or identity response won out while "the master" was away. Remember, the partial selves function in order to get an ego need met, and they are indeed a part of our personality. We created them because we needed them at the time. But they are *not* the true Self. And we may find that they've outlived their usefulness.

It is antitherapeutic, however, to try to rid ourselves of a partial self, even an extremely negative one. We can never rid ourselves of a part of ourself! The more we try, the more force this little self will have, and the more trouble it will give us. This phenomenon has been noted by all major psychological theories. We must, instead, integrate these little selves by a five-step process: acknowledgment or recognition, understanding, acceptance, coordination/cooperation, and synthesis.

ACKNOWLEDGMENT OR RECOGNITION

Before anything else can happen, we have to become aware of a particular subpersonality operating in/on us. A good clue is the feeling of a personality change that happens instantly, triggered by a certain event in the outer world. And there will be a pattern to it, such as "I *always* act that way around male authority figures!"

Once we see the little character and realize it has literally taken over our eyes, mouth, and ears, it helps to picture this self as a real, honest-to-goodness character. See him/her in your imagination in a costume, or uniform, with a distinct look on its face, a certain stance, a certain way of being. The more detail we have, the better. Give the little character a name. Humorous ones often are very effective: Mafia Mom, Whooshing Witch, The Great White Glub (Glub for short), Superstud, etc. You can tell, just from these few examples, how graphic and potent these names are. This recognition process gives you some distance from them so you can disidentify.

UNDERSTANDING

Once we see this little person, we must find a way to get to know it. Have a dialogue with it in your mind. Or, watch yourself acting from this characterization *with awareness*. Do whatever helps you to get to know it. Ask it what it wants, what it is trying to do for you, how it feels, where it comes from. Treat this personality exactly as you would a fascinating new person coming into your life.

Once you understand this little self, you will find, *without fail*, that it is trying to do something good for you. Sure, it's distorted. And maybe even off the wall. But it is trying in its own way to help you, because it does not trust you to help yourself in this particular situation. Part of the understanding stage is to help your little partial self gain confidence in you. Perhaps it is still very childlike. Show it that you definitely appreciate its concern, and that you can handle the situation just fine. You may even have to strike a bargain with it. And if it is a wounded self, it may need your love.

ACCEPTANCE

Acceptance springs forth spontaneously from the process of complete understanding. We begin to love and appreciate these little partial selves, for we see how in their own wounded or distorted manner, they have been struggling to help us. They have been a part of our personality structure because we have needed them, using certain defensive behaviors to keep us safe from some perceived threat. Acceptance now allows them to be seen fully in the light of day, to realize where they came from, what they are needing in order to heal, and enabling us to utilize them realistically for the tasks they are meant for. And, at the same time, acceptance allows us to keep these shadowy little characters from overstepping their bounds.

COORDINATION/COOPERATION

Once acceptance is achieved, judgment will fade away. You will see this little self as having a purpose in your personality, though misguided in its expression. And you will know when you adopted it (probably when you were a child). Now you can begin the work of personality restructuring wherein this part of yourself can begin coordinating with other parts in harmony.

This type of work immediately puts you into the fourth level of consciousness. Let's say you have a subpersonality that becomes rude and aggressive with male authority figures. "I have to teach that son-of-a-gun he can't run over me! I'll show him!" But with more Self-knowledge, you discover you also have a little part in you that sometimes becomes too submissive to a strong masculine figure, and you wind up letting him run all over you. Quite often you will find these little selves work in pairs (opposite extremes). In this stage of integration, the complementary selves can learn to work together to strike a comfortable balance regarding this type of situation.

SYNTHESIS

A synthesis occurs when you no longer feel any need for a subpersonality to help you out with a theme, such as "male authority figures in my life." Once you have become completely balanced and comfortable with this type of person, there is no longer a need to put energy into the concept of male authority figure. You will just *be* someone who relates to persons in those roles as easily as you would with anyone else. The split no longer exists; you have integrated a segment of yourself. The way you will know this stage is by the *absence* of energy (interest or reaction) in the entire subject.

Emotional overreaction is always the clue that we are operating from a partial self whose true needs are still unconscious. The original pain from the unfinished business of the past must be allowed to express its rage or grief. Then the overreaction will subside. The true Self has no need to overreact to anything. It knows who it is, and lives from the standpoint of Reality, and not from a wounded ego who was hurt in years past.

Subpersonalities are *re-minders*. They are set off by particular circumstances in our lives, and they will always represent a pattern. Each time one pops up, it gives us another chance to see the truth about this particular predicament we are caught up in. Re-minders offer us another chance to complete a little piece of hurt feelings or illusion operant within the personality. We can appreciate them for the opportunity they give us to become whole.

What has been described here is the process of *dis-identifying* from these little subpersonalities and *re-identifying* with the true Self.

This five-step process encompasses three movements.

1. Observation: I have you.
2. Dis-Identification: And I am not you.
3. Re-Identification: I am pure consciousness and the impulse to act as my true Self (Self-realization).

The words "I am" are potent words;
be careful what you hitch them to.
The thing you're claiming has a way
of reaching back and claiming you.[1]

— A. L. KITSELMAN

The basis of all Self-realization and inner freedom is dis-
identification. We are dominated by what our self becomes
identified with, and we can direct and use whatever we dis-
identify from.[2]

— ROBERTO ASSAGIOLI

So now we will examine the therapeutic tasks involved at each level of polarization, exploring in detail how to work with ourselves or others when they are stuck at a certain level. In this section, I will be speaking a lot about therapists and their clients, and I will use the word "client" often for the person seeking help. However, these principles and the work suggested hold true for all people.

Before we begin, it is crucial to point out that particular people are never consistently stuck at any *one* level. Depending on the external predicaments they are caught up in, they can be stuck in level one at one time, level two at another, and level three at some other time. We all, however, usually have a certain preferable mode of "stuckness." In this sense, you can categorize people by their usual behavior. But I caution you in trying to make this model too rigid. As Alan Watts said once: "Human nature is wiggly." Any theory of personality that tries to set generalized rules in concrete has to be illusory. Each person will demonstrate to you his or her unique way of operating in life. You must have the eyes to perceive this uniqueness.

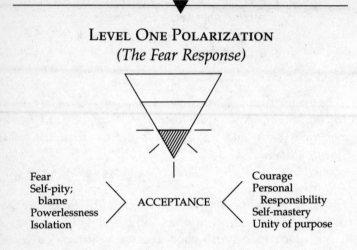

LEVEL ONE POLARIZATION
(The Fear Response)

Fear		Courage
Self-pity;		Personal
blame	ACCEPTANCE	Responsibility
Powerlessness		Self-mastery
Isolation		Unity of purpose

Allow your eyes to glance over the above words, which symbolize the essence of the predicament of a person stuck in level one polarity. This is an *intuitive* process, so do not attempt to analyze or separate out any portion of this word picture. Just let it have its way with you for a few moments. Allow the pattern and feeling tone of this person to come in on you. When you begin to "feel" this, let a symbol come into your mind that represents this unique individual. In so doing, you will get a sense of how to proceed with someone who is stuck at level one. (And counselors can ask these clients to go inward and image a symbol for themselves.)

This person is caught in the illusion of separateness and isolation, having no sense of connectedness with humanity—no sense of purpose or meaning in life, no reference group to belong to. This person will be angry or depressed, exhibiting a great need to control life, or just to go passive and withdraw. Since she is connecting with the outer world solely through fear and impotence, she feels paranoid about life and the people in it. Her experience has taught her that this is a dangerous and unpredictable world, and she must not let herself be vulnerable. This belief resides in her subconscious mind, no doubt rooted in some early childhood wound, determining the way she experiences her reality. Because of this belief structure, you can be sure this *is* indeed her reality.

Often you will notice that this person or client has a retentive stance in life—holding on, holding in. Body movements will usually be stereotyped or restricted. The person may suffer from constipation or lower back problems, or trouble with the legs and feet . . . in other words, her foundation. These level one energies are tied to the anal/ adrenal area of expression. The person will be either a withdrawer or a fighter, depending upon the particular personality style.

A reformer would argue with this person about her reality and try to convince her to believe the way the counselor (or teacher, mentor, parent, or spouse) does, leading to more polarization and increased resistance. A typical reformer response would sound like this: "That's not really how your life is; you are just imagining it." Or "I hear you saying you are a victim of your life, and that is simply not true."

A Transformer goes with the resistance and unhinges this person's defense mechanism, freeing her energy to explore other possibilities a little further down the line. "It's as though everything around you just doesn't seem to work out. I can hear your desperation." Or "I sense you are really afraid you don't have much power over your life. That must feel awful."

Entering into the person's reality with her does not mean you believe it to be the whole truth; it means you believe she believes it to be the whole truth . . . using *her* world view as the starting point from whence to launch the therapeutic process. Then you can lead her into a wider, more realistic and hopeful world as she gradually begins to trust that you do indeed understand how she feels.

Empathy and self-disclosure[3] are two counselor traits

that are very helpful with this kind of client. Especially share any times that you have felt these paranoid feelings about your own life, if you can be genuinely sincere about it. And your mode of communication should match the client's as much as possible. If the person or client talks in terms of problem-solving and goals, you do the same. If she shares a lot of feelings and emotions, or talks in metaphors or images, follow her lead as much as possible. Your communication is your tool for blending into her reality. This builds rapport.

HEALING

And your first task with this type of person is to establish rapport. And it may take a while. A statement like "I really do believe you when you say you are miserable and life seems to be just awful for you" will lead to her opening up and trusting you, consequently expanding her world a tiny bit to now include you. Her wounded heart can open and she can release her tears or anger.

The main task at this level is to assist the one seeking help in expressing her pent-up feelings and expanding her viewpoint and discovering that it's safe to do so. In other words, you will use level seven force to counteract the constricted negative side of level one force. Level seven teaches that we are a part of a larger whole, and we each have a unique purpose here. Further, there have indeed been times (and will be again) when we have used ourselves creatively, following the will of our nature, and that we *can* be safe and feel united with a larger energy that gives us a sense of belonging. It teaches us to release the fear we are holding on to and to have faith in the total process of humanness, even when security, pleasure, or self-esteem of the lower self are threatened.

You must impart this knowledge concretely, not abstractly. One way is by creating a way for her to talk about some of her successes in life, no matter how small. "What have you done in life that you are proud of?" or "What has happened in your life that has made you feel good?'' Help her to see the conditions that led up to this success. Point out to her that she can have this kind of result again if she can understand the process. Then you can always go back to these recalled successes when she moves into spaces of hopelessness.

Concreteness is crucial. Most people stuck at level one will not understand a mini-lecture about cosmic consciousness, but they will understand the principle of love and of feeling their own power, if you can help them recall times they've been able to be real. When you understand the principles to work with, it will occur to you naturally and easily what to do and say with each individual person. And even though the work may sometimes seem slow (after all, these people are often limited in their ability to explore), you will succeed.

Someone who is trapped in a fear response needs to discover that she is not alone and that life is worth living. She needs to feel that even her suffering can have a purpose. She must tediously begin expanding her point of view so that her experiences can broaden. This person must be emotionally supported and understood while she ventures out and finds her group or her place in the sun.

As this person begins to venture out, your task is to help her do it gradually, with as little risk as possible. Encourage her to expand, but avoid extremely scary things at first. Slowly desensitize her to the fear of new experiences by helping her pick new situations that will be fairly safe and easy. If you want to put her in a counseling group, for instance, make sure it will be a group on her level, with people who are somewhat like her. Putting her with others too dissimilar will make her feel even more alienated. You are dealing with the polarity struggle between powerlessness and an appropriate sense of power and connectedness with others.

As you talk with her, implant the realization that we have created our past and will therefore create our future.

The task here is to help her to see specifically how she has created her past by the choices she's made, given how she viewed the world at the time. If she goes back and recalls the exact points in time when she made choices that she now views as mistakes, she will see that *given* how she was perceiving her alternatives, she made exactly the right choice each time. This awareness will often relieve her guilt feelings entirely.

In fact, take a little time right now and recall a choice you once made, seeing yourself at the decision-making point in time and space (e.g., that day I was in the parking lot about to get in my car when I suddenly realized I had to move out of this city). Be this specific about the point in time and review how you were perceiving your world then, the choices you felt you had, the people in the predicament with you, etc., and you will see what I mean. It was exactly the correct choice *then*. (Certainly, now that you are several years older, and several degrees wiser, you would do differently, but this is irrelevant because it is not reality.) Work with fourth and fifth force. This will model love and forgiveness, and the use of the creative imagination.

After rapport is established and the past has been reviewed somewhat, study Exercise #8, "Transforming Resentments" (p. 267), and lead your client through this process however many times are necessary. Begin with *self*-forgiveness. Her energy that was utilized to hold on to resentments needs to be freed up for moving forward in life.

Once past resentments are dealt with and have been cleared out, she must learn a new skill so as not to build them up again: the use of the observer self that can watch without judgment what she does *as she is doing it*. In counseling sessions, practice the observer self exercises in Appendix 1. As she discovers how she has chosen the past by her reactions to others and to situations, she will gain confidence in choosing her present (which creates her future) choices. She will realize she is free to choose safety if she wishes, or she can risk at her own pace. She *must* learn to do this consciously, rather than seeing herself as a victim of life. You must help her transcend any feelings of victimhood, because this is the enemy of personal freedom.

Victimhood is only perceived as reality when we are operating from a mechanical consciousness without awareness. When we learn to be aware, we cannot be a victim of anything: We are *creators* of our lives, not victims. If you are a therapist, teach this to your client.

For a homework assignment, ask her to walk around for fifteen minutes each day for a week observing her actions, feelings, and thoughts, and asking, "How am I setting this one up?" or "How have I attracted this to myself?" And get honest. Be insistent and firm about honesty. It's exciting to really get to know yourself. You must model this enthusiasm and faith in the process of awakening.

This client has to learn how to stay in the here and now rather than spending so much time catastrophizing about the future or worrying about the past. For awareness on this, have her draw on a piece of paper three circles of varying sizes to show how much of her energy she spends in the past, present, or future.[4]

A healing involvement in the present looks like this:

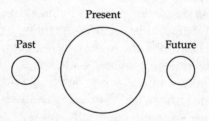

Self-defeating drawings would have much larger circles for the past and/or future and small ones for the present. The relative size of the circle will give you information about where she expends her energy.

Emotional/sensual awareness (level two consciousness) is a wonderful way to guide this client up a notch. As we begin to live more from our actual experiences, we make better contact with our repressed feelings and with the world and we can let go of the paranoid delusions we are creating with our thoughts.

▲ **The body knows, and the soul knows; only our intellects can lie.**

When our true feelings are suppressed, we get completely out of touch with our real needs. So we will go after symbolic needs, such as food, alcohol, etc. They do not fulfill us, because they are false needs. I don't really need that food or that drink; I need safety or love. But now our minds are telling us an untruth, so we begin to create a false reality, getting further away from our real needs. Helping yourself or someone else get in touch with *real* feelings, *real* needs, is a healing event. A felt shift of energy occurs.

STAGES OF THE HEALING PROCESS FOR LEVEL ONE POLARIZATION

1. *Empathic Listening.* Begin by listening to your client, entering into her reality, slowly forming a bond. Always believe your client! Never argue with her about how she sees things. Just listen, empathize, and if you want, add some things from how you see your world, if you think she can relate to them. Otherwise, don't confuse her by bringing in too much about yourself, especially at first.

Draw out your client's "story" or personal myth as a way of establishing rapport. This will give you a sense of how she perceives herself and responds habitually to her universe. It will also enable her to vent some pent-up energy. As you learn her patterns of thinking, feeling, and acting, you will be able to assess how to enter into her life therapeutically.

2. *Releasing constricted energy.* Once rapport is established, help her begin to release the pent-up emotions that have built up from past unfinished and misunderstood situations. Emptying the painful emotions, letting go of guilt and resentments, and building self-acceptance and forgiveness will be the main tasks. (See Exercises 8, 9, 11, and 13 on pp. 267, 270, 273, and 276 as especially valid for this stage.)

3. *Attributing meaning and purpose to the past.* As your client brings up this old material, help her redefine her past with purpose and meaning. Everything that has happened to her was for a reason. And it all makes sense now, if together you can both look at the patterns and events through the lens of understanding and acceptance. Help her see that given how she viewed the situation at the time, there were no mistakes, that she is not to blame.

4. *Transforming.* Once the more remedial work is done, you can begin guiding your client to higher levels of functioning by connecting her with the more integrated true Self. She must begin by utilizing the here and now appropriately. The observer self (Exercise 5, p. 262) will give her a larger perspective on her activities, helping her transcend judging herself negatively and seeing the world through the distortion of fear. "Seeing Yourself Completely" (Exercise 13, p. 276) will give her a larger, more loving perspective on herself. "Evoking an Ideal Model" (Exercise 15, p. 279) will enable her to begin practicing how to be in the world in a way that is effective and desirable. This will, in turn, build her self esteem. "Invoking a Positive Quality" (Exercise 16, p. 281) will teach your client how to work with the positive side of a negative habit pattern, and will also give her a great sense of accomplishment and order in following the instructions and experiencing the results.

5. *Right action.* Emphasis should be placed upon the client's everyday life; the actions, feelings, and thoughts she is consciously choosing to focus on will be examined and corrected by right action—doing *the next right thing.* She can begin practicing harmlessness and processing with you the

situations occurring in her life that are troublesome or exciting for her to share. She will have some successes to report. In this work, be sure to continue to build up her successes and work with the failures, redefining them as tests.

6. *Transpersonal focusing.* As therapy progresses successfully, gradually guide your client out of herself into serving another. Help her discover her particular strengths and talents in serving. No matter how small, each of us has something worthwhile to give another. This is how we learn to be part of a whole, relieving isolation and feelings of meaninglessness.

7. *Disengaging.* Toward the end of the process, begin acknowledging more and more your client's own personal power, disallowing dependency on you and transferring her dependency to a larger group or activity. Help substitute interdependence for dependence, where others are dependent upon her sometimes. Help her understand that dependency/independency are both natural and can be used appropriately and interchangeably in life as we learn to recognize the cycles of change within ourselves.

QUESTIONS AND ANSWERS ABOUT LEVEL ONE POLARITY

QUESTION: What is addiction at the cellular level, and where did it come from?

ANSWER: Two theories explain cellular addiction best for me. Perhaps either of these will help you understand this phenomenon: (1) *Genetic memory.* This theory says we pass on to our offspring certain traits, strengths, and weaknesses. A "factor X" may or may not exist that causes a proclivity toward alcoholism or some other substance or process. Allergy and diabetes also seem to fit into this category. (2) *The Doctrine of Rebirth.* This concept is fairly new to the West, but long recognized in the East. It is beyond the scope of this book to delve deeply into the philosophy of reincarnation, but briefly, it says we have lived before in other times, as our soul seeks many experiences through various personalities in order to evolve its nature. Through many lives we build up a chain of cause and effect relationships whereby lessons are learned, or not learned, from our experiences. In future lifetimes we will be drawn toward lessons we need in order to balance everything out. According to this theory, the alcoholic would be born alcoholic with something very fundamental to work through in this life, either through a family chain of cause and effect (group karma), or personally (individual karma).

There have been some clinical studies in past life regressions that tend to support this theory.[5] Many people report having had spontaneous recall of past life events or people. Some even have abilities, such as speaking foreign languages or interpreting foreign symbols from other times or other cultures. According to this theory, the law of cause and effect is not a punitive law, but a benevolent one, offering us time and time again the opportunity to advance in the areas where defects, ignorance, or defeat reign within the personality. Our souls opt for the circumstances where the necessary lessons can be learned. Disease, in itself, is viewed as benevolent, for it brings the personality face-to-face with the urge of the soul. Its objective is coming from a Higher Purpose, such as getting the attention of the personality in order to correct something within the person that is illusory. Or the disease can serve as a teacher to someone else in the life of the sick one. Coping with alcoholism would be a seedbed of knowledge about the lower self and its desires. Transforming this addiction would lead to the development of many beautiful, soul-enriching qualities.

The doctrine of rebirth is often confused with the idea of transmigration of souls, the view that people become animals, insects, or inert matter as punishment for wrongs. Personally, I consider this to be a false theory because it violates the natural process of evolution, taking us backward instead of forward. We are evolving, not devolving! We *can* get stuck. But it is unlikely, since we are human, that there would be lessons of a *non*human nature to learn.

QUESTION: I am comfortable with genetic theories, but the idea of reincarnation scares me. I've noticed, though, that I'm fascinated with the subject. What do you suggest I do to help me believe in it?

ANSWER: Instead of trying to believe in a particular philosophy, I would suggest that you examine the facts you already *know* about human experience. Then be sure you hold a philosophy of life that is large enough to contain what you know. A philosophy of life always underpins our knowledge and experiences. Sometimes we are living out of a philosophy that we have never even verbalized. Have you ever had an experience that does not fit into this particular time frame? Or does your intuition tell you there has been something before your birth that is influencing you? If the doctrine of rebirth fascinates you, by all means study it. If it is a truth for you, your study will set off a spark deep in the place where you know. If not, you can reject it, or simply suspend judgment.

QUESTION: Can a person be addicted at the cellular level and be further along than level one emotionally or mentally?

ANSWER: Yes. I have worked with people where this was the case. It depends on how highly advanced the soul was when it fell into the alcoholism. We can progress and fall back, progress and fall back . . . at least at the current level of human existence as we are experiencing it. (I don't know yet what happens to superhumans.) The way you can tell if people have progressed above the first level of consciousness is that they will recognize truth at the higher levels. It won't be like talking to a blank wall when you speak of a higher Self, service to humanity, or following the soul's urge.

These people are, to me, the most beautiful and touching to be involved with, because they know on a very deep level the trouble they are in, and they have a desperate desire to rise above their dependence. They usually do not feel they are victims and realize they must take responsibility for their own health or lack of it. They know intuitively that they are more than their bodies.

Intervention begins at whatever level the client is showing the most symptoms. Then we facilitate the progress upward. When people realize they are spiritual beings, their higher centers begin to open, and a new kind of energy is available. (Not really new at all; it's been there all along, just unrealized.)

> The "higher circuits" already exist in the human personality, as does the subconscious, determining a lot of our pain and joy. Peak experiences, creativity, aestheticism and spirituality are functions of these higher energies. These levels are the natural flow toward the realization of our emerging perfection.[6]
>
> —A. H. MASLOW

When I work with a person stuck at levels one or two, it helps to remember that emotion follows thought. And thought, fueled by emotion (energy), manifests in the physical world. "As a man thinketh *in his heart,* so is he." Synthesizing the mind and heart (what the person thinks and feels become one) creates a healing event in the life of a person in conflict.

▲ **Emotion follows thought.**

QUESTION: So you are saying that addiction at the cellular level can come from the past, even before birth, or it can come from falling all the way down through the dimensions during one's lifetime, all the way down to the physical level. Is that right?

ANSWER: Exactly. And I would speculate—and this is pure speculation—that if one falls all the way down to the cellular level during this lifetime, and then begets children, the children may inherit the weakness. Food for thought.

QUESTION: Does it fit into your philosophy, then, to say that addiction is a disease?

ANSWER: Certainly, a disease on many levels. Look at the word *disease*. It means lack of ease. I would define disease as a conflict between the soul and the personality, which can never be eradicated by merely directing curative measures toward the body alone. It requires a spiritual, mental, and emotional effort as well.

Focusing purely on physical cures falls into the trap of materialism, believing we are *only* a body. This is why we've not progressed very far in eradicating alcoholism. We only superficially repair damage, leaving the cause still operative in the person. In fact, apparent physical recovery can even be harmful as it hides from the person the true cause of the problem and enables him or her to fall short of discovering the deeper aspects of renewed health. If we were called upon to continue working at the higher levels for total cure, we would discover those deeper aspects.

Disease is our teacher, and if we rightly interpret its message, we are guided to an awareness of a virtue we are being asked to develop by our higher Self. Suffering is a corrective that points out a lesson we have failed to learn, and it will continue to reappear (maybe in varied forms) until we learn what we came here to learn. Once we get it, we no longer need the suffering. And, in fact, we can prevent or divert suffering or disease when we realize at its onset what is actually happening. As long as we still have physical life, no matter how diseased we become, we can know our soul is still not without hope. We, as one Humanity, can advance beyond our stuck point by making our disease and dysfunction conscious, and through our very experience of it, learn of its nature and its cure. In this way we serve the whole.

LEVEL TWO POLARIZATION
(The Passion Response)

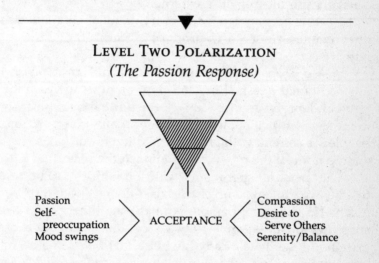

Passion
Self-
   preoccupation
Mood swings

> ACCEPTANCE <

Compassion
Desire to
   Serve Others
Serenity/Balance

Again, do not attempt to analyze or dissect the above words. Let them wash over you as an intuitive response emerges within you toward a person stuck at this level of consciousness. Then, slowly, allow this person to come into focus and let a symbol representing this unique person come into your mind. This symbol will contain the energy and the meaning of the whole truth of that person. Use this information to guide you in your work with yourself or with another.

For therapists, this is the client who is addicted to seeking sensation (or avoiding it, if too much pain has been experienced at the emotional level). In fact, this client *defines* himself by the degree or type of sensation he is feeling (or missing). When he is not high on something or someone, he

feels depressed or dead. At the extreme end of the continuum, this becomes the manic/depressive syndrome (a combination of physical and emotional imbalance). Mood swings
are a fact of life for this client, as though his life is lived on a
pendulum, swinging from one end to the other, needing
constant stimuli from the external world. Often this client
will have experimented with every kind of mood-altering
phenomenon rumored to produce a "turn on" that he can
find.

Please keep in mind, I'm talking about an *addiction* to
this emotional quest. It is natural for all of us to yearn for a
transcendent experience, as we are spiritual beings seeking
to merge with that something greater than we are. But most
people are content with gradual evolution toward these highs
and do not feel the urgent need to push the river.

This person experiments with life with the same furor
that he experiments with chemicals. Often he even flirts with
death. He has untold amounts of pent-up energy, restless-
ness, nervousness, and is always on the move. He avoids
learning to meditate or anything else that helps him be still.
Yet, this is exactly what he needs to learn, to balance out
some of this supercharged energy he is attempting to handle.
He will talk to you in emotional/feeling language, as though
his whole world is viewed from the level of sensation: "That
felt awful to me." "I'm bored stiff." "Boy, what a thrill." "I
had a big blowout last night." "Life is flat, dull. I may as well
be dead." It is as though this person needs a way to blow off
steam—he produces so much of it.

The starting point in the work of balancing our emotional states is self-observation, the work of the observer self.
Can I observe my emotional state as I am experiencing the
emotion and ask what brought it on? In what connection did
it arise? If I can learn to do this, I can begin to bring my
emotions into alignment with my higher Self.

People who are trapped in their emotions are stuck in
the past. In fact, many people continually nurture a great
reservoir of unhappiness from their past. It takes a great deal

of personal work to clear out these habitual responses. Such people are used to feeling unhappy, which of course only gives rise to continual negative feelings. We must eventually cancel out our past and not allow it to control us. But before we can believe it possible to let go of the past, we must learn we have control over the present. And we begin this by learning to watch our habitual ways of responding to stimuli coming from outside us or from our own thoughts and beliefs. Our habitual negative responses, based on a lack of understanding of life, are creating the emotional imbalances we get caught up in.

So, level two addictions are the *misuse* of the emotional energy. Emotion is our way of experiencing feeling/motivation. It is our love energy. But this second force without the balance of sixth force is love turned to its extravagance—lust. The rules of lust are: "If a little bit is good, more will be better," and "I don't care what tomorrow brings; I'll just have all I can get right now." Love and attending to the now are natural. Lust and addiction to instant gratification are natural urges turned to their opposites, which will eventually lead to pain.

When we seek pleasure solely from the things of life, only one of two possibilities can result: satiation or frustration. And enough of either leads to hopelessness. The first time I try a sensational gourmet delight I am thrilled by its taste. The second time, I still am, maybe. But what happens if I eat the same menu several times in a row? I become satiated. It has lost its allure. In fact, I can even become repulsed by the thought of this once-cherished flavor. Satiation feels awful, because of the letdown. Something I thought would "give it to me" no longer does. And recalling the first thrilling exposure to this delight makes me feel even worse. What happened? Is something wrong with me? Can I never be satisfied? So the message my organism records (the sense awareness) is that nothing lasts; everything fun eventually fades away. Nothing is worth going for. I can never be happy.

On the other hand, if I continually seek out a certain

delight and discover I cannot find it, or if I find poor substitutes but not the real thing, I cannot satisfy my desire. Then I continually long for it, pitying myself that I cannot have it. And, in my imagination, this desired object becomes the grand unreachable perfection that I now compare my ordinary experiences with and find wanting. Frustration is the result.

Both satiation and frustration are ways to experience failure and hopelessness. They are an inability to be present to my real existence. Through making these processes *conscious*, I can let go of my need to reexperience over and over again the same gourmet delight. It is now possible for me to flow with my present experience, whatever it may be, trusting that the future will bring more diverse and pleasant experiences.

People polarized at level two can turn sour in another way (besides seeking the highs from objects in life). They can also become emotionally attached to causes and ideals, over-aggrandizing their values. When they cannot live up to the exaggerated ideal, they create suffering for themselves and others. This is a misuse of the beautiful spiritual devotion that resides at level six. At level two we are devoted to a *fragment* of truth and we tend to exaggerate its importance; we absolutize it. This leads to dogmatism, fanaticism, arrogance, closed-mindedness, or even cruelty. All these qualities, of course, are the very opposite of love and compassion. The little cause, especially if it is designed to serve humankind, becomes a way to feel self-righteous. And the human dignity of an individual not worshiping the same cause can be compromised or brutally ignored. Extremism will eventually turn to its opposite, always.

In the area of child abuse, there are many heartbreaking examples of this kind of distortion of truth. I once knew a preacher who tied his children to the tabletop for hours at a time and wouldn't let their feet touch the floor as punishment for disregarding "God's rules." The earth, to him, had become so evil, he didn't want his children's feet to get dirty. What we label child abuse, he called righteousness.

So, how do we help this person? Shaming someone for his excesses or mandating him to stop some behavior leads to more abuse. Experience has taught us that trying to prematurely force one's lower self away from an addiction always fails. Apparently, the person still needs the experience in order to learn something about life or about himself. Does this mean we encourage the continued abuse? It seems that either way becomes a trap for the therapist or helper. This whole question of guiding clients toward transcendence of lower-self excesses is indeed a very big issue for those in the chemical addictions field. It's the very core of their work. I have devoted much time and thought to this question, as I'm quite sure many of you have. And I don't pretend to have a formula that is foolproof for working in this area. The following information helped me to understand this client and greatly assisted me in feeling less urgency to *fix* him, or to blame myself when I couldn't. So, even though it is not a panacea, I offer it to you as a helpful suggestion.

First of all, people living at level two consciousness tend to fall into two categories: One type seems to be "young" and inexperienced in the worldly life, as though his soul just hasn't had enough of certain sensations and events. This person is still at the stage of development where he is diving down *into* the world, craving more of life's experiences. Classical Buddhist psychology (Abhidharma) provides a good source of practical wisdom for this type of client when he suffers from his experiencing. The work of "mindfulness" gradually removes the energy from the coveted source of pleasure. The person continues to involve in the excessive behavior, and is sometimes even encouraged to exaggerate it but only with awareness. He watches himself nonjudg-mentally as he indulges himself. He does not judge; he watches.

> *Mindfulness is bare attention, or keeping present, with accurate, non-discursive registering of the situation taking place, without any reaction to the situation through mental evaluation, comment, labeling, behaving. It is deliberate observation of the body processes, emotions, and thoughts as one is engaged in the activity.*[7]
>
> —*NYAROPONIKA THERA*

Thera speaks of our everyday activities as being like events occurring in a dark room cluttered with garbage, where a large portion of our affairs occur in a twilight state of semiconsciousness. In this sleep state, unwholesome, neurotic behavior can thrive without our having to take responsibility for it. Ignorance and lack of awareness settle in the mind like dust that accumulates year after year, reducing the living space in the room.

If we are fascinated by an experience, we will continue to crave it—even a negative one—until we experience it fully with total involvement. Mindfulness is a technique that can lead us out of a negative compulsion because it allows us to be *totally* involved without guilt, so we can simply satiate. When we judge a behavior to be bad, we turned our attention away from the event as we were doing it. Consequently, we never let ourselves complete the experiencing. We went through the motions in a robotlike fashion without taking responsibility for our actions, without making conscious what we were doing. Remember, we are here to make it all conscious. Mindfulness focuses our attention totally on the action, enabling us to complete it. When something is completed, we are literally finished with it, so it no longer requires our energy. Now we know it. And when we know something, it fades away, and our mind moves on to master something else.

As the one seeking help gains proficiency in utilizing this method of watching, he will discover for himself that healthy mental states are antagonistic to unhealthy ones. They cannot reside in the same space. And he will gradually learn to substitute the positive counterpart for the unhealthy behavior when he is not caught up in the negative side. When the negative side *is* operating, he uses mindfulness again. For example, when he overeats, he watches himself without judgment. When he is not overeating, he practices moderation in diet, choosing behaviors that lead to healthy food selection and eating habits—such as substituting non-eating activities, breathing adequately, trying new, healthier foods, being around nutrition-conscious people—and he is mindful of all this as well.

We must realize in working with the mindfulness technique that this is a gradual, slow-moving process, carefully supervised, which sometimes takes several years. But eventually, the technique of mindfulness shifts us from unconscious to conscious living.

The other type of person in this category seems to be "burnt out" on already having passed through so many years of excessive living. He knows about the world and is feeling somewhat defeated, or perhaps the best description is tired. You will sense that he is begging you to help him quit indulging himself. The pleasure is long gone and really holds no appeal for him, yet he still seems stuck, like a broken record, in some defeating habit pattern. He isn't just saying these things, either. He really is *through*, but hasn't the motivation, the strength, or the skill to stop doing his mechanistic dance and move forward.

This man is on the way *up* and *out*. He needs to transcend his behavior. A seed thought for him (and you, to assist him) is:

▲ **The Self is greater than its conditions.**

And the way of negation will be this person's path. He doesn't need mindfulness to watch his excesses and run them out. They no longer hold any fascination for him.

Instead, he needs to practice denial of the experience, gradually learning to withdraw this behavior pattern from the world of the senses. With your help, or the help of others you refer him to, he will respond to meditation, yoga, spiritual knowledge about the senses. He will be willing to practice the rewards of aloneness, or communing with others who are choosing a life devoid of this excess. This is a difficult path, but one many of our most saintly people have traveled. And one must be ready and prepared for it. Practiced prematurely, when there is still a strong fascination with the behavior in question, it will only lead to downfall.

The path of negation is a true spiritual path, but only when experiencing is *completed*. Otherwise, it becomes a false teaching that bids us to leave our physical senses before we have learned how to use them properly. For example, a person does not go from unhealthy sex to no sex. If he attempts celibacy prematurely, he merely carries his misunderstanding and frustrated needs into his celibate life with him, manifesting neurosis. If one is unable to achieve balance of the appetites through spiritual practices, such as meditation, then he or she must travel from unhealthy to healthy sexual encounters, then evolve gradually into a celibate state, if this is so desired by the higher Self. These matters are *states of mind*, levels of consciousness we reach through personal evolution—*not* physical events that are achieved. Spiritually and psychologically we cannot pretend to be where we are *not*. Only the lower self can pretend! The true Self just *is*.

Again, this is a very touchy subject, one containing many fears and controversies. We are talking of the split most of us feel between our animal nature and our spiritual nature, as though the two are poles apart. It helps resolve the duality if we remember that we do not denigrate our animal nature simply because it is like a high-spirited young colt, wild and unbroken. Its vital energy is God-given; its nature is to be full of life. Instead, we attempt to give this creature the room it needs to be itself, while all the time exposing it to the more domestic life of the trained animal. And we do this with love. Often we are so frightened by the raw force of our passions that, in our fear, we attempt to flee madly from our unpurified nature. It is a far sounder policy, however, to equilibrate the battling forces within us by learning to understand both sides of our nature, experimenting a little here, a little there, *with awareness*, until we discover the energy is balancing or transmuting to its positive counterpart, and our unruly team of passions calms down.

Our greatest teachers have taught us not to fear plunging into life. We are here to experience and to gain knowledge, which can only be done through facing realities and seeking to our utmost the truth of human nature and of this universe we populate.[8]

The pleasure and pain we experience as second force become the data for developing level six consciousness—a merging of love and wisdom that inspires us and eventually leads us to the world of inner sensing and true and *felt* compassion.

STAGES OF THE HEALING PROCESS FOR LEVEL TWO POLARIZATION

1. *Nonjudgmental listening.* Listen to your client without judgment as he describes to you his excessive behavior. Once you have really heard him, ask him this: "Do you *experience* the behavior as a problem?" (Some people complain about an excess they are involved in, because they feel they ought to, but they really delight in it and are not about to give it up.) "You talk about this as though it should be a problem, but let me ask you again, do you actually *experience* it as a problem?" If the truthful answer is "No," then I would invite you to work with your client on discovering why he needs to complain about it. Whose voice is inside him serving as "the judge"? Is it Dad, Mom, the church? Who is disapproving?

If the answer is "Yes," he is having a great deal of trouble with this, and you believe him, you can begin helping him transform his behavior, either through the way of mindfulness or the path of negation.

If the client is ambivalent about whether or not he is "through" with this experience, have him begin practicing mindfulness as a part of his life-style and evoking whichever positive qualities he desires to manifest (see Exercise 16, p. 281). And you will see a gradual change in the energy attached to this behavior. This approach requires patience, monitoring, journal-keeping, and nonjudgmentalness on both your parts. But it is highly effective.

2. *Bibliotherapy.* Reading materials that contain transformational ideas can be an important adjunct to this client's therapy. The Bibliography in this book would be a good start. Also, you can visit a well-stocked New Age bookstore for the latest in scientific, mystical, and transformational materials. Most of them will also have large sections on addiction and self-help. Browse around and let the books pick you!

Avoid literature that is preachy or judgmental. This client needs to *understand* his addictions, not flee from them or go underground with them out of shame. He is seeking transformation, which can only come from a seedbed of self-love. Self-hatred leads to increased energy in the undesired behavior or to "symptom substitution"; one negative behavior may disappear, only to have another take its place. For example, a person may quit drinking alcohol but begin to act out sexually or overeat. And an added burden of guilt now takes him down instead of up.

3. *Proactive focusing.* Therapy sessions do not need to focus continually on the negative side of the excessive behavior. Gradually withdraw the energy from the negative and stress its positive opposite. (See Exercise 16, p. 281.) What virtue is attempting to emerge in your client that would naturally solve this problem? If it is moderation, concentrate on time and exercises developing this quality. If it is patience, utilize theory and techniques that breed serenity, a slowing down, and steadfastness in thought and action. Always allow

the client to work with you in defining the positive opposite quality. To me, the opposite of excess might be moderation. To another, it might be learning to appreciate whatever one is involved in at the moment (impartiality). We are working with qualities, not quantities. Qualities are part of our true nature, gifts of the higher Self. Consequently, we cannot know these about another person, as they are invisible and belong to this one person's particular evolutionary schema, not ours. Remember, we are individualized souls, each one evolving toward his or her unique perfection.

4. *Thematic life history.* When the person you are helping is beginning to experience results in transforming the excessive behavior, have him write a life history of this particular indulgence so he can gain a clear understanding of the lesson he was learning from this particular difficulty. This will be a theme-centered life history, not a general one. Once he discovers the purpose of his affliction, he will be able to love himself in spite of it and finally let go of it forever. During this stage, if he feels he has harmed another by his past behavior, or feels the need of forgiveness from someone, you can help him resolve this—either directly with the person involved, or symbolically in imagery or Gestalt work. (See Exercise 8, "Transforming Resentments," p. 267, for one way to work with unfinished business from the past.)

5. *Connecting mind and heart.* Pent-up feelings held over from our past must be released in a safe and loving setting before the emotional body can settle down and heal. We must learn to trust our feeling nature and allow it to teach us how it heals by going into our feelings, and not by attempting to avoid, deny, or "fix" them. Carl Jung taught: "It's not out, but *through* that we heal."

This truth has been borne out by my experiential work of the past twenty years with clients and workshop participants. A deep catharsis will come in waves that will last about ten minutes or so. People who can hold steady while another releases deep emotional pain are truly therapeutic agents, because they are no longer afraid of their own emotional pain. Allow those who ask you for help to cry, rage, scream, or otherwise express what's bothering them. In fact, encourage these feelings to come out, and no matter what comes, remain nonjudgmental. This is true empathy.

Therapists and treatment programs that offer forms of breath work, music therapy, movement, deep body work, artwork, psychodrama, inner child work, or other experiential psychotherapies that focus on feelings and bring them to the surface are effective in the task of accessing and releasing deeply repressed issues. Programs that only intellectualize the healing process are fairly useless in the long run. Their clients will usually experience symptom substitution.

Utilize Gendlin's method of "Focusing on a Feeling" (Exercise 9, p. 270) as a way of aiding this client in learning about his feelings. He will begin noticing when and how feelings occur in him, how he uses feelings. Once these feelings are expressed, you can teach your client or friend to breathe deeply and evenly, using centering and meditative techniques to bring about a balancing of necessary emotions that habitually run rampant. Once he learns to understand and accept his feeling nature, help him discover ways to tie meaning to the feeling reactions. He can also learn to use his mind to control his feelings when appropriate. A good use of restraint and reserve can be excellent qualities for this person to develop. You can teach him to evoke these qualities (see Exercise 16, p. 281). But first, the feelings must be emptied out.

6. *Transpersonal focusing.* Transmuting passion to compassion requires a training ground for this switch in emphasis to occur. Have your client begin to serve others in some movement, group, or cause he believes in. Remember, this person is naturally devotional by long association with his emotional nature. He will benefit greatly by having something or someone to concentrate upon besides himself. Self-preoccupation has been one of his main difficulties in life, holding back his progress. An excellent positive quality for

him to develop is nonattachment, or self-forgetfulness. (See Exercise 16, p. 281.) His use of the observer self will serve as a guide for balancing extremes and seeing the world more clearly. Also, learning to get messages from his higher Self will enable him to learn the difference between acting creatively in life and overreacting emotionally from outworn, exaggerated negative habit patterns.

7. *Meditation.* Teach this client a simple form of meditation. Learning to still the mind for short periods every day can become a lifelong practice that eventually balances excess energy and emotions.

QUESTIONS AND ANSWERS ABOUT LEVEL TWO POLARITY

QUESTION: I think level six is about the energies that inspire us. How does devotion fit with inspiration?

ANSWER: The inspired person is elevated to truth about the Self and our correct relation to the universal scheme. This means he has transcended limited sense awareness. He gets his "data" from the inner world of wisdom, and he is perfectly focused on devotion to one aim only—that of serving his master, the higher Self. We can think of this higher authority as God, the Source, or any projection of a master. An intense devotion to the Totality of all-that-we-are is more integrative than being fanatically devoted to an earthly cause, a fragment of truth, such as Presbyterianism, vegetarianism, meditation, even world peace, or eradication of hunger or disease. All of these are worthy, high causes, of course, but still only serve particles of universal need. I am saying they are fragments of the truth that are appropriate for persons at certain times, but *not* for everyone at every stage of unfoldment. They are means, not ends. And, as stated earlier, partial truths can become dogma or pet projects that limit our vision and cause us to emotionally overreact in certain situations, losing sight sometimes of the higher, more synthesized Truth which will always supersede the lower truth; it takes it into itself.

These partial truths do lead us to the higher, however, unless we become stuck and addicted to the lesser ones. This is the teaching about not laying false idols before us. Devotion is a lofty calling, if the devotion is not carrying us off to worship another human being, and therefore giving our power away in codependence. Pure devotion to the teachings of one's higher Self leads to a balancing of the qualities of love and wisdom. Sixth force does not merely know Truth; it *feels* it as well. It is the emotions of the Spirit.

QUESTION: How are we to know whether someone needs more digging into the earth experiences, or whether to work on transcending them? Seems to me, we have to make a judgment here in order to know which way to guide.

ANSWER: I never feel I can make this judgment, but my client can. He has to be taught this point of view first, of course, or he may not have enough understanding to contemplate his life from the standpoint of cause and effect or his soul's growth. People usually know where they are on their path, if you know the right questions to ask them. "What do you want?" is a very good question to ask, for instance. Has he truly had enough of a certain experience? Usually, suffering will make it so. If so, help him transmute the energy from this negative one to a more rewarding, total one. Is he seeking balance, peace, or Self-knowledge? If he truly is tired of bogging down in the same old mess, perhaps he genuinely is seeking to negate this particular behavior by turning the attention in another direction. He either will or he won't change the behavior. If he cannot seem to change, he needs the mindfulness approach so he can learn to drop judgment and shame.

The soul has to complete its human experience before it is ready to transcend into unity with the higher Self. But there comes a point on our path where we pass the nadir of the descent into matter and begin the path of return. To attempt to escape from our experiences before we have learned our lessons is to evade our training. We must *fulfill* the conditions of liberation from the trials of life, which means we shirk nothing we are to learn.

▲ **We can only leave behind us what we have mastered, balanced, or outgrown.**

If any experience is still hanging around incomplete, a portion of our energy will constantly feel pulled backward, seeking to complete the experience.

Pretending we know something we don't is another way we try to short-circuit our training. But this only leads to unripe ideals not grounded in our experience and does not make us better teachers. This is what Jesus called the unprofitable servant. We attain by the process of *natural growth*, not by repression, avoidance, or denial.

QUESTION: It seems to me that all chemical addictions are level two addictions. They are, just by their nature, aren't they?

ANSWER: No. Some people are more addicted to physical safety or mental ideas of themselves than they are to seeking highs. Not all addicts are the emotional/relational type. Chemical addiction can occur at any level as a substitute for not getting that particular set of developmental needs met. I do believe that level two addicts come to our attention more frequently, however. They are often extroverted, charismatic, fun-loving, gregarious, exciting to be with . . . out there where the people and the action are . . . . living it up.

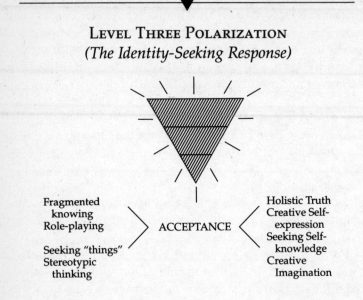

LEVEL THREE POLARIZATION
(The Identity-Seeking Response)

Fragmented
knowing
Role-playing

Seeking "things"
Stereotypic
thinking

> ACCEPTANCE <

Holistic Truth
Creative Self-
expression
Seeking Self-
knowledge
Creative
Imagination

As you glance at the above word picture, let your intuition tap into the essence of this client who is so starved for approval and lost in her search for Self. Absolutely caught up in how others see her, she is nervous, outer-directed, and uncentered, feeling at the mercy of whoever chooses to define her. Close your eyes, relax, and allow a symbol to come into your mind for this client. See her with your inner eye, and let the symbol give you the key to her essence.

As you will recall, this is the level of consciousness where the mental life becomes activated. This person is becoming quite sophisticated, as she now has at her disposal the full functioning of the physical/instinctual, the emotional/relational, and now the mental centers. This is the level just before the personality becomes integrated and highly organized, designed to be the servant of the higher Self.

The mental aspect of the personality is the energy that gathers facts from life. It is still contaminated by emotional attachments, but the intellect is coming to the forefront. It sees things in fragments, rather than as wholes. It is caught up in the particular part of experience that contains the ego gratification sought at the moment. But it is beginning to cognate and attempting to make sense of its world by the use of logic.

Concepts at this level are born from sense experience in life. Those self-concepts fueled by emotional energy are the addictions at this level of consciousness. For instance, if I have always idolized movie stars and beauty queens, I will experience an ego boost every time someone calls me glamorous or beautiful. If I have valued great scholars, my ego will light up when I accomplish tasks pertaining to the intellect. At this level, without its higher level five counterpart, I will glorify the identity life gives me. I am enslaved by public opinion, and other people's approval of me is my addiction. When I have it, I am at ease; when I don't have it or doubt it, I am distressed. I have made the outer world of experience my god because I've given it power over me.

When we evolve naturally, this is the level where our whole organism begins to develop its Self-definition. Paradoxically, it is often through experiencing the not-self that we learn who the Self is. Since we live in a world of duality, we learn by experiencing opposites. I may try on certain roles, job titles, and characterizations during my life, only to discover after practicing them for a while that they were someone else's idea of who I was. They were not a true part of myself. Not one of us can learn without times of trial and error, confusions between fact and fantasy, or other tests that take us away from ourselves. Our day-to-day experiences are our practice field. The true test for us is to rediscover, over and over again, the truth behind the veil of illusion.

By using fifth force, which completes level three, we will uncover the wholeness that contains the fragment of life we were fixated on at the lower level. This lower self fixation, of course, takes us away from ourselves. A person can never find her true identity as long as she totally defines herself by a fragment of the outer life. She will become less and less authentic as she focuses on being like others want her to be. These are the "shoulds" and "ought tos" we've often found so troublesome. A woman becomes the leader of her organization because "she just couldn't say no," when in reality she is a shy person who serves better than leads. Or she might join a social group because "everyone she admires belongs to it," when in fact, the goals and functions of the group do not interest her. In this level three reality, her self-esteem suffers every time she receives a slight or an insult from another—especially if the slight deprives her of her status or role in life.

Alcoholics stuck at the third level of consciousness have often been leaders in their professional careers, or have had honors, power, or money. Listen to them and you will hear much talk about past accomplishments or important people they have known. They cannot see beyond the fragmented reality this honor actually represented when they did have it. They are stuck in limited thinking and stuck in the past. They are dangerously addicted to identities that reside outside themselves.

Level five consciousness is the higher Self's mind. It sees Reality all in one piece, comprehending the whole Truth. It can grasp the unity of things, because it is part of the *essence* of the person. It can broaden the mind and carve out a variety of paths in life, paths that match the true Self's urges for expression. It is not stuck in compulsive conformity or limited thinking. It is imaginative and creative. Fifth force can contemplate life, then fix in the mind a perfected image or thought that comes from the true Self, and finally mold that perfected mental construct into a correct action.

Level three consciousness sees the fact about a thing devoid of its meaning. Fifth level consciousness relates the meaning to the fact. For instance, I bring you a bouquet of flowers as a gift. Level three consciousness will have the facts about which flowers last the longest, which are in season, how big the bouquet is, how much it cost. Level five consciousness will understand what the gift of flowers symbolizes for you, their meaning in your life. Level three knows facts; level five understands the essence of the matter.

In teaching this person to use her mental powers and the creative imagination, you will need to direct her away from piecemeal thinking into holistic thinking. She will need to study her life and comprehend its meaning. Meaning in action. And she must learn to direct thought toward the dictates of her true Self. Once she gets a glimpse of the powers of her mind and *realizes* that thought is creative, she will become more inner-directed and less concerned with the outside world's approval. On the surface this may seem to be irresponsible, but quite the opposite is true: She will be becoming responsible for herself, *claiming* herself for all the world to see. Thoughts from the higher mind can lead her outside the boundaries of her ego to a more loving, more integrated expression. She will become a model for others, a conscious co-creator.

STAGES OF THE HEALING PROCESS FOR LEVEL THREE POLARIZATION

1. *Reality testing.* In listening to this person describe her failures (according to society's or her family's standards), you can begin wedging a space between her idea of what ought to be and how the experience actually felt. Example: "Father wanted me to study medicine, and I've failed miserably by flunking premed classes." You ask: "Were your premed classes interesting to you?" "Do you want to be a doctor?" Help her to see there may be a discrepancy between her idea of medical training and how it actually felt to her.

Actual experience is our teacher, but only if we have our mental self tuned into the experience to draw a conclusion and comprehend its meaning. Experiencing without being able to attribute meaning to the experience leads nowhere but to repeating the same old patterns. So we begin connecting the experience in the world with the ideas that fit the experience. We look for patterns, themes, pictures, associa-

tions, wishes, hopes, dreams. In a therapy session, the
therapist will begin tying together the client's miscreations
of the past with the potentials for creating the future of her
choice.

The observer self is paramount to reality-testing. Please
refer to the sections of this book that speak of the observer
self, including Exercises 4 and 5 (pp. 259–264). Offer seed
thoughts that will lead the client to more knowledge about
who she is. She will catch them, if they strike a chord. Levels
three, four, and five are activated while this work is being
done. The pendulum will swing between three and five, with
four used to provide the balance between self-acceptance and
self-criticism. As more understanding and acceptance of life
emerge, move to the next step.

2. *Evoke an ideal model.* At this stage I like to teach my
clients to become acquainted and identified with their higher
Self. One way to do this is explained and experienced in
Exercise 15, p. 279. Once they have a clear picture of what
their higher Self looks like, they can practice responding to
situations as this wise Self. When confronted with an emo-
tion-packed negative situation, your client can learn to say to
herself, "What would higher Self do now?," then picture it,
and act accordingly.

3. *Practice "as if."* Support practicing the true Self in
action in the person's daily life. If this is a bank clerk yearning
to paint pictures, help support her creative urge to paint. If
she is a quiet, shy woman who has been pushing herself into
leadership roles or aggressive jobs, help her acknowledge
her truer nature. Provide her with reading materials and
models that reinforce her quieter side, while at the same time
encouraging some growth of her more assertive, outgoing
potential. If she feels awkward practicing the new roles,
remind her to act "as if" she already *is* this new self, and to
begin picturing herself being the new way. This is how truth
becomes manifest.

Please note, there is a big difference in pretending we
are someone we are not, and practicing "as if" we've already

achieved a desired quality we are learning to manifest. The former is phony, unconscious, and repressive, leading to more false personality; the latter is done, *with awareness*, as constructive work-on-ourselves that leads to Self-creation.

4. *Mental transformation.* As clients begin to express themselves more creatively in the world, they seem encouraged about life. They are extremely ripe for mental transformation. I like to implant seed thoughts containing transformation energy . . . thoughts that shock the consciousness into new ways of perceiving reality. (Thoughts like: "You are not who you think you are." "Quit trying to control everything and you will master life." "Yes, love even *that!*" "The person with the most authority is the least authoritarian." "The less I need approval from others, the more I receive it." "This game is a lot bigger than we ever imagined.") The sentences marked as seed thoughts throughout this book can serve toward this aim.

The true Self stands between the outer and inner worlds, both making up a certain kind of reality. The outer world offers knowledge gained from the senses; the inner world contains all of the knowledge gained from the intuition. All of us are somewhere on the continuum of learning to let go of the outer world's dominance over us. And as we accomplish this, the sensual knowledge we've experienced passes into us as internal experience.

All of us are existing within a certain ratio between these two realities. We learn that the outer life does not satisfy the deepest yearnings within us. And we begin to awaken to a different kind of knowledge—*understanding*, rather than just knowing facts. Seed thoughts carry transformation energy and produce understanding. They are the "ahas" we experience during moments of enlightenment. And it is at this level three/five that the client or person seeking help can begin making the shift from being guided solely by her senses to being guided by her inner truth.

5. *Provocative questions.* Provocative questions provide an excellent tool for mental transformation. These are ques-

tions that, on the surface, appear mundane, but contain deep spiritual significance. Some of the most fruitful questions I've used are: "Who are you?" "Where do you come from?" "Where are you going?" "What are you here for?" "What quality is trying to emerge in you?" "How did you manage to attract *this* experience to yourself?" "What are you doing?"

6. *Thought is creative.* Therapists have noted that once a client realizes that her thoughts are creating her reality, she is awakening to the inner life, which means she is becoming dominated by her soul's purpose rather than society's wishes for her. She is now ready to begin replacing habitual programs and tapes with the creative thoughts she wants to rule her life.

▲ **Whatever we feed to our minds and then nurture will grow!**

And this maxim applies to both positive and negative thoughts. Until we arrive at this level of consciousness, we are powerless over our minds, victimized by unmonitored thoughts that rush in from everywhere. I am constantly asking my clients, "Where did that thought come from?" Until we gain knowledge and control over our minds, we will not discover the real solution to our difficulties. The correct answer always lies in the direction of knowing ourselves, which leads to a change in consciousness. As long as a person is turned outward and believes the problem and the solution lie out there somewhere, she is caught in the world of appearances, cutting off the possibility of inner change.

A therapist's task at this level is to help her client feel that there is more to life than what is apparent to the physical senses, that deeper meanings and interpretations are possible. Then an openness and a sense of wonder can occur. Also, a person can bear up under tremendous difficulties if she knows there is meaning in the suffering. It gives her a sense of purpose larger than herself—transcendence. She will see that the outer world needs adapting to. And we must become proficient at doing this when it is appropriate. But she will understand now that the real truth of Self-transformation lies within. I realized a long time ago that it is not what happens to me in life that determines who I am. It's how I react to it. I create my personal melodramas and then become the leading lady.

As the true Self emerges and your client realizes that her mind is creating the life she is seeking, she will undergo a redefinition of Self that can be both exhilarating and frightening. She is discovering her power. She will look at the ways she's been defining herself with new understanding. The "I am" statements she's been making have been *literally* creating her reality: "I can never do this. . . ." "I am never like that. . . ." "I am always such and such. . . ." "Sorry, that's just how I am." All such statements are viewed by *you* as limiting concepts, identifications that are keeping her *down*, structuring her reality. And she now begins practicing their opposites: "I am free to change how I am." She learns to disidentify with self-defeating patterns of thought.

7. *Letting go of limitation.* Dealing with the pain and fear that result in letting go of the past and opening to the present is the crux of the therapeutic process. Your skills at listening, empathizing, encouraging, softening, and staying truthful will be your instruments of healing for this person.

In more detail, here is what is happening. As your client or friend begins to affirm what she believes she can achieve, or even what she desires to achieve, remnants left over from the past dwelling in the subconscious recesses pop up and unbalance her. Fears she thought she'd left behind reappear, doubts that seem elementary pervade her awareness. Even new fears she didn't even know she had come to the surface and must be observed and equilibrated.

But as Jesus said: "Get thee behind me, Satan!" (limitation). We do not give our fears power over us; we just acknowledge them and allow them to pass on by. We don't identify with them; we just say, "Well, there goes *that* one!" They are only there because we've allowed them to exist. Blocked energy is limitation—the fear of releasing something we do not understand. And since we won't bring it out and look at it, it remains misunderstood and, consequently, very powerful. Once the fearsome thing is seen through the eyes of observer self and comprehended for what it really is, limitation vanishes. Neutralized through understanding, the fears are transcended. They become the force behind the positive quality hidden underneath the limitation. Negativity is merely the opposite of a positive potential, unrealized because the negative has held us under its spell.

Once examined, my jealousy of someone else turns out to be a misconception of my own power and beauty. My fear of rejection is merely an inability to know my own self-sufficiency, to recognize my ability to validate myself. I forgot that I am part of you and you, me. I thought I was separate and alone.

Level three consciousness is where we learn to analyze fragments of reality, making sense of the pieces of life. Level five consciousness means contemplating and understanding the whole concept in question. The unenlightened scientific mind operates at level three; the enlightened one at level five. For example, at level three, an investigator might become preoccupied with measuring the number of eyeblinks that correlate with certain levels of anxiety. He might even spend his entire career focusing on this subject and argue that his findings *define* anxiety in human personality. You might browse through the indexes in a psychology department library and look at the myriad research topics that have preoccupied our behavioral scientific minds. You will come away feeling that if you added it all up together, it still would not make a whole human being. And you'd be right!

Without level five's comprehensive, intuitive understanding of the whole picture, level three consciousness becomes a string of irrelevant data. Level five transcends limitation, placing the data gathered at level three within the context of the nature, meaning, and purpose of anxiety in the personality, the uniqueness of the person experiencing the anxiety, and the conditions within which this personality is functioning in time and space. When we become preoccupied with fragments, we lose sight of the whole. Level three is logical, analytical thinking (left-brained dominance). Level five is creative, intuitive thinking (right-brained). The two working in cooperation with one another provide a science based on truth. Intelligent persons stuck at level three often become chemically addicted, due to the frustration and outright despair of trying to figure out the world based on fragments of unrelated data. Three books on this subject you might find useful are *Zen and the Art of Motorcycle Maintenance*, *The Crack in the Cosmic Egg*, and *The Tao of Physics*. (See Bibliography.)

QUESTIONS AND ANSWERS ABOUT LEVEL THREE POLARIZATION

QUESTION: I'm a little confused about the difference between level three knowledge and the understanding or comprehending that happens at level five. Can you elaborate on this?

ANSWER: Third level knowledge gathers facts from the external world with little awareness, or even interest, in what all these fragments actually mean at a deeper level. This type of knowledge is usually not grounded in the person's experience, but comes instead from stereotypic values external to the person. These values are simply memorized and often become unexamined belief systems. Third level discriminates and makes a lot of judgments, preferring one thing over another. It is thinking based on *separating*, rather than uniting.

Fifth level consciousness, on the other hand, sees all of life as a "teaching" and is gathering its "data" from the inner world. Consequently, this person can sleep on the ground or on a fine silk sofa and love either experience equally. He can live in a shack or in a mansion and find Truth in each experience. He can be impartial because his main concern is the quality of experience for his soul's sake, not the quantity of the possessions of life. Everything becomes grist for the mill for the real work of life, Self-creation. You can see that this leads to freedom from ego control. Level three knowledge is still very egoistic; level five has transcended the ego. Level five produces a comprehensive, nonjudgmental understanding of the whole, an inner quality derived from a high level of being. At level five we create whole new responses.

QUESTION: When I am operating at level three, is level two or one still active in me as well?

ANSWER: Yes. Level three, or our solar plexus center, is the container of all unassimilated "stuff" from the lower levels. All three levels are operating. But the mind is the highest, most integrated of the three; consequently, the mental life contains the emotional/relational and the physical/instinctual. The level three stage of development is designed to make us masters of the outer life by the proper use of the intellect—what Western psychologists call an integrated personality.

But we've been talking about the *traps* of the third level without the help of level five consciousness—polarization. This then becomes the ego's search for its definition. But unfortunately, the ego always looks outward. This is its undoing, for the outside world can really never define us. We are not of this world. "The world" is something we are *doing*; not something we *are*. We are in it, but we are something other. We are seeds sown into the earth; some by the wayside, some on shallow ground, some amidst the thorns, and some in good soil—depending upon our willingness to know and live in Truth. (See Matthew 13:1–23.)

QUESTION: If the outside world is only appearances, what is the purpose of it? Does it have a purpose? Or is it all just one great big mistake?

ANSWER: The outside world, our world, provides us the mirror or context within which we experience our consciousness—the tension we push against so we can exist and experience this existence. Our particular circumstances are the reality we have created by the level of consciousness we are living in. Through interaction with our world, we learn and we grow. We can actually see what we are doing. We can even delight in the experiencing! Life is our teacher. Someone once said, "Circumstance is another word for God."

QUESTION: And how does level four enter into this particular duality of three/five?

ANSWER: When we begin operating on level three without a conscious shock (an idea or experience that mentally transforms us), we stagnate at this level. We have a well-defined personality containing a physical, emotional, and mental component, but view external life as the whole truth. People stuck at level three are ego-dominated and hardly sense a deeper meaning in life, that "something else" we know resides within, the life of the Spirit. Consequently, they are determined by whatever facts life deals them. In the parable of the sower referred to above, they would be a seed sown by the wayside. Truth was offered them and they didn't understand, so the fowls devoured the seed.

If a higher Truth awakens in them, like "There really is something bigger than myself" or "Even *this* has a meaning," they will begin to use the observer self, who can rise above its conditions and see them in the context of a bigger picture. In so doing, fourth force comes into play, and forgiveness and acceptance begin to occur. Harmonizing the energies of levels three and five is its function here.

As we experience harmony and acceptance of level four consciousness, we begin to have the ability to examine ourselves without judgment. Only then can we arrive at understanding. Otherwise, we still have to hide the "despicable" parts of ourselves from our own conscious awareness. Judgment separates and keeps us stuck. Often I've heard clients say, "I just can't look at that, it's too awful." Or, "I wouldn't be able to stand myself if this were seen." This fear that we are rotten at the core is the main stumbling block to Self-knowledge, especially for alcoholics, who as a rule are very sensitive and conscientious people. Fourth force dissolves judgment, creating openness and a willingness to see both sides of the pole, the positive and the negative as well. Then a thing can be accepted . . . in its wholeness.

Transformation: Entering the World of Synthesis

Everyone should know that since creation no other person ever was like him. Had there been such another, there would be no need for him to be . . . each is called to perfect his unique qualities. . . .[1]

—BA'AL SHEM TOV

Each of us is perfectly designed to be one of a kind. Many of us forget this as we continually seek out people to copy and to please. The realization that we are indeed unique and each have a significant purpose for being here is quite an awakening. It fills our lives with a deep sense of meaning.

When any of us becomes hooked on a self-defeating addiction, however, we've lost touch with the true Self and have gotten off our path, out of step with our sacred intentions. We've become entangled in a web of neediness that is sapping us of our very life force. Our energies, designed for Self-creation, are being wasted in the pursuit of alcohol, drugs, codependent relationships, overeating, compulsive romanticism or sexual acting out, workaholism, obsessive worrying, or some other process addiction that keeps us distracted. We begin to show signs of extremism or imbalance that makes others nervous and uneasy when they relate to us. We all seek to avoid people who seem to pull on us neurotically or become irrational when their particular form of addictive behavior strikes. And we feel sad and lonely, and sometimes terrified, when, once more, some dire consequence of our own excesses must be faced. Another broken relationship, thousands more dollars and valuable time spent in a treatment center, another jobless and income-bare period—and on and on goes the misery.

✴ **All human misery is a result of the soul's inability to express its purpose through us.**

Waking up from our fog and facing our misery is a very demanding task, requiring great strength of soul. Frankly, most people never make the decision to wake up and go that final round. Once we do wake up, though, we no longer find conformity to irrelevant standards rewarding enough to keep us going. We have even learned, perhaps, to "go with the flow." But still, another step is needed before we can all return "Home," to that place of serenity within. It requires more than mere spontaneity to end our old unfulfilling ways; we must turn in a new direction and begin all over again. We must now learn to swim upstream. Our little personal wills must align with the will of a Higher Power. To awaken fully, we have no choice but to surrender—to "let go and let God."

Abstinence from a troublesome chemical or addictive process is extremely difficult and demands a deep commitment to change. And abstinence is only the beginning of a new life. But to what end? What is it that we all hunger so for as we journey along this path, separate and together, awakened or not? This question is a crucial one if we are ever to reach our unique potential or aid others in realizing theirs. We need more understanding and confirmation of a philosophy based on the whole truth about human nature and how we evolve and heal, not just the facts about the form an addiction takes.

Many try to intellectualize their way out of an addiction, leaving the emotional wounds unaccessed and unhealed. Even treatment programs often fall short, rarely even attempting to empty their clients of long-held childhood hurts. And seldom does anyone help us know that we are more than mere egos butting up against one condition after another in our daily routines. Not only our egos, but our very souls require nurturing and healing. To heal our addictions and turn in the direction of the true Self, we must work with both the ego and the soul. We must include the whole Self in recovery, for it is the inner healer.

Looking more closely, then, at who we really are, we see that this journey beyond addictive living follows a natural progression from identification with our little ego self to identification with our root consciousness, the whole and higher Self. And this journey unfolds along three dimensions of human growth.

THE PERSONAL DIMENSION

We must all begin by being selfish. This focused pursuit of self-understanding and personal goals enables us to form an increasingly well-integrated, creative personality that can enter into relationships with others in a loving manner. And as we discover, through the trials and delights of living, what we are really like, we really *do* appear self-centered. We are preoccupied with thinking about ourselves, talking about ourselves, and often totally caught up in our own ego needs. But is this wrong, really? How else are we going to learn who we are?

Selfishness is a stepping stone to Self-ness. We cannot give to someone else something we do not ourselves possess. So we must develop a Self before we can give this Self to others. Viewed this way, maybe we can forgive ourselves and each other for times of myopic self-preoccupation and move on away from the past.

THE INTERPERSONAL DIMENSION

This stage begins to unfold naturally as we learn to know and trust ourselves, because now we begin attracting others to us. We become relational. We fall in love. Or we become conscious of our responsibility within a family or a group. And then entirely interactional goals and aspirations arise which create new learning situations. Becoming interdependent, instead of too dependent or too aloof, is the next training ground our evolving soul encounters. Intimacy and isolation issues are dealt with, creating the melodramas that often require family therapy, relationship counseling, or group work.

At this stage we learn to own and express our resentments or needs to our close associates so they won't build up inside us. We learn to process our feelings with honesty and forthrightness, letting go of the need to blame others.

THE TRANSPERSONAL DIMENSION

Once our personalities are fairly well developed (healthy body, balanced emotions, and sane thoughts), and once our relationships form and flow with confidence, our consciousness is no longer so captivated by the pains and pleasures of ego. Now we begin moving beyond our idiosyncratic point of view into a larger realm of consciousness: identification with Humanity. For the first time, gratifying our needs becomes secondary to the desire to serve others. We yearn to express our unique talents in the world for the good of others, not just for personal acclaim. This ushers in a stream of energy from the subconscious mind, the higher Self that brings us spiritual stature and seeks completion of the true Self in the expression of Its life's work, which is service.

Most recovering alcoholics I've known have a strong sense of the superconscious or a Higher Power. Many have experienced "peak experiences"[2] where the Self feels uplifted by an overwhelming sense of gratitude, meaning, and purpose. These are moments of bliss when we realize we really *are* connected to a spiritual source. Psychic or religious experiences accompany this stage. These phenomena *are* of this world, a natural part of our humanness; at some point we will all experience some aspect of the transpersonal dimension. Our awareness will expand to a more universal viewpoint, and we'll realize we are more than what we look like. And this feels good, because we stop taking our little ego selves so seriously. Our attitude becomes one of forgiveness and compassion for ourselves and others, as we begin to realize that our circumstances are merely the trials our soul deliberately seeks out for its own development, so we can serve better. Our circumstances, in other words, are the teacher we must and *will* attract in order to overcome our illusions and our fears.

In the transpersonal dimension, we seek more than anything else clarity of vision and the sense of freedom and harmony that comes from transcending our ego's limited point of view. At this more integrated level of consciousness, attachment to addictions becomes painfully limiting, and just plain boring. Our addictions are now experienced as distractions from our important purpose in life. This is the dimension of growth that imbues our life with spiritual force and purpose, a more certain direction, and lots of creative expression for the making of the Self. It feels like coming home.

Twelve-Step Recovery Programs

Anyone familiar with the Alcoholics Anonymous and other addiction recovery programs recognizes immediately that they contain the progression from surrender of the little self to identification with the higher Self, moving through stages of personal and interpersonal work toward service to fellow addicts. What a gift. Here is a natural path that leads to freedom from addiction and a sense of purpose in life. As direct spin-offs of AA, we now have a host of "Anonymous" recovery programs and self-help groups for all the other identifiable addictions. We owe deep gratitude to the pioneers of this potent and effective self-help movement.

It is no secret, however, that many recovering from any form of addiction intellectualize the twelve-step program, rather than committing to the real work of facing and transcending the lower self. These people are attempting to control their addiction rather than transforming it. Their energy is stuck in focusing on the addiction of choice, even though they are now abstinent. They have blocked at the third step. They think they have indeed "turned their lives over to God as they understand Him," but they truly still lack faith. They have not been able to trust they can really let go and take a good, long, honest look at themselves, which is what naturally happens when people enter upon the work of the fourth and fifth steps. In AA, these people are referred to as "dry drunks." They still have the same personality structure as they did before they quit drinking—still the same defenses, the same way of viewing life and themselves. The only difference is they no longer drink alcohol.

There are many abstinent alcoholics, however, who get bored with this way of living. They can see other possibilities and are willing to take the risk required for further growth, even though they may not realize yet just how to do this.

Let's take a deeper look at the transformation process a recovering alcoholic undergoes when this person truly commits to the path of inner development. It can serve as a model for all people struggling with addictions, or unhealthy craving of any kind, not to mention all people wanting to consciously evolve.

There are certain prerequisites—a mental preparation—that precede entering upon the path to Self-knowledge and Self-creation. These resemble preparing the soil for a bountiful crop, natural work that must be done before a crop comes to a healthy fruition. Sometimes we don't know *how* we know, but we do know what must be done before this work can come fully forth. Sometimes this knowing comes from having become awakened enough to begin following the intuition. Attending workshops and lectures or reading books that open our minds can be another way we sometimes "prepare the soil."

The people who venture beyond the mere control of an addiction have prepared their minds. They realize they are still focusing on the disease, rather than learning the conditions of health that are its opposite. Recovering addicts still focusing on the disease are continuing to live in the past. And though they feel good about maintaining their abstinence, they are still not learning how to live a life based on the principles of health. Consequently, what's really happening is they are no longer sick, but they are not yet well. They are in a never-never land in between illness and health that, quite frankly, feels dull and uninteresting. There is a lot of grief and depression that comes from having given up all one's ways to "kick up one's heels" in life. This is the basic problem of dry drunks. They're no longer having fun. Living has become a *sobering* experience.

So we begin our transformation work with people in recovery by helping them wake up to who they really are, *beyond just being abstinent.* The first realization that must come is one that serves the purpose of relieving guilt:

✷ **All my experiences, including my years of active addiction, have been for a reason. They have afforded me the grounding for understanding human suffering. Now I am prepared for a life of service on the path of the heart.**

In other words, this first realization *heals.* It helps people who want to go forward, to realize they have done their homework. After this seed thought sinks in, here are the beliefs they must now acknowledge before the total twelve-step process can unfold:

1. There is something higher (or wiser) than ego residing *within us*.

2. We are all evolving toward more and more completion.

3. Others have gone before who can serve as guides.

4. We can do it, too.

5. This path is predictable in principle, only varied in form.

6. We are co-creators with the Higher Power; we have our part to do.

7. And, finally, surrender to a Higher Power happens from within. We focus inwardly to find the wise, all-knowing Power; we no longer look outside ourselves for "the answer."

From these beliefs, the soil is now prepared for the next realization.

---

* I am creating my future today by the choices I am making *now*. And I have a wise Self within that will guide me to the next right step, if I will be still and listen.

Having had these two realizations, people will begin to see that, *in the moment*, they always have two choices: They can opt for the life-producing choice or the death-producing one, right now.

And next, we realize something very simple:

---

* The higher Self never leaves us with a destructive choice.

So now we move through the twelve steps, seeking the constructive choice every step of the way.

The Twelve Steps as a Spiritual Path and a Guide for the Transformer

Paradoxically, when we succeed in turning our lives over to a Higher Power, the first revelation that comes is that we, alone, control our personal choices. As seekers of the Truth, we discover we are existing within the universal mind of God, the source of all things manifest and unmanifest. We will draw into our own personal reality as much of this giant, limitless mind as we can conceive. So now, rather than passively turning ourselves over to a Power in the sky separate and apart from us, we realize this process of surrender is an active, powerful, *positive* statement about our Self. We know now that we are creators-in-miniature, and we are turning our little, limited ego self over to the greater Self that resides *within us*, the Self that is connected to the Source of all things. Consequently, the first stage on any path of Self-realization is surrender, correctly understood.

The following annotated material quotes from the twelve steps of AA: (And remember as you read along, if alcohol is not your problem, substitute some compulsion or unwanted behavior that is.)

1. "Admitted we"—our egos—"were powerless over alcohol—that our lives had become unmanageable"—under the control of the ego.

2. "Came to believe that a Power greater than ourselves"—greater than our ego—"could restore us to sanity." This is the correct use of the power of mind—utilizing a transforming belief that a Power greater than our ego resides within us; we don't have to give ourselves away to some external authority (I call this "cosmic codependence!").

3. "Made a decision"—again the power of mind—"to turn our will and our lives over to the care of God as we understand Him."

The first three steps can be restated to mean: In the past

we've allowed an addicted partial self to rule us, and it cannot control its cravings. We are now putting a stop to this dictatorship and will allow a more integrated Self within us to take over. This Self, our essence, is identical to God's essence, and is really our true and rightful Self. So, we are not giving away our power. We are accepting it by becoming identified with who we really are.

Each one of us today is the result of how we've made use of our minds either consciously or unconsciously. We are, *now*, what we've thought! The answer to what we will be in the future is contained in how we think and what we believe in the present. We now realize that when we operate from our Self, our true identity, all is one. We have aligned ourselves with universal law.

The second stage of the path of Self-realization will always be concerned with purification. Now that we are thinking correctly, we have created an inner environment of malleable, fertile soil ready to bear healthy fruit.

All experiences are connected and valuable, even the negative ones. Consequently, we will be required to undergo an internal and external catharsis. No more evasion of personal responsibility for our life. As Socrates said, "The place to study is where you are."

✴ **We now realize life must flow harmoniously from experience to experience.**

The twelve steps continue to show us the way:

4. We "made a searching and fearless moral inventory of ourselves." We cleared out the past, redefining our actions and reactions toward ourselves and others according to right thinking, and released any pent-up emotion that is blocking our progress, which will include forgiveness of ourselves and significant others.

5. "Admitted to God, to ourselves, and to another hu-

man being the exact nature of our wrongs." Doing this enables us to take full responsibility for ourselves. It is extremely difficult to continue self-defeating patterns when we've confessed these problems to others. The very act of externalizing these realizations through verbalization is healing *in itself*, for it clarifies, concretizes, and focuses us on Truth, enabling us to move beyond irrational thoughts (what AA calls "stinking thinking").

6. "We're entirely ready to have God remove all these defects of character." Again, this is a statement of the power of the Self, not a passive giving in to some super energy source separate and apart from us. It means choosing consciously to purge ourselves from our wrong thinking, feeling, and acting, putting our true Self in charge, for it is aligned with the Higher Power.

When we commit to this inner movement of purification, the higher Self descends and cleans out anything negative that cannot be contained within its brilliance, drawing its energy from the Higher Power. Therefore, we can expect this to be a very painful stage on the path, yet permanently rewarding.

What we are seeking are not drastic measures of discipline, but gentle, effective ways of eliminating vices and faults. The discipline should be fairly effortless. Extremes revert to their opposites. Self-violence and fads should be avoided at all costs. Again, to quote Socrates, "In all things, not too much." Moderation is the desired quality seeking expression—especially for recovering addicts.

First comes the body. We seek a healthy, balanced diet, exercise, and quiet times of prayer/meditation. The diet should contain the nutrients that the body is deficient in from the former life-style of addiction. Fresh vegetables, herbs, vitamins, and minerals, and good sources of protein must replenish the body's depleted energies. Sugars, white flour, heavy carbohydrate junk foods, cigarettes, and caffeine must be curtailed, gently . . . with love.[3]

Physical exercise can be natural, fun, and practiced

daily. Violent and unaccustomed exercise programs exhaust and hurt you and should be avoided, for they are an act of intemperance. Someone once asked a Greek philosopher to go to see a famous athlete who could swim like a fish, jump like a deer, and run like a hare, to which he declined, saying: "I do not wish to imitate the animals; but if you know of someone I could see who thinks like a God, I will go." The seeker on the path exercises not to become a famous athlete but to enter upon a pleasant routine of aesthetic expression.

And finally, the body needs peace and quiet. Ex-addicts are learning to live comfortably with their energies. They are tired of the swings from high to low; they need *contact* with their Higher Power, not just a realization of it. Instead of looking to the outside world for excitement, they now desire peace, courage, security, a sense of purpose, loving relationships, altruistic quests, and a sense of well-being.

As they rework their past and discover the defeating patterns of interpersonal relating they've been involved in unconsciously, they seek a new way of belonging to a group. Seekers do not usually become joiners. They maintain their individuality, thinking their own thoughts and feeling personally responsible for building their own lives. But they do benefit greatly from a support group of seekers like themselves to bolster mutual courage. In this way, they can begin to work out their emotional and mental levels of relating with truthfulness, and practice a selfless sharing of themselves with others.

The twelve steps show us the way to interpersonal growth:

7. As our courage mounts we will truly be ready to "humbly ask God to remove all our shortcomings." This can be a painful and dangerous move to make if we're not prepared for the havoc wreaked when this purifying Higher Power begins to move through us. But if we are sincere in our desire to become more advanced members of the human

race, and if we are somewhat prepared for what this request actually entails, we will welcome the opportunity to work on ourselves that this step brings.

And now we will be entering the interpersonal area of growth, the area of right relationship, where we learn to face up to the responsibility of human sharing in the here and now. We are training to become co-workers in the master plan for Humanity by first getting our own relationships in order.

8. "We made a list of all persons we've harmed and became willing to make amends." Making amends does not mean mumbling a superficial "I'm sorry." It means transforming our ordinary mode of involvement with another. First, we redefine our relationships realistically, letting go of the ones that cannot work for us, and committing to the ones that matter. Then we begin the arduous task of learning to communicate.

9. "Making direct amends to such people wherever possible, except when to do so would injure them or others." We must refine and practice the virtue of discrimination. We don't just walk about venting and sharing our past with others for our sake. Every interpersonal situation contains a whole *gestalt*, an entire perspective that must be acknowledged. We learn to be sensitive to the entire group we might affect by an indiscriminate need to confess or cathart. Some people cannot deal with our past mistakes and weaknesses which involved them, for they are not ready to deal with their own—and maybe for a good reason. Sometimes we must do this work alone, even though it involves another.

10. "Continued to take personal inventory and when we were wrong promptly admitted it." Now we are shifting the emphasis to living in the here and now. Self-analysis, emotional clearing, and right thinking have brought us to the place where we can begin living our life consciously moment by moment, as we experience it. We can reprogram our minds with character traits we wish to develop. We can draw to us the personal qualities we've sought: perseverance,

lovingness, tranquillity, poise, detachment from results, sense of humor, personal harmony, mastery over unhealthy appetites, ways to go beyond worry and fear, enthusiasm, and the development of any creative endeavor we wish to pursue.

Now, in all our comings and goings, our observer self is operative. It will guide us to the truth point in any experience, in any condition in which we find ourselves. We will find the truth and live by it.

The next stage on the path will be concerned with learning to listen to our higher Self, our contact with the Higher Power. We must now develop our ability to discover experientially "that which cannot be written about." In the midst of our active, daily lives we must learn to listen for the truth, moment by moment, which will enter into our consciousness quietly when we are open to receiving it.

---

* **Since the here and now is "the vanishing point" in time, we are merely going with the flow when we are fully present in the now.**

---

11. We "sought through prayer and meditation to improve our conscious contact with God as we understand Him, praying only for knowledge of His will for us and the power to carry that out."

This deep serenity arises from a holistic understanding of universal truth, of the rightness of life and the laws that govern it. This is the stage of comprehension and Self-creative expression. None of us are victims of our conditions. Everything unfolds as it should. Happiness comes from within, the result of spiritual unfoldment.

And there is no blame: We all get exactly what we earn, the "good" with the "bad." There is no way we can avoid our just desserts. At this stage on our journey we learn to understand the law of karma—the immutable balancing law of cause and effect. By proper study and discipline, we can master our personal chain of cause and effect events by the practice of harmlessness.[4] By refusing to think, feel, or act in any manner that produces harm to our Self or another, we begin to live rightly. Staying constantly in tune with an inner voice that quietly guides us (the voice of our intuition), and making note of the comments of our observer self, we begin to master our life.

Patience now becomes an active ingredient in our personality—an attitude that recognizes that in the fullness of time everything works according to law. Another virtue we develop during this stage is the ability to conserve all our energy for the purpose of living life consciously. Seekers learn to do the tasks of life by the simplest, most direct means, to live by the simplest codes; they do not get caught up in negative emotions or situations that deflect their peace of mind and sense of direction. They learn to discriminate between necessary and unnecessary action, feeling, and thought. We begin to notice in them a quality of poise and loving nonattachment. At this stage on the path, the addictive life-style has been transcended. The voice of the higher Self is now easily discerned, for they've become attentive listeners to the voice within. They are developing the advanced skill of living and loving wisely.

At this point on the path another paradox occurs. Seekers' personalities become subservient to the rule of the higher Self. The inner life dominates. And though inward they go, the *outward* urge toward service to others draws them into their expression. Now the ego cannot be boss, for it is not expansive enough to live within the transpersonal consciousness—beyond the personal. By its very definition, the ego lives for the personal. Those who pursue the path beyond this point are searching for the mystery of the inner life and can only use the higher values in their acting, feeling, and thinking. The ordinary *personal* mind will now be of very little service, the lower-self emotions of very little value. The observer self watches these lower drives, acknowledges them, and allows them to pass on by, giving them no energy. "Ah, yes, and there goes *that* one." (Dis-identification.)

People who have gone past the personal difficulties of the addictive life by having done the work at the personal and interpersonal levels will tell you they have discovered that the search for personal gratification is not enough. Living solely for ego pleasure is a base and shallow experience. They come to the realization that our mortal actions, feelings, and ideas produce an outer world of calculating minds, politics, and institutions that, in the long run, are meaningless symbols for the building of false personality. Focusing on outer ego gratifications leads to more and more ego difficulties. More pitting oneself against others in useless competition, more frustration, more power needs, more demands made upon the Self, more comparisons, more duality, more addiction.

---

* **On the path to Self-creation the ego must be transcended. But it can only be transcended by working through its needs at the personal and interpersonal levels—*not* by denial or attempting to bypass them.**

We will find ourselves, again and again, at the very same place of personal work we failed to complete, until we work through it to a point of understanding and acceptance. This is how the law of transcendence works.

But when we truly earn the right to live in the transpersonal realm, we become a valuable server of Humanity. The transpersonal dimension is nothing exotic or unusual. It is the natural result of right action, right feeling, and right thought. It is the *overflowing* of a full and rich consciousness, of needs fulfilled and transcended, of satisfaction, contentment, and wisdom—total acceptance of the human condition—and a realization that the Self is larger than its conditions.

12. "Having had a spiritual awakening as the result of these steps, we tried to carry this message to alcoholics, and *to practice these principles* in all our affairs." (Italics mine.)

And practicing the principles is the key; serving others is the natural by-product. The seeker is now a model of authentic being, no longer governed by subpersonalities struggling incessantly to meet conflicting ego needs. There is an intrinsic validity in all that the person does. Energy that was used to gain personal gratification becomes redirected toward serving the good of others.

Persons living at the transpersonal level vary in their area of service. Some are qualified to serve individuals or small groups of fellow travelers—such as counselors, group leaders, householders, or organizers of small, purposeful establishments. Some are designed for larger work—serving humanity on a national or planetary level. The area of service depends upon the person's natural abilities, latent talents, and desires. One area is just as important as the other, only different in scale or design. At this level there is no comparison or rating-sheet mentality. Each one of us operates from our own unique and rightful expression, authentically. And sacrifice is no longer a negative word.

The Transmutations

Controlling is holding on; transforming is release!

Transmutations are not controls. When something transmutes into something else a literal change of structure has taken place. From biochemical factors to philosophies of life, we are no longer the same.

Consequently, when our energy is not being dissipated in negativity, activities (outer or inner) that block or distort the authentic activities of the true Self, the positive quality just naturally emerges and begins expressing itself. Some of the signs that we are truly being guided by the Higher Power are the following observable shifts.

FEAR IS TRANSMUTED INTO COURAGE

Fear is an ego defense based on illusion. Once we look our fears squarely in the face, we find that they are simply negative expressions of positive traits trying to express themselves. When we understand the nature of these fears and clear up the wrong thinking they represent, we begin risking new action and opting for innovative choices.

For instance, I fear you because I think you are more important than me (illusion). Transmuted, this becomes the courage to express my own equal importance. I fear a situation because I believe I'm a bad person if I fail (illusion). Transmuted, this is the opportunity to accept my weaknesses and my strengths realistically and to follow my own path. Or, I'm afraid to look at a part of myself, because if I acknowledge it I will have to see myself as "bad" (illusion). Transmuted, this becomes the chance to see myself as I really am—partially unawakened and still needing more experiences to become enlightened. Once we get the picture of who we truly are, self-doubt diminishes, and fear becomes an irrelevant issue. When life comes in on us, we go inward and find the key.

SELF-PITY AND BLAME SHIFT TO A DESIRE TO TAKE PERSONAL RESPONSIBILITY FOR OUR LIFE

Seeing ourselves as victims of our situations is a debilitating point of view based on illusion rather than truth. We are totally responsible for our personal circumstances and for the people we attract to us. These external forces in our lives are merely reflections of our inner state of mind and our current level of evolution. Learning to say "I chose to do this, given the options I felt I had," or "Here's how I set this one up" grants us freedom.

Because we have created our past by our moment-by-moment choices, it follows logically that we are also creating our future by the choices we make now. There is a direct relationship between cause and effect. *We*, not someone else, are setting the chain in motion with our every thought, feeling, and action. There is no blame. If we hadn't needed the experience, we wouldn't have chosen it.

Conscious action (personal choice) rather than unconscious *re*action (putting ourselves to sleep and allowing fate to choose for us) is the key to freedom. Blessed relief from the shackles of victimhood!

People who've experienced early childhood abuse balk at this truth about victimhood, arguing that little children do not choose their fate. And from the ego's limited intellect, this is true. The metaphysical soul, however, opted to enter fully into this family dysfunction—to take on the suffering so it could know it, and therefore *heal* it. This is love in action. A sacrifice is made in the early life for a later healing of an entire family lineage.

Powerlessness is transmuted into empowerment

As we begin to experience ourselves as having chosen our lives, we realize we are perfectly free to make any changes we really want to make in our thinking, our feelings, or in our actions. At this stage, we can't maintain depression. Nor can we abuse. Our spiritual will becomes operative, directing us now toward integration and authentic power. A sense of joy and fascination replaces feelings of impotence and fear. We now begin directing our lives toward meaningful events that lead to higher purpose, moving further away from dominance by the little ego selves. Feelings of isolation fade as we expand ourselves into the whole of community.

PASSION IS TRANSMUTED INTO COMPASSION

When we become involved in the art of Self-creating, passions become our teachers. They lead us to the outside world where we look for something we never find. Passion gets hooked on diversity, absolutizing every little experience, thinking each is essential. Now we realize there is another way. We can turn inward. When we do, love is there. We begin seeing ourselves through the eyes of acceptance rather than the voice of judgment. We can understand, as we look deeper, how we've gotten where we are; and we can comprehend the hardness of our life, the sadness of our mistakes. We develop compassion, the place in our hearts where emotion and realization merge.

As we develop this for ourselves, it begins spilling out to others. We love and see others as we love and see ourselves. Compassion is feeling, but it is not ego-involved feeling. It stands on the sidelines and weeps for humankind. Then it moves in and acts, where it can, for others. It draws diversity back into itself, realizing the unity behind everything.

SELF-PREOCCUPATION SHIFTS INTO AN ASPIRATION TO SERVE HUMANITY

Now we have the tools for serving others. We feel for ourselves, and we feel for life. We've learned that gratification comes from within, not from all the various objects and people in the outside world. We've tried that already, hardly leaving a stone unturned. It simply doesn't work. Perhaps it is originally in self-defense that we turn to serving others for our means of true gratification. But it is a kind of work that eventually leads us beyond ourselves, and we learn a truth: I am only truly joyful when I am experiencing myself connecting with my brothers and sisters through mutual sharing, love, and purpose. Giving myself away gives me back to myself tenfold.

EXAGGERATED MOOD SWINGS BALANCE INTO A STATE OF SERENITY

Now I can work with the law of polarity and neutralize its energetic force. Before, I was a victim of my moods, going from depression to elation, depending upon what the outside world brought into my consciousness. Now *I* am in the driver's seat. I can use my moods, my feelings, my highs or my lows for experiencing the full gamut of my humanness. And when I start going too low, I can remember who I really am and get outside my absurd preoccupation with misery. I can serve. I can be still. I can pull toward the center. I can become fully present in nature and allow her to show me her multifaceted radiant perfection. When I feel elated, I can enjoy it fully, not needing it to last, but appreciating the moment for what it has to offer.

My faith is now in the process of life itself. I know other true moments of joy will occur; I don't have to hang on to this one. I feel serene. All of it is okay—even the hard times. They are taking me exactly where I need to be, showing me what I need to know.

FRAGMENTED KNOWLEDGE IS TRANSMUTED INTO HOLISTIC TRUTH

While we are still dominated by our little egos, we fall in love with our ideas and our ability to become an "expert" in various segments of outer life. I may recount to you great academic victories in the art of loving, without knowing the slightest about the nature of love or of the human being experiencing it.

Fragments of truth can create illusions and divisiveness. Learning to see the whole picture of the nature and purpose of something within the life context of a human being leads to great leaps of wisdom. This is the difference between the scientist and the wise person: A scientist *can* be a wise person; but a wise person is never *merely* an objective investigator of facts.

PLAYACTING GRADUALLY SHIFTS INTO EXPRESSING OUR AUTHENTIC NATURE

Until we know who we are, we play roles, trying on first this one, then that. And often, we discover we are filling our lives with meaningless pap, involving ourselves in events that have nothing to do with the development of our true essence. Once we are on the path, we begin showing the world who we really are, even if this true Self looks different from others. We develop the courage to be who we are.

DESIRE FOR EXTERNAL THINGS IS TRANSMUTED INTO SEEKING SELF-KNOWLEDGE

Once we truly begin seeking truth, our teachers appear in varied forms. Self-knowledge is by its nature transforming, and we are on our way. Our energy is no longer so tied up in searching for things to gratify our sense of identity. We are finding our true Self. The most exhilarating safari we will ever take, the journey into Self!

People who are on the path, being guided by their Higher Power, do not benefit from programs, even AA groups, that are still focusing on the negative storyline. They must avoid being stuck in obsessively talking about the past, their fears, mistakes, diseases, and instead focus on programs that teach about the Self, how to go within, release the past, and learn about the higher Self, a future Self ready to emerge. It teaches you from within how to take on its qualities and expand into its identity. Recovery programs become *dis*covery programs. Seekers are no longer working on staying sober. They are searching for truth of the Self, and determined to find it.

A nonseeker cannot recognize a seeker. But seekers *can* recognize each other. Seekers must be strong enough to resist the criticisms of nonseekers. Seekers *do* appear "different" and are often misunderstood by nonseekers. They must accept this reality and search out persons of like mind for validation and support.

Seekers are Transformers.

In Conclusion: A Message to Transformers

We see now that the artistry of Self-creation provides the ability to live in the now with fascination and hope—a life turned on to continual new possibilities and now abstinent from debilitating addictions. Who needs them?

Seeing our predicaments as "mistakes" becomes an irrelevant concept. We no longer need guilt in our lives. We view our own Self-made choices as serving a positive purpose in our development. If we have harmed others by our choices, we make amends, forgive ourselves, and let go. God forgives, why shouldn't we? Our only responsibility is to stay conscious, to *stay awake*, so that we will understand the significance of our choices and the purpose they are serving . . . not repeating ad infinitum situations that lead nowhere.

Realization of the Self is an attitude that views life as a teacher and ourselves as co-creators of this life—co-creators with an energy so fine, so immensely wondrous, it defies description. And yet, we are a part of this amazing energy. We are designed in its image.

Self-realization is complete understanding and acceptance of the human experience. Awareness and a willingness to work on ourselves provide the springboard for this inward, upward journey that takes us first *into* ourselves and finally beyond ourselves in service of others.

A Transformer is a true people-helper, a guide to this natural process of unfoldment—not an expert, not a judge, but a guide. Real helpers are fellow travelers, who invite others to discover the meaning of their suffering, relieve suffering wherever they can, but who resist interfering with another's free will. This means viewing abstinence from an addiction or neurosis as each individual's responsibility. It

247

means that we're all responsible for all our own thoughts, feelings, and actions. And that's only the beginning of a very exciting journey.

If we go through life caught in addictions or irresponsible behavior, caught up in fear, passion, and desire for status, we find we are misusing our life force, depleting this precious energy designed for the creation of our very Self. Once we transcend these more personalistic levels, by drawing to ourselves the creative energies from the higher centers—no longer polarizing earth and heaven or form and essence—we move beyond ego-dominance to become aligned with our soul's purpose. Our addicted selves, the mechanistic fragments of our personality, increasingly give way to this more integrated Self as our knowledge and conscious experiencing expands and unfolds.

Once we release in us this powerful energy source, our root-consciousness, we are being who we truly are. Then, the question becomes one of having the courage to continue living according to *our* grain instead of someone else's idea of it. And if we opt for this grand experience, we discover the greatest "high" of all. We truly begin to live.

Transformers never fear working on themselves, for it is through their own trials of balancing the higher forces with the lower, earthy self that they have grounded their knowledge of the human endeavor in truth. Their deepest yearning is the urge toward Self-creation.

I challenge you to a deeper life, and for the sake of those you serve to seek a stronger bond with your own soul so that you will continually bring new truths to light and help fit others for the living and understanding of these truths.

—*A TIBETAN MASTER*

A Word on Unity

In this book, I have attempted, through words, to unveil the mystery of the twofold nature of our consciousness, the higher Self and the lower. But words can only imply the majesty of our human spirit. When we turn within to find the amazing spiritual powers of the mind, the heart, and the body, we must become wordless. Our dualistic mortal mind really cannot define the unitary immortal Self. Understanding this is the beginning of true knowledge.

The theoretical portions of this book have presented a dualistic model of humankind in the mode of the third level of consciousness. In order to understand the outer world of experience, we dissect life, studying it piece by piece—for it is in so doing that we, the "scientists," discover our core. By going down, down, involving in life, we use logic, making finer and finer distinctions, separating, analyzing, so as to know what is what.

Going down into diversity, studying the "many" piece by piece, is the work of the intellect—the logical left brain, which belongs to the outer world. Reaching for the unity, the Oneness that has no boundaries, beyond dissection, is the work of the higher mind, the intuition—the fifth level of consciousness belonging to the inner world of wisdom. This is the function of the right brain—the relational mind, the one that "thinks" in wholes.

And if we reflect for a minute about how our life *really* works, we will see immediately that the holistic mode (which can *include* the left brain's analysis, but is not limited by it) fits our experiences more accurately than does the dissecting separate mode. When I fall in love, can I tell you exactly *when* in time it happened? Was it Wednesday at 2:10? Can I tell you the distinct steps I followed to make this occur? And do I love him for his bone structure, his eye color, the shape of his nose or feet? Or do I love him for that "certain quality" that defies description? When I feel joyous or depressed, can I pinpoint in time and space the exact event that created this state of mind? Did joyousness strike me at 4:03 A.M.? Of course not. We don't experience our lives in discrete units. I flow from feeling happy to feeling unhappy, but I cannot say exactly when the changeover took place—because *they are not two things—they are one.* They gradually merge into one another, with no clear-cut boundaries.

> *And Jesus said to them: When you make the two one, and when you make the inner as the outer, and the outer as the inner, and the above as the below . . . then you shall enter the Kingdom.*
>
> —THE GOSPEL ACCORDING TO ST. THOMAS

Unless we realize this unity, reaching for the Oneness *behind* the polarities, we are still misunderstanding. And we will continue to live in misery—going from extreme to extreme, loving the one and hating the other, searching for the answer. But the minute we find it, it will switch to its opposite, and off we will go again searching once more for the truth. And again, we're stuck in the discomfort of duality. For each of us intuitively knows that "the two must eventually become one."

The most important matters in life cannot be dissected and made distinct. This separative mode of thinking may be utilitarian, but it is *not* the truth. The truth defies analysis. Duality is a myth. The wise person drops judgmentalness, drops distinctions, and lives like a little child—in a relational world with no boundaries. This is the promise of the future, and one we all hold dear to our hearts.

> *In the ancient temple of Serapis at Alexandria stood a gigantic image of the weeping god. His body was fashioned out of the twigs and branches of the trees; his hair was grass and grain; his eyes were precious stones; his garments were made of metal; and his body was over-cloaked in the skins of animals. He was crowned with the feathers of birds; flowers bloomed in his hands; and insects gathered honey from his mantle. This weeping god upon whose head light shone down through the open roof of the temple, is [Humanity itself], the symbol of all nature, who bears within him all questions and all answers*
>
> *He is, of all creatures, the most mysterious. . . .*[1]
>
> —MANLY P. HALL

Appendix 1
Guided Imagery Exercises for Transformers

The following guided imagery exercises will aid you in your work in transformation. These imageries from the creative imagination tap into the powerful depths of the unconscious mind. Throughout Book Two, I have referred to some of these exercises as they relate to specific tasks at different levels. In addition to using the individual exercises for purposes I have indicated, you will find that some of these exercises will be "longtime companions," practices you will do repeatedly in your life as a Transformer.

Here are a few suggestions that will help to make this work a useful, safe, and positive experience:

1. If you have never done guided imagery or worked with the powerful imagination, please experience these techniques with a friend or therapist yourself before you attempt using them with others. Or you can tape them in your own voice and play them back to yourself. This is very powerful. Having experienced them yourself will activate your own imagination and intuition in guiding someone else. Otherwise, the exercises will come across as superficial, your timing might be off, or you could get into difficulty with them. It will also enrich the experience of your clients or students.

2. Any imagery of *ascension* will take the person doing the exercise into the superconscious realm. And, conversely, any symbolism of *descent* will move the client into the subconscious. The superconscious is seldom scary and usually produces very beautiful, high experiences. But the subconscious

251

can be extremely dark and sometimes frightening. People may show resistance in viewing whatever is trying to emerge from the dark recesses of their minds. You can provide a symbol for them to use in their imagery as tools of protection—a light, a cord to pull to bring themselves up, a suit of armor to wear, a sword, whatever they feel they need. This may overcome the resistance. If not, do not push it. If the issue is an important one, you can be sure another time will come when the person will be more ready to work on this particular problem.

3. Always end trips into the lower unconscious, or subconscious, with a positive experience. Surround the "evil" with love or light. Tell it you are going to try to understand it and grant it its wishes in an appropriate way. Allow it to run away or dissipate. Or leave it behind and come "up and out." If it gets really uncomfortable, surround yourself or your client with love and light. Never leave yourself or anyone else down in the subconscious in the midst of a negative experience.

4. In the guiding instructions of the exercises to follow, a series of dots (. . .) represent a five to ten second pause, unless otherwise specified.

5. Symbols are carriers of meaning and energy. They show us the causative level of the issue they represent. They are agents of transformation and extremely potent, providing the missing piece in our struggle for wholeness. Working at the symbolic level of a problem often produces amazingly rapid results. You must be prepared for this and trust the process. Symbols have personal meaning to each individual, depending on his or her own unique life history. Therefore, please avoid interpreting anyone else's symbolic relationships. Interpretation should be a nondirective process, asking the person to tell you what it means to him or her. This holds true for interpreting your own symbols as well. Trust your own meanings over anyone else's interpretations (including universal meanings from books on symbolism).

6. Study each exercise in its *entirety* and familiarize your-

self with the steps to follow before you guide anyone through one of these experiences.

7. Your voice quality and instructions should not impede the meditative process of each exercise. All guided imagery exercises should be read by someone with a calm, neutral, and pleasant voice. Or you can record them for yourself. The quality of the voice is a very important factor in the meditative process.

8. These imagery exercises can be used over and over. The imagery will change each time, which will indicate movement of the psyche.

I have been doing this work for years, and to my knowledge, I have never seen any harm come from working with the unconscious, only powerful, positive growth. But I've always followed these guidelines I am sharing with you. One can seldom get into trouble when feeling sincere love and empathy for others. The rule I use for myself is: "All the work I do is designed to lead to a furthering of truth, goodness, and beauty."

EXERCISE 1 ▲　　▲　　▲　　▲　　▲　　▲

Getting a Message from the Higher Self

PURPOSE: Use this exercise to get an answer to a problem from the superconscious mind, when problem-solving at the conscious level has been unsuccessful.

INSTRUCTIONS TO GUIDE: Begin by helping the person phrase his question properly and have him write it down.

Tell him that in a minute you will be guiding him through a meditative process that will enable him to get a message from his higher Self. The message will be coming in a symbolic form and he must wait with the attitude of a moviegoer awaiting the picture to come on the screen—expectantly, but with no anxiety. Tell him he is *not* the projectionist. It will not be his responsibility to make the picture come on the screen. Now, guide your client in the following manner:

GUIDED IMAGERY EXERCISE: "Close your eyes and become aware of your breathing. Begin letting go of the tension in your body and feel yourself relaxing . . . letting go. Allow your breathing to become balanced and calm . . . realize that gravity will hold you . . . let go . . . relax. . . .

"Focus on your body and notice any physical sensations you are having. . . . Now, ask your body to become perfectly relaxed and still. . . .

"Focus on your emotions and notice any movement you are feeling . . . especially in the heart or the solar plexus. . . . Now, ask your emotions to become calm . . . like a lake with no ripples.

"Focus on your mind and notice any thoughts you are having. Just be aware of your thoughts for a while. . . . Ask your active mind to be quiet. . . . Experience the stillness . . . the silence. . . .

"Now imagine yourself sitting here inside a warm, beautiful bubble of rose-colored light. Just feel the pleasant, safe warmth. And above your head, at the top of the bubble, picture a brilliant star . . . shining its radiance down upon you. . . . This star is your higher Self. Know that your higher Self wants to communicate with you. It is the voice of your very soul. It will speak to you in symbols. . . . Experience this beautiful star for a moment, and tell it you are open to receiving its message. . . . Now, ask your higher Self whatever question you wish to ask it. Phrase it carefully so that you can understand the answer when it comes. . . .

"Now sit still and wait for the answer. When the symbol

appears, take whatever it is as your message, and then thank your higher Self for this meaningful gift."

Note: If the client balks and does not seem to be receiving an answer after a minute or so, say to him, "Take whatever comes when you hear my hand clap," and clap loudly. Then ask, "What did you get?"

PROCESSING: When the client tells you the symbol, have him work with it in this way: Write or draw it on a piece of paper and *immediately* write down any descriptive words or sentences that he associates with this particular symbol. The client is not to be concerned at this point with the question he asked. He is just working now with the interpretation of the symbol—what it means to *him*, not to anyone else.

When your client has run out of things to write about his symbol, have him take a look at what he has written and apply this knowledge to the question that he asked his higher Self. He will probably see his answer clearly.

Ponder together the answer your client received. If the symbolism was too abstruse, he can go back to his higher Self to ask for a clarification symbol. Or he can ask to be shown a picture of how he would be acting in his daily life if he were *doing* the answer to his question. Use your own imagination and intuition in processing this exercise with your client. Be sure he understands how his answer applies to his daily life.

Note: Since the higher Self does not work in the dimension of time, the client needs to be aware that he must use practical discrimination about when and how to apply the solution he has received—such as putting off a decision until an appropriate time, making arrangements for persons dependent on himself, gathering more material resources before following guidance. Messages from the higher Self are answers at a more abstract level than living in this world. And, since we *do* live in the ordinary world, we must always use our practical nature along with our higher nature in determining our life's decisions.

EXERCISE 2 ▲   ▲   ▲   ▲   ▲   ▲

Centering

PURPOSE: Use this exercise to bring consciousness back into the body, in the center where it belongs, attached to the true Self.

Anytime we feel caught up in a situation where our emotions are beginning to rock around, we will notice a strange shift in consciousness has occurred. Our consciousness has left us and gone over and attached itself to the someone or something that is upsetting us. We have literally lost ourselves for the time being, and have given away our power. Consequently, we cannot think straight; we cannot control our emotions; and our body even feels out of hand. We've become obsessed! Before we can resolve this intolerable situation, we must get hold of ourself again.

For instance, you are having lunch with your boss and she is telling you she is removing you from the project you've been working on. She is putting you in charge of something else. But you hear a threat. Your consciousness runs off. It "sees" a perfect, ideal person replacing you and the project working better without you. You are off somewhere in a corner no longer being noticed, making less money, being told you are not needed anymore, etc., etc., etc. The whole time your boss is talking to you, you are not at home. Your imagination is running wild.

GUIDED EXERCISE: "Close your eyes for a moment and picture yourself being out there in the other person or thing . . . literally. *See* your consciousness over there in the other or scurrying around the scene that is upsetting you. . . .

"Now gradually, in your mind's eye, picture yourself (your observer self who is aware of this predicament just now) tossing a rope out to your consciousness over there and lassoing it. . . . Very slowly now, bring it back in toward the center of your body, put it in its rightful place within you. Feel this happening as you do it."

PROCESSING: If you or your client is successful, she will experience a calming down, a settling in, a lightening up, and a letting go of anxiety and fear. She will be home again.

Once this happens, have her check out her body, her emotions, and her mental attitude. If this process has worked, she will discover that she is feeling fine and thinking sanely. Now, you can deal with the issue realistically as the two of you process this together. Your client will know exactly what to do, and her response will match the reality of the situation.

If the exercise did not work, the processing must include gaining insight into the difficulty or resistance that occurred. The exercise can be tried again, or modified to better fit the client's needs.

EXERCISE 3 ▲　　▲　　▲　　▲　　▲　　▲

Following the Drink

> *The man takes a drink*
> *The drink takes a drink*
> *The drink takes the man. . . .*

PURPOSE: Use this exercise to give yourself or others permission to experience the craving *in their mind.*

Most alcoholics, when recovering from their addiction, experience times of craving, or building toward a "slip." When these times occur, it is helpful to have the client talk about them and make the cravings explicit. Often they are ashamed of these desires and are hesitant to discuss them, so they may need prompting.

Something experienced on the symbolic level (in the mind, in dreams) is truly experienced. And often, this inner dreamwork completes the experience. When this happens, it will keep the behavior from manifesting on the physical plane. The symbolic experience discharges the pent-up energy that is getting built up around the subject of returning to the addicted behavior.

INSTRUCTIONS TO GUIDE: After discussing with your client or friend his craving, or his fantasizing about returning to the addicted behavior, ask him to close his eyes, relax, and begin to see himself in his mind's eye in the scene he wishes to be in—a bar, a party, a sexual liaison. Have him begin to describe it in flowery detail, letting his imagination run wild and living it through. Have him exaggerate the high, the delights that he imagines.

Example: "I'm in this bar having two double scotches, one right after the other, and I look great! I'm dressed to the hilt, my hair is perfect, I'm really grand. A gorgeous lady comes over and joins me. We begin to kid around, really getting high on each other. I order another drink, and we dance a while. Then we leave together." Have him continue his fantasy on through the entire evening. And on into the waking up the next morning: the hangover, the remorse, the rest of the next day, all the consequences.

Don't allow the fantasy to end until the consequences of the drinking have also been experienced. Follow it completely through. Keep asking questions that elicit the whole experience. If the client wants to kid himself by trying to stop while it's all still pleasant, prod him on into the day after or beyond, until he experiences his compulsive, slavelike addictive behavior returning on him. Then process this experience extensively, drawing him out about *all* his feelings, ideas, plans.

PROCESSING: Make a realistic plan for the next several days to ensure a support system for your client, if you sense he is really about to slip. Do not act alarmed or judgmental. Be supportive of the progress he has made and how natural it is to have fantasies about returning to the addictive behavior.

Note: Your client may need to grieve about giving up the addiction. Sometimes the fantasizing is a way of getting in touch with the pain of the loss. Be very sensitive to him. That bottle may have been his best friend.

EXERCISE 4 ▲ ▲ ▲ ▲ ▲ ▲

(For use in groups) Observer Self

PURPOSE: Use this exercise to help people learn they have a consciousness level that can rise above their predicaments and see things clearly and comprehensively. This profound exercise leads to a practical use of the emotions and the observer self-consciousness in sticky situations where confrontations or negative experiences are occurring.

INSTRUCTIONS TO GUIDE: Have group members each choose a partner and decide who will be A and who will be B. Give the following instructions:

1. "All who are A, I would like for you to think of a situation that has occurred in your life recently that you still have some energy in that made you mad or hurt your feelings . . . some kind of negative experience you felt you had to really process or deal with."

2. "Now, tell this story to your partner as vividly as you can recall it. It's okay to get back into the feelings . . . in fact, it's even advisable. And partners—B's—all you do is listen and empathize, as if you are simply a sympathetic friend. You can say a few supportive words now and then, but basically, remain non-verbal."

Allow five minutes for this . . . or go a little longer if your intuition says to.

3. "Now, stop wherever you are in your story. Just cut it off for now. And those of you who are B's, if you will, please tell a story that has happened to you lately that made you upset, and A's, listen to them in the way you've just been listened to."

Allow another five minutes or so.

4. "Now, stop again, wherever you are in your story . . . just stop for now. And, all A's, those of you who shared your story first, I want you to go back now and tell your *same* story again while B listens.

"Only this time, you must tell it in the third person, using your first name, and the pronoun he or she. Imagine you are watching the scene on a soap opera. You may not use the word 'I,' and partners, please monitor this. . . . If they say 'I,' they are getting re-identified, so move in and stop them. Just tell the story, purely and simply, in the third person."

Allow four minutes. It shouldn't take as long because there will be less justifying and less emotional involvement.

5. "Stop, please, wherever you are in your story. And now, A's, you listen while B's tell their story in the third person. Remember, don't let them use the word 'I.' "

Again, allow four minutes or so.

6. "Please stop now, and let me have your attention. Take a minute or two to appreciate your partner. Then come out of your pairs and all process this together in the large group."

PROCESSING: Group leader, use blackboard or newsprint pad that is divided into two columns like this:

PERSONAL SELF (Ego)	IMPERSONAL SELF (Observer)

From the group, draw out the descriptions from each state—"I" and "He/She"—from the experience they just had with their partner. Allow them to volunteer this information by raising their hands: "Who is willing to share how that was for them? What differences did you notice when you told your story in 'I' language versus how you were when you told it in third person?"

Some types of answers will be: "In 'I,' I was very emotional, very angry. In the third person, it seemed rather humorous that I got so hot over something so ridiculous." On the board under PERSONAL SELF write "emotionally upset." Under IMPERSONAL SELF write "humor" and "unemotional" or "less emotional." Another example might be: "In 'I' self I felt intensely concerned about proving my point. In 'he/she,' it didn't matter so much." In the first column, you write "need to justify or prove point" and in the second column, "less intensity in proving point." Use your imagination to draw these dualistic states of consciousness for comparison, but be sure to stick to the facts of what they are reporting.

The idea is for them to see that the personal self is stuck in ego needs and cannot see the larger picture. It comes from a fragment of truth, while the impersonal and higher Self can see the situation holistically and without ego involvement. The higher Self, as observer, is in the situation and above it at the same time. The lower self (ego) is totally caught up in its own perspective.

Point to be made: Emotional overreactions clue us that we are stuck in our ego. We need to stop at a time like that and observe what is going on with us. It will show us something about our personality structure, which is being offered a chance to grow beyond a weakness. Perhaps I need to have the power. Maybe I'm overly invested in a certain outcome. Perhaps I'm protecting an image of myself.

Note: Sometimes someone will report a higher-Self emotional reaction, such as reacting to a child or animal being abused. Remind the group that the higher Self reacts to injustice, but it still does not *over*react. *Over*reaction is the key. Would *everybody* have felt rejected or hurt by that? If not, then it is probably an ego need rather than objecting justifiably to an inhuman act.

EXERCISE 5 ▲　　▲　　▲　　▲　　▲　　▲

Observer Self

PURPOSE: Use this exercise when you feel it is important for the person you're working with to get outside her emotional reaction to a situation and see it from a wider point of view (from the standpoint of Reality rather than from the personal reality).

INSTRUCTIONS TO GUIDE: Ask your client or friend to close her eyes and picture herself totally involved in an emotional scene that is representative of some current problem. After she has gone inward and become silent, and you sense she is picturing the scene, guide her with these types of statements, spoken quietly and unobtrusively.

GUIDED IMAGERY EXERCISE: "Be aware of how you are feeling as you involve in this scene. . . . Notice the look on your face and on the faces of those involved with you. . . . Be aware of the kind of energy that is in the air as you involve in this. . . . Notice your body movements. . . . Be aware of the intentions of yourself and others involved . . . the message you're trying to get across to the other(s). . . . Now, just *feel* for a moment the very *essence* of this experience, as though it's happening right now. . . . Just be with that for a while. . . ." (Put on some quiet meditative music at this point, if possible.)

"Now, rise above yourself. . . . All the way up into the sky . . . look down on the scene you left behind and see it in its entirety. . . . Notice what you are doing. . . . Notice how the other(s) are reacting to you. . . . Be aware of the context within which this scene is occurring . . . the role you and others are playing out, the place it's happening . . . this particular time in history . . . in the city where you live . . . this culture . . . this age. . . .

"Now, very slowly allow yourself to descend back into the scene you've been witnessing. . . . Reenter your body and begin acting out this scene based on what you saw from above. . . . Notice any changes you are making in how you are relating to this situation. . . . Notice any changes in others. . . . Be aware of how your body now looks and feels. . . . Be aware of any insights into the situation you are having. . . . Be especially aware of the needs the other(s) have, or what is motivating their behavior, and notice your reactions to them now. . . .

"Allow this scene to come to an end in whatever way you wish to resolve the matter for now. . . .

"Slowly open your eyes and come back here with me."

PROCESSING: In processing this experience, pay special attention to the difference in how the person you are guiding felt from above as compared to being totally involved down below. Point out that the uninvolved (higher) Self had the most loving responses. (Often we confuse passionate emotional involvement—that we feel when we are attached and needy—with love.)

EXERCISE 6 ▲ ▲ ▲ ▲ ▲ ▲

I Am Aware

PURPOSE: Use this exercise to explore ways in which you or your clients are unconscious of how they use their awareness continuum to select what they do and do not attend to in life. Sometime spend a whole session with your client exploring his continuum of awareness. The more sensitively we can become tuned into the subtle energies within and around us, the more fully we are participating in life and the art of Self-creation.

INSTRUCTIONS TO GUIDE: First of all, teach him that we can only be aware of (1) inner states or feelings, (2) outer objects contacted by our senses, or (3) mind activity. And we can only be aware of one thing at a time. (If I am focusing on an inner feeling, I will be oblivious to an outside noise or color or smell—unless, of course, they become so overwhelming they shift my awareness to them. In that case, I will no longer be aware of my inner feelings.)

GUIDED EXERCISE: Ask your client to close his eyes, and give him some time to relax.

"Notice your breath as it goes in and out of your body. . . . Now, gently begin to balance out your breathing . . . feel yourself letting go . . . calming down . . . centering.

"Follow the awareness. Stay with it. . . . What's happening now?" (Keep client in his awareness and just follow it for a while.)

"Now, I want you to become aware of any sounds you hear. Just notice for a while." (Allow client to report out loud what he is hearing. . . .)

"Now, shift to any smell you are experiencing . . . any light you are aware of . . . color . . . how it feels to be touching something. . . ." (Your client can open his eyes during this part, as he is using his external awareness continuum.) "Just follow your awareness for a while and report to me what your senses are picking up. . . .

"Now, close your eyes, and go up into your mind and become aware of any thoughts you are having . . . any activity in your mind . . . and report to me. Such as: 'I'm aware I am worrying about tomorrow . . . ,' or, 'I'm aware my mind is jumping all around.' Now, just be with your mind activity for a while. Watch the content of your mind. . . ." (Longer pause.)

"Now, slowly open your eyes and come back here with me . . . and let's talk about what you learned about your awareness."

PROCESSING: Allow the person you are guiding to discuss this experience fully with you. Emphasize any new learning about himself that he discovered, such as how much he uses one kind of awareness almost exclusively.

Note: When observing mind activity, notice that the activities all end with *ing* . . . recalling, worrying, planning, thinking . . . as they are all here-and-now activities. Point this out to your client.

Homework assignment: Ask your client to spend ten minutes each day for a week following his awareness, as he did in this exercise, then write in his journal what he discovers. This is excellent training for becoming an artist of Self-creation. Artists are keenly aware people.

EXERCISE 7 ▲ ▲ ▲ ▲ ▲ ▲

Reverberation! (An Exercise in Empathy)

PURPOSE: Use this exercise when clarity on some pressing issue is needed.

INSTRUCTIONS TO GUIDE: Sit face-to-face with your client, closely, so that you can hold hands. Now, say to her: "Let's each close our eyes for a few moments and focus on allowing the highest good from this session together."

Now, both of you close your eyes and go into this meditative state together. (Counselor focuses on being an instrument for client's highest good. After a few moments, counselor breaks the meditative state by slowly withdrawing hands and opening eyes.)

Quietly invite the client now to begin telling you the problem in all its ramifications. As she shares, you remain silent . . . *completely* silent . . . except for spontaneous, simple statements that keep her speaking, like "I understand," or "Please elaborate." Nonverbal empathy, such as head nods, smiles, and warm facial expressions are permissible and even desirable.

When the person you are guiding has stated the problem completely, ask her to sit quietly for a while and write down her own observations and solutions to the problem. While she is doing this, you write down your impressions of the client's situation and possible solutions.

Tell her to use whatever impressions come in while doing this written assignment. *Anything* that comes through the senses or the intuition should be put on paper. This is very important because we want the intuition to work.

For example, a feeling of repulsion or excitement might occur as the client is stating something. Or an image, a picture, or a symbol might come into the mind. Or a flash of insight might hit, with a creative solution to the situation. An old memory or an old association may emerge. Anything can be used. But it is important that each of you do your own written impressions silently, with no feedback from the other.

PROCESSING: When she is completely finished, take turns sharing what you have written. Let her share first. The two of you process this together.

Now, the session progresses as usual, using the material that has surfaced from this exercise as the content of the session.

Note: You will find that the nonverbal contact with the client with instruction to focus on the highest good, and the silent period that comes while writing down what is coming through the consciousness, will give each of you a profound contact with your higher Self.

EXERCISE 8 ▲ ▲ ▲ ▲ ▲ ▲

(For use with individuals or groups) Transforming Resentments[1]

PURPOSE: Use this exercise to release energy tied up in past resentments and repressed anger, or any other type of emotional "unfinished business." Use after rapport is established and the client is fully ready to work on himself.

INSTRUCTIONS TO GUIDE: If you are doing this exercise in groups, divide the group into A's and B's. Briefly outline the role of the teller and of the listener. Make sure everybody understands they will have a chance to take both roles. (Make sure to tell the listener to take notes, enough to describe each specific situation for recall later.)

GUIDED IMAGERY EXERCISE: "Close your eyes and take a few deep breaths.

"In your mind's eye, reflect rapidly back over your life of relationships and situations, and become aware of any angry, hurt, or resentful feelings that you have toward particular people or places.

"Now, begin telling me (or listener) who or what you feel resentment toward. List them out loud. (Listener, take notes so you can read them back later.)

"Open your eyes, and one by one we are going to put these people here in this empty chair and begin telling them *specifically* what we resent, or what feels unfinished that is painful to you."

Say to the client:

1. "See the person clearly in the chair. Describe to me what they are wearing, the look on their face, the attitude they are projecting, etc. See them clearly.

2. "As I (or your listener) call out each specific event you recalled, please begin telling them what you resent. Just spell them out one at a time. Don't worry if you are not being rational about it. Don't worry about feeling justified. Feelings are feelings. Just express them.

3. "Now begin telling them what you would rather have had from them . . . what you wish they had done or been. It's okay to feel sadness or regret. Just tell them.

4. "When you feel done with this, close your eyes and begin breathing evenly, slowly relaxing yourself." (Therapist, put music on with low volume, as background music. Allow silence to pervade the room except for the music. The music needs to be meditative and melodic, with no words, very quiet, and not disruptive.)[2]

5. As music plays and relaxation occurs, tell your client

to picture himself and the one he is resenting sitting together surrounded in rose-colored light. "Just be in that space together for a minute or two. Now, when it feels right, begin telling the person you resent that you release him or her with love and you surround him or her with light . . . that you surround the *two* of you in the light of compassion, together . . . that you are ready to let go of the past and be with this person in whatever way the universe sees fit. . . .

6. "Now, gently tell the other person anything about him- or herself that you appreciate."

7. Wait quietly with your client until you sense an inner change of mood occur. If forgiveness and letting go clearly happen, your client will sigh, feel lighter, smile, or weep quietly with a kind of quiet joy. If forgiveness does not occur, you will sense nothing is happening, in which case you invite your client to go back to Step 2 and bring up other resentments or feelings that have not yet been shared, then proceed through the steps again. Or you can do this at another session.

Note: *Do not use music until Step 4*, because the earlier steps are to come from the personal self, with ego energy. The music evokes the transpersonal Self.

PROCESSING: Ask client to check and see how his body is feeling. Are there any pent-up emotions still being felt? If so, have him gently breathe in and out a few times to balance the feelings. Or, if he's on the verge of some expression (tears, anger) encourage him to go on into the feeling and let it express.

Let him know it's okay if he couldn't let go and forgive, or whatever. Help him realize that these things have their own timing. Allow him to talk about his experience until the energy seems to balance. Then remind him this can be tried again later.

EXERCISE 9 ▲   ▲   ▲   ▲   ▲   ▲

Focusing on a Feeling

PURPOSE: This exercise allows you or your clients to become aware of feelings in the physical body and to connect the feeling with its meaning, so the emotional wound can heal.

INSTRUCTIONS TO GUIDE: When your client expresses something you sense must have feeling accompanying it, ask her if she is experiencing a feeling somewhere in her body as she talks. If she says no, then just continue listening to her. If she says yes, have her point to where the feeling is located.

Then ask her to close her eyes and go to the feeling, focusing her entire attention there. Have her watch the feeling to see what happens, reporting to you as she notices changes. Stay with her, following the feeling wherever it wants to go.

Often the feeling will dissolve when noticed, and you can share this insight with your client: "It only wanted you to notice it. Now it can go away." Or, sometimes the feeling will become intensified. If so, have her focus on the feeling. *Stay with it.* If she tries to leave, keep bringing her back.

As it intensifies, allow the feeling to speak. *Not* the intellect, the feeling. The feeling has a voice. "Let it talk to you."

As the feeling speaks its mind, help your client express the feeling—cry, moan, yell, whatever is asking to be expressed. If there is no emotional release, have your client ask the feeling what it needs in order to let go and then follow the feeling's instructions.

Example: The feeling might say, "I need to be alone with you to experience this." Or, "I need for you to express this directly to your father." Or, "I need permission to express myself."

PROCESSING: Once the feeling is out, go back and make sure there is only relief and serenity left. If something else remains that needs to be dealt with, go for it in the same manner as you did the first one.

Note: When a feeling is willing to dialogue with its host, you might find it useful to have it tell its body and its mind what it needs from them. Often we gain insight when we see how our different selves are working or not working together. For example, my emotions once told my mind to quit giving them so much data to process. My emotions felt they had to block off a lot of feeling because they couldn't handle all the thoughts that came in. And my emotions told my body they wanted to color my body some beautiful colors, because my body was too devoid of feeling sometimes, too aligned with my mental life. This insight has helped me greatly in aligning my physical, emotional, and mental selves.

Eugene Gendlin's book, *Focusing*, is an excellent source for this process. (See Bibliography.)

EXERCISE **10** ▲ ▲ ▲ ▲ ▲ ▲

Going into the Silence

PURPOSE: Use this exercise in mindfulness whenever you or a client need to gain understanding of a particular difficulty. You can use it to gain a sense of level five consciousness. You can use this exercise to practice mindfulness with no particular goal in mind.

GUIDED EXERCISE: "Sit in a quiet place, pleasant and warm. Close your eyes and begin feeling yourself relax. . . .

Let go of the tension in your body. . . . Realize that gravity will hold you. . . . Just sit . . . just be.

"Take a few quiet, even breaths." (Long pause.)

"In your mind's eye, imagine you are going inward toward the center of your being. Deeper and deeper . . . inward . . . inward . . . down into the center . . . where all truth resides. . . .

"Everything is totally still . . . stillness . . . complete silence . . . silent stillness. . . ." (Long pause.)

"Be here now . . . absorb the silence . . . feel its weight. . . ."

(Allow two minutes to pass with no sound.)

"Now allow the silence to speak . . . to show you who you are . . . what you need to know. . . ."

(Allow another two minutes to pass or however long your intuition says your client needs. Do not allow your own anxiety or impatience to rule you. Stay tuned in to your client's experience, and you will know exactly when to speak.)

"Now, slowly allow yourself to ascend back out to the surface of yourself. . . . Slowly come back here with me. . . ."

PROCESSING: When the client is back and his eyes are open, ask him to tell you what he learned, and process it together.

This exercise can be practiced repeatedly as a daily meditation and can be done alone.

EXERCISE 11 ▲ ▲ ▲ ▲ ▲ ▲

Becoming a Being of Light

PURPOSE: This imagery will aid you or your clients in experiencing a moment of enlightenment, all the way into the cellular level of your being.

INSTRUCTIONS TO GUIDE: Ask your client to stand quietly, closing her eyes for a while, and begin to breathe with balanced breath . . . *in* to the count of four, *out* to the count of four . . . to feel herself relaxing and letting go.

GUIDED IMAGERY EXPERIENCE: "Realize that gravity will hold you. Spread your feet apart about fourteen inches and feel your weight balancing between your legs. Bend your knees a little so that you can sway like a tree in a gentle wind.

"Now become aware of your body, standing here so gracefully, and realize it is a vessel of supreme beauty and bliss, casting the light of the Spirit as a lamp reflects the luminosity of its indwelling flame. Realize that your expression is the workings of the gods. . . . The joy of life channels through you into a world that needs your light. Be this Godself. Be this bliss . . . this joy . . . this consciousness. . . . Feel yourself to be light, transparent, and filled with the flow of universal love and confidence . . . You are a being of light." (Long pause.)

"Now open your eyes and walk around in this newfound state of consciousness . . . being truly who you are at the highest possible level. Stay very close to your experience, and *realize* this truth. . . ."

PROCESSING: After a few minutes of this, have your client share with you what this experience was like, what insights she gained, what feelings she experienced.

EXERCISE 12 ▲   ▲   ▲   ▲   ▲   ▲

Enlightening

PURPOSE: Use this exercise for clearing emotional energy or physical pain that is stuck in the body. You can use this same exercise to go to a place in the body where a physical problem is occurring. For example, tightness in the neck, a nervous stomach, etc. The point is to have the client *personify* the feeling or physical ailment, experience it, and have a conversation with it in order to understand it.

INSTRUCTIONS TO GUIDE: Use quiet, meditative music. Ask your client to close his eyes and begin relaxing, noticing his breath as he breathes in and out. Then have him begin balancing his breath . . . breathe *in* to the count of four, breathe *out* to the count of four.

GUIDED EXERCISE: "Notice any tension or pain anywhere in your body. . . . Gradually breathe your breath into these tense parts, breathing out the tension. . . . Feel yourself letting go. . . . more and more . . . let go."
     When you feel your client is really inward, continue:
     "Now, in your imagination, see yourself standing at the top of a staircase looking down at seven steps. You are going to descend to the bottom, knowing that there you will be completely relaxed. Now you are going down: 1 . . . 2 . . . 3 . . . 4 . . . 5 . . . 6 . . . 7. . . ." (Note: When counting keep your voice even, with same amount of time between each count.)
     "Now you are at the bottom, and you see yourself standing there with the lantern of consciousness in your hand. You are going to go down into your emotional space. Please point for me where that is in your body . . . the place where you feel the emotion." (The person you are guiding will point, probably to the solar plexus or the chest.)

"Okay, now in your right hand is your lantern of consciousness, shining its clear light. And in your left hand is a cord you can pull anytime you wish to be lifted up out of the emotional place you are going to. So you are safe and protected, and everything is fine. Now you are going into the emotional place. . . . See in there . . . and tell me what your emotion looks like. . . . What is it? (The person will report a thing, or a symbol.) . . . Give the feeling a name. (Long pause.)

"Now, ask your symbol what it needs and tell me what it says. . . . Call it by its name."

As he is reporting what the emotion needs, ask him if he is experiencing any feeling right now. If yes, have him express the feeling . . . tears, anger, whatever. If the client is *not* feeling anything, continue with the exercise. Now ask him:

"Who does your emotion need this from? . . . And how can your emotion get it?"

Follow his train of thought and experience, and logically lead him on to conclusion, getting as much data from the emotion as you can, and getting out as much feeling as the client is in touch with. When you sense all has been brought into the light and seen clearly, say this to your client or friend:

"Now, picture the emotion standing there with the full light of consciousness shining its light upon it, feeling its warmth, and surrounding it with love and appreciation. And begin ascending back up the seven steps to the top, counting slowly from 7 to 1, and end the experience any way you wish."

When it feels right, ask him to come back to the room, to experience his body on the floor (or in the chair), and slowly to open his eyes.

PROCESSING: Process this experience with the person you've been guiding, having him write down any significant insights that occurred.

Always end by shining the light of consciousness on it, encircling it with love and appreciation. This work is occurring on the symbolic level, which is *the causative level*. It will have far-reaching effects on the consciousness of your client, even though sometimes he cannot verbalize completely what happened.

You can trust the process.

EXERCISE 13 ▲   ▲   ▲   ▲   ▲   ▲

Seeing Yourself Completely

PURPOSE: Use this exercise for aiding clients or persons seeking help in achieving fourth level consciousness . . . loving acceptance of themselves as they are.

INSTRUCTIONS TO GUIDE: Use background music, soft, meditative.

GUIDED IMAGERY EXERCISE: "Stand quietly, erect, centered. Close your eyes and breathe deeply a few times to relax. Experience yourself in an egg-shaped bubble of soft rose-colored light. Above your head, about eighteen inches, resides your higher Self. Picture it as a shining star, pouring its warmth and brilliance down upon you.

"Now, begin reflecting on your past. Just let it float by you as if on ticker tape. See it without judgment . . . just warmth. . . . Now, ask yourself if there is anything *about yourself* you've gained from your past that you would like to keep. . . . Say them out loud. . . ."

(Guide, record them.)

"Now, see yourself in the future at whatever time you choose as manifesting these qualities you wish to keep and this life-style you dream of. . . . See yourself doing it and being it in all its clarity. . . .

"When you are ready, come back here to this room with me."

PROCESSING: Process this experience with your client, attributing patterns, meaning, or dealing with any unfinished emotion. If something emerges that is too much to work on in one session, make a note to follow up at another time.

EXERCISE 14 ▲ ▲ ▲ ▲ ▲ ▲

Nature of Resistance

PURPOSE: Use this exercise when resistance is present in your own life or in the therapy session. Resistance will also be present in the processing. Work *with* the resistance, not against it. And drop the content of the personal work that created the resistance until you are clear on what the resistance is. Study this exercise carefully before attempting to use it.

INSTRUCTIONS TO GUIDE: Transformers do not abruptly press themselves or persons they guide past a point of resistance. They view resistance as a gift to be respected. They do believe, however, that it is their obligation to help discover where the resistance is coming from, in themselves as well as in others.

GUIDED IMAGERY EXERCISE: When you sense resistance, begin by pointing out to the person you're guiding (or to yourself) that you are perceiving her objections as resistance. Ask the client what it feels like. If she affirms that it is indeed some sort of blockage to a particular aspect of personal work, ask her if she would like to explore where the resistance is coming from.

Explain that it can be a message from her lower self, having its basis in fear. Or it can be a message from her higher Self, as a way to step down her energy, which the higher Self senses is moving too rapidly. In order to determine from which unconscious mind the block is being constructed (the subconscious or the superconscious), the Transformer asks the client or friend to close her eyes and breathe a while (to relax the body). When you feel she is somewhat relaxed, say:

"Now, very spontaneously, allow an image to come into your mind that symbolizes your resistance. . . ."

When she has a symbol, ask her to describe it in detail. If the symbol is representative of anything that is down, heavy, dark, or thick, it will be from the subconscious (fear-based). Examples: a dark wall with no windows, black mud covering the entrance to something, heavy weights bolting a door, a "No Exit" sign beside one spelling "Danger." Or sometimes the subconscious images will be shadows, murkiness, thick, dark clouds, or other amorphous substances that block our vision.

If, on the other hand, the image is one from the higher Self, it will be one of a master, a teacher, guide, or Christ figure, usually robed in white, or beautiful or aged, representing strength, purity, or wisdom. Or often it will be a symbol of a cross, a rose, a serpent encircling a staff, a crown, a field of green grass, a brilliant light, or some type of religious symbol. It will be white, golden, yellow, or shades of blue, violet, or rose. All of these are symbols from the superconscious mind, the home of the higher Self.

If the subconscious is blocking, ask the person you are guiding if she would be willing to talk about her fear. See what guarantees she would need for safety or comfort in order to proceed. If she resists, let it go. (If the pattern is significant, you can bet the issue will resurface for another chance to be worked through.)

If the superconscious is blocking, tell her to respect her higher Self's wishes and follow its guidance. It knows more about what's better for her than you do. If your client asks you why her higher Self would be blocking a piece of personal work, you can share with her the knowledge that her higher Self (for some reason) knows she is not ready yet to deal with this particular issue in life. Perhaps it would require certain moves in her circumstances that would adversely affect innocent persons. Or it might give the client or friend too much to deal with right now, which might produce discouragement on the path, or some kind of breakdown.

PROCESSING: Give the person you are guiding permission to resist, even to hold up on processing. (Most often, this permission will paradoxically cause her to want to talk about the experience.) When processing, be sure to help the person ascertain whether the resistance was from the higher or lower self.

EXERCISE 15 ▲ ▲ ▲ ▲ ▲ ▲

Evoking an Ideal Model

PURPOSE: Use this exercise to get yourself or your client in touch with his higher Self, or some other ideal model needed to help integrate his personality or achieve a desired behavior.

INSTRUCTIONS TO GUIDE: Take some time to put the person you are guiding in a quiet, relaxed state. Then have him begin visualizing himself walking down a corridor of a museum, slowly approaching a statue that is emerging in the distance.

"As you are approaching this statue, you are beginning to see its form emerge, and you realize this is your higher Self! (If it is another ideal model you want him to identify with, such as his playful self or his responsible self, or more archetypally, a god/goddess, or his other half—or divine partner, substitute here.)

"Be aware of what this higher Self looks like, its stance . . . the expression on its face . . . its attire . . . experience its essence for a moment . . . discover how you feel in its presence. Now, just allow yourself to be there in the presence of this statue for a moment and experience a relationship with it. . . . Now slowly move toward this glorious statue, allowing yourself to come closer and closer, staying in touch with how you feel . . . and merge with this Self, coming down off your pedestal and moving around as this Self. . . . Discover how it feels to be walking in its feet, moving its arms, breathing its breath . . . just being this Self.

"Now imagine you, as your higher Self, are returning back to your pedestal to take your stance once again, and slowly experience yourself as you are now stepping out of its form and standing in front of it once again. . . . Your higher Self is now giving you a gift to use whenever you need it for strength, courage, or loving action. See the gift being handed to you, accept it . . . and in your own way thank your higher Self for this wondrous gift and take a few moments in silence to assimilate this experience." (Long pause.)

"Now, slowly return to the room here with me by experiencing yourself sitting in the chair, becoming aware of your body. . . . Now, slowly open your eyes when you feel ready."

PROCESSING: Take a few minutes to process this experience with your client or friend. Make sure you ask questions about the main points you have covered in this imagery. The main purpose is to be sure your client emerges with a clear picture of this Self, in detail, the *essence* of this Self, and a clear understanding of what the gift means for him in his everyday life.

EXERCISE 16 ▲   ▲   ▲   ▲   ▲   ▲

Invoking a Positive Quality[3]

PURPOSE: Use this exercise when a client (or you) seems stuck in a negative characteristic way of behaving, feeling, or thinking, and is willing to really work on opening to a new possibility.

INSTRUCTIONS TO GUIDE: First, clearly define the negative quality she seeks to transform. Let's say for example, that it is extravagance. The person you are guiding will need to contemplate what its opposite would be for her. After careful thought and discussion with you, she chooses simplicity as the desired trait she feels would counteract her wasteful extravagance.

The essence of simplicity, an archetype, must now be planted in her consciousness and prepared to manifest. Once the preparation is properly instigated, it will manifest naturally, with absolutely no effort. Here are some suggested ways to do this. (You may think of others that will work just as well.)

1. Have your client or friend meditate on the word *simplicity* and discover for herself its nature. She should do this for perhaps a week, writing down the insights and feelings she has concerning the concept.

2. Tell her to ask her higher Self for a symbol for this

quality. The symbol, then, will provide more information on the essence of simplicity. She can invoke the symbol, as well as the word, in her consciousness several times a day—call it out, reflect on it, see the symbol in her mind's eye, etc.

3. In her everyday life, your friend or client can begin talking about the quality to her friends, declaring her intention to develop it in her character. This grounds the thought in reality, giving the unconscious mind a chance to believe it and to *cause* it to happen.

4. She can begin acting "as if" she possesses this quality—imaging the archetype of simplicity overshadowing her, and doing things that are representative of this quality's nature. You do not need to suggest what these actions might be. It is better to allow her own creativity to work on it. She will find that she does things she wouldn't have dreamed of as this quality comes alive in her, *as* her. It will feel like magic!

5. She can write the word several times a day or make cards or artistic renditions of it and place them around her room or office.

For your aid in teaching clients or others seeking guidance to invoke positive qualities, here is a listing of the qualities that have emerged most often from persons using this technique:

> *acceptance, appreciation, aspiration, authenticity, beauty, being, belonging, calmness, centeredness, childlikeness, compassion, comradeship, concreteness, courage, creativity, curiosity, daring, decisiveness, detachment, determination, discipline, discretion, discrimination, ease, empathy, endurance, enthusiasm, faith, freedom, friendliness, generosity, genuineness, good-heartedness, grace, harmlessness, harmony, humility, humor, initiative, integration, integrity, leadership, light, love, mutuality, nonattachment, order, patience, peacefulness, persistence, position, positiveness, power, purity, reality, re-*

sponsibility, serenity, service, significance, silence, simplicity, stability, synthesis, thoughtfulness, tolerance, trust, truth, understanding, unity, vitality, wholeness, will, wisdom, wonder.

PROCESSING: When your client or friend begins speaking of the positive quality or qualities she's invoking, it is good to help her discover and name its opposite and how that plays out in her life. These qualities tend to come paired with their opposites. And remember, let your *client* name its opposite, not you. This is crucial.

Appendix 2
A Model of Human Nature

FORCE	COGNITION	QUALITY		BASIC URGE	PITFALL	INTEGRATION
7th The Love of God (Self)	Intuition	Spiritual Love/Will (Being)		Unity Consciousness	(Indiscriminate Use of Will)	Will
6th The Love of Life	Inspiration	Love/Wisdom (Higher Emotions)		Compassion/Aspiration to Serve	(Overidentification with Humanity's Suffering)	Appetites/Emotions
5th The Love of Truth	Creative Imagination	Creative Intelligence (Higher Mind)		Understanding/Self-Creative Expression	(Abstraction)	Intellect
4th Awakening	Harmonizing Higher with Lower Nature	Harmony Through Conflict		Acceptance Harmonizing	(Attachment to Conflict)	Self-Creation
3rd The Will to Know	Self-Definition	Analysis/Comparison (Concrete Mind)		Identity-Seeking	(Fragmentation)	Right Thought
2nd The Will to Feel	Self-Gratification	Pleasure/Devotion (Emotional/Relational)		Passion	(Duality)	Right Feeling
1st The Will to Live	Self-Preservation	Order (Physical/Instinctual)		Fear	(Isolation)	Right Action

HIGHER POWER

Transpersonal Dimension (Beyond Time) — Domain of Essence — Inner World of Wisdom

Personal Dimension (Time)

Outer World of Experience — Domain of Ego

BEING

BECOMING

Key

Our Many Selves — Integration

* Higher Self
True Self
Observer Self
Partial Selves

Appendix 3
The Transmutations
(Working with the Polarities)

BEING
Love/Will Merge:
Courage to Be; Unity;
Personal Responsibility;
Self-Mastery;
Intuition;
The Love of God (Self)

THE WILL TO FEEL
(Ruled by Passions;
Self-Preoccupation;
Exaggerated Mood Swings.)

THE WILL TO KNOW
(Mind Ruled by Fragmented
Half-Truths; Role Playing;
Desire for Status/"Things.")

7

2   3

4
ACCEPTANCE

5   6

1

THINKING
Truth Activates:
Holistic Comprehension
Creative Imagination
Self-Creative Expression
Desire for Self-Knowledge
The Love of Truth

FEELING
Love/Wisdom Merge:
Compassion; Aspiration to
Serve Others; Serenity;
Inspiration;
The Love of Life

THE WILL TO LIVE
(Fear; Isolation;
Self-Pity and
Blame;
Powerlessness.)

Notes

INTRODUCTION

1. Abraham H. Maslow, *The Farther Reaches of Human Nature* (New York: Viking Press, 1971), pp. 281–82.

2. Marilyn Ferguson, *The Aquarian Conspiracy: Personal & Social Transformation in the '80's* (Los Angeles: J. P. Tarcher, 1980).

3. See Fritjof Capra, *The Tao of Physics* (Boulder, CO: Shambhala Press, 1975) and *The Turning Point* (New York: Simon & Schuster, 1982).

4. Jean Houston, *The Possible Human: A Course in Extending Your Physical, Mental and Creative Abilities* (Los Angeles: J. P. Tarcher, 1982), p. 217.

5. Fred Alan Wolf, *Taking the Quantum Leap* (New York: Harper & Row, 1988).

6. Fritjof Capra, *The Turning Point* (New York: Simon & Schuster, 1982).

7. Modern thinkers such as David Bohm, F. David Peat, Rupert Sheldrake, Fred Alan Wolf, Gary Zukav, Ken Wilber, Stanislav Grof, Charles Tart, Deepak Chopra, Larry Dossey, and David Spangler express theoretical viewpoints that agree with Capra on this point.

8. Jane English, "Science and Transformation: Levels of Reality in Science and in Consciousness." Unpublished paper: 867 Arlington Ave., Berkeley, CA 94707.

9. Abraham H. Maslow, *Toward a Psychology of Being* (Princeton, NJ: Van Nostrand Co., 1962).

10. Richard Selzer, *Mortal Lessons* (New York: Simon & Schuster, 1976).

11. A special appreciation is extended to Harper & Row, Publishers, Inc. for granting permission to quote extensively from Satprem's *Sri Aurobindo, or the Adventure of Consciousness*, 1968.

12. Research on human brain functioning has led to the discovery that we have basically two modes of thinking available to us, emanating from two distinct hemispheres of the brain, one that processes ordinary sensory data in a logical, linear fashion, and the other that intuitively transforms ordinary data into new creations—one that "analyzes over time"; the other that "synthesizes over space" (J. Levy, Cal. Tech. researcher).

The left brain is our computer. It reasons, organizes incoming data, using speech and concrete, materialized facts for its explanation of reality. This verbal brain dominates most of us most of the time, not because it is the best, but because it has been granted the seat of honor in most institutions of learning. It is the *valued* mode of thinking in the West.

The right brain has been devalued, for it is nonrational. It "sees" in wholes. Something "feels" right or wrong, and it cannot explain it. It thinks all-at-once, has flashes of insight based on intuition, and creatively involves with life through meditation, movement, creative inspiration, and intuition. It has been equated with negativity, femininity, emotionalism, the dark, and the moon. In contrast, the left brain has been equated with masculinity, positiveness, the sun, rationality, and being conscious—as though it is "right," and the right brain is "wrong."

The left brain controls the right side of the body, and the right brain, the left side of the body.

Following are some of the common parallels that are made of left-brain and right-brain functioning that will familiarize you with these two modes of knowing.

RIGHT-BRAIN	LEFT-BRAIN
emotion	reason
intuition	intellect
Yin	Yang
abstract	concrete
dark	light
feminine	masculine
free-association	directed thought
divergent	convergent
simultaneous	successive
relational	analytic
nonlineal	lineal
subjective	objective
multiple	sequential
night	day

For those of you wishing to pursue the study of split-brain research, I recommend the following:

Robert Ornstein, *The Psychology of Consciousness*, 2nd ed. rev. (New York: Harcourt Brace Jovanovich, 1977).

S. J. Dimond and J. G. Beaumont, *Hemisphere Function in the Human Brain* (New York: Wiley, 1974).

The works of R. W. Sperry, California Institute of Technology, Dept. of Psychobiology.

M. Gazzaniga, "The Split Brain in Man," in *Perception: Mechanisms and Models*. R. Held and W. Richards, eds., (San Francisco: W. H. Freeman, 1972).

J. Jaynes, *The Origin of Consciousness in the Breakdown of the Bicameral Mind* (Boston: Houghton Mifflin, 1976).

13. This is Thomas Kuhn's concept, from his book *The Structure of Scientific Revolutions* (Chicago: University of Chicago Press, 1962).

INTRODUCTION: TRANSFORMERS, WHO ARE THEY?

1. Alexis Edwards, "Guidelines," a Findhorn publication, 1971. This quotation was slightly altered by its author in 1979.
2. Adapted from R. Assagioli, *Psychosynthesis* (New York: Penguin Books, 1976).

CHAPTER 1
THE PRINCIPLES OF SELF-CREATION

1. Bobby Bridger, personal friend, poet, and epic balladeer, wrote these words to his song "Heal in the Wisdom," from his album of the same name. His work captures the essence of the coming age. Reproduced by permission of the author © 1981 Stareyes, ASCAP.
2. G. Jampolsky, *Love Is Letting Go of Fear* (New York: Bantam Books, 1979).
3. The following is a synopsis of Carl Jung's thoughts about the Self as described in Stephen Hoeller's book, *The Gnostic Jung and the Seven Sermons to the Dead* (Wheaton, IL: Theosophical Publishing House, 1982).
4. A. Guillaumont, H.-CH. Puech, and G. Quispel, trans., *The Gospel According to Thomas* (New York: Harper & Row, 1959), Logion 45.
5. M. Naimy, *The Book of Mirdad* (New York: Penguin Books, 1962).
6. Thaddeus Golas, *The Lazy Man's Guide to Enlightenment* (New York: Bantam Books, 1972).
7. See *New Pathways in Psychology: Maslow and the Post-Freudian Revolution,* by Colin Wilson (New York: Taplinger, 1972), for an expansion of this idea.

CHAPTER 3
HOW ADDICTION UNFOLDS IN THE PERSONALITY

1. Suggested readings:
Sigmund Freud, "The Ego and the Id," *The Standard Edition of the Complete Psychological Works of Sigmund Freud,* Vol. 19, James Strachey, ed. (London: Hogarth Press, 1953–1964).
Karen Horney, *The Neurotic Personality of Our Time* (New York: Norton, 1968).
Carl Jung, *The Collected Works of C. G. Jung,* Vol. 9, Part 1, "The Archetypes and the Collective Unconscious," Bollingen Series XX (Princeton, NJ: Princeton University Press, 1968).
H. S. Sullivan, *The Interpersonal Theory of Psychiatry* (New York: Norton, 1953).

CHAPTER 4
HARMONY CONSCIOUSNESS: TURNING THE INSIDE OUT

1. Ken Wilber, "Psychologie Perennis: The Spectrum of Consciousness," *Journal of Transpersonal Psychology,* Vol. 7 (1975), No. 2: 121.

2. Alice A. Bailey, *Glamour: A World Problem* (New York: Lucis Press, 1950).

3. Karmic Balancing—In Hindu philosophy, the Law of Karma is the Law of Retribution, which balances out everything in the universe, based on the Law of Energy. Everything must finally come to the zero point, where no energy remains in an event, either positive or negative. This law has been interpreted in the Judeo-Christian religion in a judgmental manner, "an eye for an eye" and "as ye sow, so shall ye reap." But the Law of Karma was never intended to be construed as punishment. It has nothing to do with morality; it is a fact of nature, as evidenced in the law of physics that states "for every force, there is an equal and opposite force that counteracts it."

Hindu philosophy teaches that we reincarnate in order to balance experiences and relationships that still contain energy, either positive or negative. A person will return to make positive an unfinished negative experience—or to complete a positive experience to which the person is still attached. According to this law, if a person dies addicted to something (cigarettes, alcohol, etc.), the soul will seek ways to reembody in order to complete the addiction. Some say the soul becomes earthbound, literally "hanging around" persons who are addicted to a particular attachment. Or it will choose another lifetime addicted to the same substance.

"Karmic balancing" explains why we are sometimes receiving a negative or positive experience in this life that we feel we do not deserve. If we were able to view the whole picture of our soul's entire evolutionary process we would be able to observe the balancing that is presently occurring.

4. In Eastern philosophy, the three aspects of the higher nature are called Satchitananda—*sat* means "truth," *chit* means "consciousness," and *ananda* means "bliss."

5. Swami Rama, R. Ballentine, and Swami Ajaya, *Yoga and Psychotherapy: The Evolution of Consciousness* (Glenview, IL: Himalayan Institute, 1976), p. 222.

6. As quoted on page 54 of *Yoga and Psychotherapy*. The original research referred to is the following: Frank Waters, *The Book of Hopi* (New York: Ballantine Books, 1963), pp. 10–11.

CHAPTER 5
BEING: A DESCRIPTION OF THE HIGHER SELF

1. Maurice Nicoll, *The Mark* (London & Dulverton: Watkins, 1981), p. 20.

CHAPTER 6
A MODEL OF TRANSCENDENCE

1. The practice of harmlessness is a self-discipline, practiced moment by moment by not allowing ourselves to say, think, or perform any actions that produce harm to any living creature. You can see how this will dissolve karmic predicaments, because it sets up no new negative causes.

BOOK TWO
INTRODUCTION

1. Yatri, *Unknown Man* (New York: Simon & Schuster, 1988), p. 169.

CHAPTER 7
UTILIZING THE HIGHER KNOWLEDGE

1. As told in *Emotion to Enlightenment,* by Swami Rama and Swami Ajaya (Honesdale, PA: Himalayan Institute, 1976).

2. Annie Besant, *The Seven Principles in Man* (Wheaton, IL: Theosophical Publishing House, 1972), p. 30.

3. My thanks to Anne Hubbell Maiden, who gave us this Govinda quote in a Psychosynthesis workshop in California in 1980. In our group's study of resistance, many of the seed thoughts given in this book were clarified.

4. Elisabeth Haich, *Initiation* (Palo Alto, CA: Seed Center, 1974), p. 366.

5. Sri Krishna Prem and Sri Madhava Ashish, *Man, the Measure of All Things* (Wheaton, IL: Theosophical Publishing House, 1969), p. 23.

6. Franz Pfeiffer, *Meister Eckhart,* Vol. 1 and 2 (New York: Gordon Press, 1977).

7. Matthew Fox was publicly silenced by the Vatican as of December 15, 1988, for one year by the Congregation for the Doctrine of Faith, headed by Cardinal Joseph Ratzinger. Until 1965, this office had been known for centuries as the Holy Office of the Roman Inquisition. Matthew Fox, "the accused," was never given the opportunity to respond to the charges against him—as occurs in all Inquisitional events.

CHAPTER 8
THE TRANSFORMER'S HEALING FUNCTION

1. A. L. Kitselman, now deceased, was a teacher from New York who developed a theory called E-Therapy. To my knowledge, his works were never published.

2. Roberto Assagioli, *Psychosynthesis* (New York: Penguin Books, 1976).

3. See Jacquelyn Small, *Becoming Naturally Therapeutic* (New York: Bantam Books, 1990), especially the chapter on Empathy and Self-disclosure.

4. A special thanks to my friend, Dr. Art Brownell, for this concept.

5. Those of you wishing to become familiar with the scientific exploration of the Doctrine of Rebirth will be interested in reading *Reincarnation: An East-West Anthology,* Joseph Head and S. L. Cranston, eds. (Wheaton, IL: Theosophical Publishing House, 1968). Especially of interest will be pages 285–304, "Scientists and Psychologists on Reincarnation."

6. Abraham H. Maslow, *The Farther Reaches of Human Nature* (New York: Viking Press, 1971).

7. Nyaroponika Thera, *The Power of Mindfulness* (San Francisco: Unity Press, 1972).

8. Read *Narcissus and Goldmund*, by Hermann Hesse (New York: Bantam Books, 1971), for a profound statement about following the path of the senses as a way toward truth.

CHAPTER 9
TRANSFORMATION: ENTERING THE WORLD OF SYNTHESIS

1. Quote from the Jewish mystic Ba'al Shem Tov in *The Torah, Genesis, A Modern Commentary*, by W. Gunther Plaut (New York: Union of American Hebrew Congregations, 1974).

2. Abraham H. Maslow, *Religion, Values and Peak Experiences* (New York: Viking Press, 1970), pp. 59–68.

3. Natural food grocery stores offer a variety of coffee and sugar substitute products that are delicious *and* nutritious. Also, several herbal tea companies offer rich, full-bodied tea blends that satisfy a craving for coffee. Food shopping patterns can change and offer an exciting new adventure. An excellent resource for a general and holistic view of nutrition and diet is *Diet and Nutrition*, by Rudolph Ballentine (Honesdale, Pennsylvania: The Himalayan Institute, 1972). Also *Laurel's Kitchen*, by Laurel Robertson, Carol Flinders, and Bronwen Godfrey, is a wonderful reference for wholesome and nutritious recipes, while also being an excellent handbook on nutrition (Berkeley, California: Nilgiri Press, 1976).

4. See Chapter 6, footnote 1.

IN CONCLUSION: A MESSAGE TO TRANSFORMERS

1. Manly P. Hall, *Self-Unfoldment by Disciplines of Self-Realization* (Los Angeles: Philosophical Research Society, 1942), p. 113.

APPENDIX 1
GUIDED IMAGERY EXERCISES FOR TRANSFORMERS

1. My special thanks to Dr. Edith Stauffer, who has served as one of my teachers, for her loving understanding of forgiveness and for helping me to formulate the *specificity* with which we must work on this task.

2. There is an increasing number of selections of music for relaxation, meditation, and guided imagery. A large selection of these tapes and records is available from Book People, Austin, TX, (512) 476-0116.

3. Adapted from Roberto Assagioli's *Psychosynthesis* (New York: Penguin Books, 1976).

Bibliography
(and suggested readings)

Alcyone (Krishnamurti). *At the Feet of the Master*. Wheaton, IL: Theosophical Publishing House, 1970.

Anonymous. *The Initiate: Some Impressions of a Great Soul*. New York: Samuel Weiser, 1977.

Assagioli, Roberto. *The Act of Will*. New York: Penguin Books, 1974.

———. *Psychosynthesis*. New York: Penguin Books, 1976.

Bailey, Alice A. *Education in the New Age*. New York: Lucis Press, 1954.

———. *Serving Humanity*. New York: Lucis Press, 1972.

Ballentine, Rudolph. *Diet and Nutrition*. Honesdale, PA: Himalayan International Institute, 1972.

Besant, Annie. *The Seven Principles of Man*. Wheaton, IL: Theosophical Publishing House, 1972.

Bradshaw, John. *Healing the Shame That Binds You*. Deerfield Beach, FL: Heath Communications, 1988.

———. *Homecoming*. New York: Bantam Books, 1990.

Brown, Molly Young. *The Unfolding Self*. Los Angeles: Psychosynthesis Press, 1983.

Capra, F. *The Tao of Physics*. Boulder, CO: Shambhala Press, 1975.

———. *The Turning Point*. New York: Simon & Schuster, 1982.

Chopra, Deepak. *Quantum Healing*. New York: Bantam Books, 1989.

Dass, Ram. *The Only Dance There Is*. New York: Doubleday, 1974.

Dass, Ram and Stephen Levine. *Grist for the Mill*. San Francisco, CA: Unity Press, 1977.

Dass, Ram and Paul Gorman. *How Can I Help? Stories and Reflections on Service*. New York: Knopf, 1985.

DeRopp, Robert. *The Master Game*. New York: Dell, 1968.

Dimond, S. J. and J. G. Beaumont. *Hemisphere Function in the Human Brain*. New York: Wiley, 1974.

Dossey, Larry. *Meaning & Medicine: A Doctor's Tales of Breakthrough and Healing*. New York: Bantam Books, 1991.

———. *Recovering the Soul: A Scientific and Spiritual Search*. New York: Bantam Books, 1990.

Eastcott, Michael. *"I," The Story of the Self*. Wheaton, IL: Theosophical Publishing House, 1979.

English, Jane. "Science and Transformation: Levels of Reality in Science and in Consciousness." Unpublished paper. 867 Arlington Ave., Berkeley, CA 94707.

Ferguson, Marilyn. *The Aquarian Conspiracy: Personal & Social Transformation in the '80's.* Los Angeles: J. P. Tarcher, 1980.

Fox, Matthew. *The Coming of the Cosmic Christ.* New York: Harper & Row, 1988.

Freud, S. "The Ego and the Id." *The Standard Edition of the Complete Psychological Works of Sigmund Freud.* Vol. 19. James Strachey, ed. London: Hogarth Press, 1953–1964.

Gawain, Shakti. *Creative Visualization.* New York: Bantam Books, 1982.

———. *Living in the Light.* New World Library, 1986.

Gazzaniga, M. "The Split Brain in Man." In *Perception: Mechanisms and Models.* Held, R. and W. Richards, eds. San Francisco, CA: W. H. Freeman, 1972.

Gendlin, Eugene. *Focusing.* New York: Everest House, 1978.

Gerard, D. L., G. Saenger, and R. Wile. "The Abstinent Alcoholic." In *Archives of General Psychiatry,* 1962, 6: 99–111.

Golas, Thaddeus. *The Lazy Man's Guide to Enlightenment.* New York: Bantam Books, 1972.

Green, Elmer and Alyce Green. *Beyond Biofeedback.* New York: Delacorte, 1977.

Guillaumont, A., H.-CH. Puech, and G. Quispel, trans. *The Gospel According to Thomas.* New York: Harper & Row, 1959.

Haich, Elisabeth. *Initiation.* Palo Alto, CA: The Seed Center, 1974.

Hall, Manly P. *Lectures on Ancient Philosophy.* Los Angeles: Philosophical Research Society, 1942.

———. *Self-Unfoldment by Disciplines of Self-Realization.* Los Angeles: Philosophical Research Society, 1942.

Harris, Barbara. *When the Twelfth Step Happens First.* Deerfield Beach, FL: Heath Communications, 1992.

Head, J. and S. L. Cranston, eds. *Reincarnation: An East-West Anthology.* Wheaton, IL: Theosophical Publishing House, 1968.

Hendricks, Gay, and Kathlyn Hendricks. *Conscious Loving: The Journey to Co-Commitment.* New York: Bantam Books, 1990.

Hesse, Hermann. *Narcissus and Goldmund.* New York: Bantam Books, 1971.

———. *Siddhartha.* New York: Farrar, Straus & Giroux, 1975.

Hoeller, Stephen. *The Gnostic Jung and the Seven Sermons to the Dead.* Wheaton, IL: Theosophical Publishing House, 1982.

Horney, Karen. *The Neurotic Personality of Our Time.* New York: Norton, 1968.

Houston, Jean. *The Possible Human: A Course in Extending Your Physical, Mental and Creative Abilities.* Los Angeles: J. P. Tarcher, 1982.

———. *The Search for the Beloved.* Los Angeles: J. P. Tarcher, 1987.

Jampolsky, Gerald. *Love Is Letting Go of Fear.* New York: Bantam Books, 1979.

Jaynes, J. *The Origin of Consciousness in the Breakdown of the Bicameral Mind.* Boston: Houghton Mifflin, 1976.

Joy, W. Brugh. *Joy's Way*. New York: St. Martin Press, 1979.

Jung, Carl. "The Archetypes and the Collective Unconscious." *The Collected Works of C. G. Jung*, Vol. 9, Part 1. Bollingen Series XX, Princeton: Princeton University Press, 1968.

Karagulla, Shafica. *Breakthrough to Creativity*. Marina del Rey, CA: DeVorss, 1967.

Keyes, Ken, Jr. *Handbook to Higher Consciousness*. Coos Bay, OR: Living Love Publications, 1972.

Kitselman, A. L. *E-Therapy*. New York: Institute of Integration.

Koile, Earl A. *Listening as a Way of Becoming*. Waco, TX: Word Books, 1977.

Kritsberg, Wayne. *The Adult Children of Alcoholics Syndrome*. Deerfield Beach, FL: Heath Communications, 1988.

Lee, John. *At My Father's Wedding*. New York: Bantam Books, 1991.

Mascaro, Juan, trans. *The Bhagavad Gita*. New York: Viking Penguin, 1962.

Maslow, Abraham H. *The Farther Reaches of Human Nature*. New York: Viking Press, 1971.

————. *Motivation and Personality*. New York: Harper & Row, 1970.

————. *Religions, Values and Peak Experiences*. New York: Viking Press, 1970.

————. *Toward a Psychology of Being*. Princeton, NJ: Van Nostrand Reinhold, 1968.

Nicoll, Maurice. *Psychological Commentaries*, Vol. 1–5 (on the teachings of G. I. Gurdjieff and P. D. Ouspensky). London: Watkins, 1975.

Ornstein, Robert. *The Psychology of Consciousness*. New York: Harcourt Brace Jovanovich, 1977.

Oyle, Irving. *The New American Medicine Show: Discovering the Healing Connection*. San Francisco, CA: Unity Press, 1979.

Paulos, Jean and Donald Stoddard. "Sugar to Booze to Blues." *Journal of Health Sciences*, Vol. 1, No. 1, 1980.

Pearce, Joseph C. *The Crack in the Cosmic Egg*. New York: Simon & Schuster, 1971.

Perls, Fritz. *Ego, Hunger and Aggression: The Beginning of Gestalt Therapy*. New York: Random House, 1969.

Pfeiffer, Franz. *Meister Eckhart*, Vol. 1 and 2. Gordon Press, 1977.

Pirsig, Robert. *Zen and the Art of Motorcycle Maintenance: An Inquiry into Values*. New York: Bantam Books, 1976.

Prem, Sri Krishna and Sri Madhava Ashish. *Man, the Measure of All Things*. Wheaton, IL: Theosophical Publishing House, 1969.

Rajneesh, Bhagwan Shree. *The Psychology of the Esoteric*. New York: Harper & Row, 1978.

Rama, Swami and Swami Ajaya (Allen Weinstock, Ph.D.). *Emotion to Enlightenment*. Honesdale, PA: Himalayan International Institute, 1976.

Rama, Swami, Swami Ajaya, and R. Ballentine. *Yoga and Psychotherapy: The Evolution of Consciousness*. Honesdale, PA: Himalayan International Institute, 1976.

Satprem. *The Mind of the Cells*. New York: Institute for Evolutionary Research, 1982.

————. *Sri Aurobindo, or the Adventure of Consciousness*. New York: Harper & Row, 1968.

Schaeffer, Brenda. *Is It Love or Is It Addiction?* New York: HarperCollins, 1987.

————. *Loving Me, Loving You: Balancing Love and Power in a Codependent World*. San Francisco: Harper San Francisco, 1991.

Selzer, Richard. *Mortal Lessons*. New York: Simon & Schuster, 1976.

Silverstein, Lee. *Consider the Alternative*. Minneapolis, MN: CompCare, 1977.

Small, Jacquelyn. *Awakening in Time: The Journey from Codependence to Co-creation*. New York: Bantam Books, 1991.

————. *Becoming Naturally Therapeutic: A Return to the True Essence of Helping*, rev. ed., New York: Bantam Books, 1991.

Small, Jacquelyn and Sidney Wolf. "Beyond Abstinence." *Alcohol, Health and Research World*, Vol. 2, No. 3. Washington, D.C.: NIAAA, 1978, pp. 34–37.

Speeth, Kathleen Riordan. *The Gurdjieff Work*. Berkeley, CA: And/Or Press, 1976.

Stewart, Rosemarie, ed. *East Meets West: The Transpersonal Approach*. Wheaton, IL: Theosophical Publishing House, 1981.

Sullivan, H. S. *The Interpersonal Theory of Psychiatry*. New York: Norton, 1953.

Tart, Charles, ed. *Transpersonal Psychologies*. New York: Harper & Row, 1977.

Taylor, Gordon Rattray. *The Natural History of the Mind*. New York: Penguin Books, 1981.

Thera, Nyaroponika. *The Power of Mindfulness*. San Francisco, CA: Unity Press, 1972.

Trungpa, Chogyam. *Cutting Through Spiritual Materialism*. Boulder, CO: Shambhala Press, 1973.

Waters, Frank. *The Book of Hopi*. New York: Ballantine Books, 1963.

Watts, Alan W. *The Wisdom of Insecurity*. New York: Random House, 1968.

Weil, Andrew. *The Natural Mind: A New Way of Looking at Drugs and the Higher Consciousness*. New York: Houghton Mifflin, 1972.

Wilber, Ken. "Psychologie Perennis: The Spectrum of Consciousness." *Journal of Transpersonal Psychology*, Vol. 7, No. 2, 1975, p. 121.

Wilson, Colin. *New Pathways in Psychology: Maslow and the Post-Freudian Revolution*. New York: Taplinger Press, 1972.

Index